CHOCTAW BY BLOOD ENROLLMENT CARDS 1898-1914

VOLUME XV

TRANSCRIBED BY

JEFF BOWEN

NATIVE STUDY
Gallipolis, Ohio
USA

Other Books and Series by Jeff Bowen

1901-1907 Native American Census Seneca, Eastern Shawnee, Miami, Modoc, Ottawa, Peoria, Quapaw, and Wyandotte Indians (Under Seneca School, Indian Territory)

1932 Census of The Standing Rock Sioux Reservation with Births And Deaths 1924-1932

Census of The Blackfeet, Montana, 1897- 1901 Expanded Edition

Eastern Cherokee by Blood, 1906-1910, Volumes I thru XIII

Choctaw of Mississippi Indian Census 1929-1932 with Births and Deaths 1924-1931 Volume I

Choctaw of Mississippi Indian Census 1933, 1934 & 1937, Supplemental Rolls to 1934 & 1935 with Births and Deaths 1932-1938, and Marriages 1936-1938 Volume II

Eastern Cherokee Census Cherokee, North Carolina 1930-1939 Census 1930-1931 with Births And Deaths 1924-1931 Taken By Agent L. W. Page Volume I

Eastern Cherokee Census Cherokee, North Carolina 1930-1939 Census 1932-1933 with Births And Deaths 1930-1932 Taken By Agent R. L. Spalsbury Volume II

Eastern Cherokee Census Cherokee, North Carolina 1930-1939 Census 1934-1937 with Births and Deaths 1925-1938 and Marriages 1936 & 1938 Taken by Agents R. L. Spalsbury And Harold W. Foght Volume III

Seminole of Florida Indian Census, 1930-1940 with Birth and Death Records, 1930-1938

Texas Cherokees 1820-1839 A Document For Litigation 1921

Choctaw By Blood Enrollment Cards 1898-1914 Volumes I thru XIV

Visit our website at **www.nativestudy.com** to learn more about these and other books and series by Jeff Bowen

Originally published:
Baltimore, Maryland
2017

Reprinted by:

Native Study LLC
Gallipolis, OH
www.nativestudy.com

Library of Congress Control Number: 2020911767

ISBN: 978-1-64968-018-1

Made in the United States of America.

**This series is dedicated to
Mike Marchi,
who keeps my spirits up.**

CREEK CENSUS.

SECOND NOTICE.

Members of the Dawes Commission will be present at the following times and places for the purpose of enrolling Creek citizens, as required by Act of Congress of June 10, 1896:

At Muskogee, Nov. 8 to 30, 1897, inclusive.
At Wagoner, Nov. 8 to 13, " inclusive.
At Eufaula, Nov. 8 to 13, " inclusive.
At Sapulpa, Nov. 15 to 20, " inclusive.
At Wetumpka, Nov. 15 to 20, " inclusive.
At Okmulgee, Nov. 22 to 30, " inclusive.

All persons who have not heretofore enrolled before the Dawes Commission should appear and enroll. Parents and guardians can enroll their families and wards.

TAMS BIXBY,
FRANK C. ARMSTRONG,
A. S. McKENNON,
THOS. B. NEEDLES,
Commissioners.

The above illustration is similar in nature to what was found throughout Indian Territory for different tribes as far as postings on bulletin boards, public centers, or wherever they could be read so people would be notified of where and when they needed to be for enrollment with the Dawes Commission.

This is a picture of the Dawes Commission at Camp Jones in Stonewall, Indian Territory on September 8, 1898.

The images below are of two of the original cards given on the microfilm. The cards given in this book have been formatted to fit on one page and still give all the information found on the original cards.

Introduction

This series of Choctaw Enrollment Cards for the Five Civilized Tribes 1898-1914 has been transcribed from National Archive Film M-1186 Rolls 39-46.

The series contains more than 6100 Choctaw enrollment cards. All of the cards list age, sex and degree of blood, the parties' Dawes Roll Numbers, and date of enrollment by the Secretary of Interior for each person. The contents also give the enrollee's parents' names as well as miscellaneous notes pertaining to the enrollee's circumstances, when needed. Most entries indicate whether or not a spouse is an Intermarried White, with the initials I.W.

Enrollment wasn't as simple a process as most would think just by going through these pages. The relationships between the Five Tribes and the Dawes Commission were weak at best. There were political battles going on between the tribes and the U.S. Government as it was, but the struggles didn't stop there. Each tribe had its own political factions pulling it from every direction. On top of everything else, people from every corner of the United States were trying to figure how to get in on the spoils (Money and Land Allotment) by means of political favor. Kent Carter, author of *The Dawes Commission*, describes the continuous effort required to enroll the different tribes and the pressure the Commission incurred from people all over the country who tried to insinuate themselves into the equation:

"In May 1896 the Dawes Commission Returned To Indian Territory for its third visit, establishing its headquarters at Vinita in the Cherokee Nation. It now had to process applications for citizenship in addition to negotiating allotment agreements; these circumstances make the narrative of events more confusing because the commission attempted the two tasks concurrently. The commissioners resumed making their usual speeches to tribal officials and public gatherings to promote negotiations, but now they inevitably had to respond to questions about how the application process for citizenship would work. They also began receiving letters from people all over the United States asking how they could 'get on the rolls' so they could 'get Indian land'."[1]

For the actual process of Choctaw enrollment, "A commission was appointed in each county of the Choctaw Nation under an act of September 18 to make separate rolls of citizens by blood, by intermarriage, and freedmen; it was to deliver them to recently elected Chief Green McCurtain by October 20, but he rejected them even before they were completed because of charges that people were being left off for political reasons. On October 30, the National Council authorized establishment of a five-member

---

1 *The Dawes Commission* by Kent Carter, page 15, para. 1

commission to revise the rolls within ten days and then directed McCurtain to turn them over to the Dawes Commission on November 11, 1896. The Choctaws hired the law firm of Stuart, Gordon, and Hailey, of South McAlester to represent the tribe at all proceedings held by the Dawes Commission,"[2] another indication that throughout the Commission's efforts there was always controversy between the tribes and the negotiators.

When completed, this multi-volume series will contain thousands of names, all of them accounted for in the indexes carefully prepared by the author. Hopefully this work will help many researchers find their ancestors and satisfy the questions that so many have had about their Native American heritage.

Jeff Bowen
Gallipolis, Ohio
NativeStudy.com

---

[2] *The Dawes Commission* by Kent Carter, page 16, para. 5

Choctaw By Blood Enrollment Cards 1898-1914

RESIDENCE: Jackson COUNTY. **Choctaw Nation** **Choctaw Roll** *(Not Including Freedmen)* CARD NO.
POST OFFICE: Mayhew, I.T. FIELD NO. 4201

Dawes' Roll No.	NAME	Relationship to Person First Named	AGE	SEX	BLOOD	TRIBAL ENROLLMENT Year	County	No.
11783 ⊗	1 Logan, Nancy 68	First Named	65	F	Full	1896	Jackson	8156
	2							
	3 ⊗No1 Died prior to September 25, 1902 not entitled to land or money (D.C. 411-1911)							
	4							
	5 ENROLLMENT OF NOS. 1 HEREON APPROVED BY THE SECRETARY OF INTERIOR Mar 10 1903							
	6							
	7							
	8							
	9							
	10							
	11							
	12							
	13							
	14							
	15							
	16							
	17							

TRIBAL ENROLLMENT OF PARENTS

Name of Father	Year	County	Name of Mother	Year	County
1 Sa-no-chee	Dead	Towson	Al-be-ho-na	Dead	Towson
2					
3					
4					
5					
6 On 1896 roll as Mrs. Logan.					
7					
8					
9					
10					
11					
12					
13					
14					
15			Date of Application for Enrollment.		Aug 30/99
16					
17					

Choctaw By Blood Enrollment Cards 1898-1914

RESIDENCE: Jacks Fork COUNTY. **Choctaw Nation**
POST OFFICE: Stringtown, I.T.

Dawes' Roll No.		NAME	Relationship to Person First Named	AGE	SEX	BLOOD	TRIBAL ENROLLMENT Year	County	No.
11784	1	Carnes, Willie 21		18	M	Full	1896	Atoka	2937
	2								
	3								
	4								
	5	ENROLLMENT							
	6	OF NOS. 1 HEREON APPROVED BY THE SECRETARY							
	7	OF INTERIOR MAR 10 1903							
	8								
	9								
	10								
	11								
	12								
	13								
	14								
	15								
	16								
	17								

TRIBAL ENROLLMENT OF PARENTS

	Name of Father	Year	County	Name of Mother	Year	County
1	Lewis Carnes	Dead	Jacks Fork	Fannie Carnes	Dead	Jacks Fork
2						
3						
4						
5						
6	On 1896 roll as Willie Carn.					
7						
8						
9						
10						
11						
12						
13						
14						
15					Date of Application for Enrollment.	Aug 30/99
16						
17						

Choctaw By Blood Enrollment Cards 1898-1914

RESIDENCE: Atoka COUNTY. **Choctaw Nation** **Choctaw Roll** *(Not Including Freedmen)* CARD NO.

POST OFFICE: Atoka, I.T. FIELD NO. 4203

Dawes' Roll No.	NAME	Relationship to Person First Named	AGE	SEX	BLOOD	TRIBAL ENROLLMENT Year	County	No.
11785	1 Thompson, Wallace 78	First Named	75	M	Full	1896	Atoka	12438
11786	2 " Elias 21	Son	18	"	"	1896	"	12439

ENROLLMENT
OF NOS. 1 and 2 HEREON
APPROVED BY THE SECRETARY
OF INTERIOR MAR 10 1903

TRIBAL ENROLLMENT OF PARENTS

	Name of Father	Year	County	Name of Mother	Year	County
1	A-ka-ne-ubbee	Dead	Kiamitia	Put-tey	Dead	Kiamitia
2	No1			Eliz. Thompson	"	Atoka

No.2 is now the husband of Lucy Folsom, a Choctaw
Indian on Choctaw card #4176 11/20/02

~~For child of No.2 see N.B. (Apr 26,1906) Card No. 176~~
~~" " " " " " (Mar 3 1905) " " 318~~

DATE OF APPLICATION FOR ENROLLMENT. Aug 30/99

Choctaw By Blood Enrollment Cards 1898-1914

RESIDENCE: Atoka COUNTY. **Choctaw Nation** **Choctaw Roll** *(Not Including Freedmen)* CARD NO.
POST OFFICE: Atoka, I.T. FIELD NO. **4204**

Dawes' Roll No.	NAME	Relationship to Person First Named	AGE	SEX	BLOOD	TRIBAL ENROLLMENT Year	County	No.
11787	1 Charleston, Martin 56	First Named	53	M	Full	1896	Atoka	2922
11788	2 " Susan 46	Wife	43	F	"	1896	"	2923
11789	3 " Marion 23	Dau	20	"	"	1896	"	2927
11790	4 " Timothy P 19	Son	16	M	"	1896	"	2924
DEAD	5 ~~" Robert B~~	~~"~~	~~13~~	~~"~~	~~"~~	~~1896~~	~~"~~	~~2925~~
11791	6 " Simeon M 12	"	9	"	"	1896	"	2926

ENROLLMENT
OF NOS. 1,2,3,4 and 6 HEREON
APPROVED BY THE SECRETARY
OF INTERIOR Mar 10 1903

No 5 hereon dismissed under order of the Commission to the Five Civilized Tribes of March 31, 1905.

TRIBAL ENROLLMENT OF PARENTS

	Name of Father	Year	County	Name of Mother	Year	County
1	Silas Charleston	Dead	Jackson	Siney Charleston	Dead	Jacks Fork
2	Un-che-ubbee	"	Jacks Fork	Meh-ta-hu-na	"	Red River
3	No1			No. 2		
4	No1			No 2		
5	~~No1~~			~~No 2~~		
6	No1			No 2		

No4 on 1896 roll as T. P. Charleston
No5 " 1896 " " R. B. "
No6 " 1896 " " S. M. "

No5 died April 28, 1900: proof of death filed Nov. 25, 1902
For child of No.3 see NB (Apr 26, 1906) Card No. 141
" " " " " " (March 3,1905) " " 1499

Date of Application for Enrollment. Aug 30/99

Choctaw By Blood Enrollment Cards 1898-1914

RESIDENCE: Atoka COUNTY. **Choctaw Nation** **Choctaw Roll** *(Not Including Freedmen)* CARD NO.
POST OFFICE: Lehigh, I.T. FIELD NO. 4205

Dawes' Roll No.	NAME	Relationship to Person First Named	AGE	SEX	BLOOD	TRIBAL ENROLLMENT Year	County	No.
11792	1 Collins, Joseph 34	First Named	31	M	Full	1896	Atoka	2947
	2							
	3							
	4							
	5							
	6							
	7							
	8							
	9							
	10							
	11							
	12							
	13							
	14							
	15							
	16							
	17							

ENROLLMENT
OF NOS. 1 HEREON
APPROVED BY THE SECRETARY
OF INTERIOR MAR 10 1903

TRIBAL ENROLLMENT OF PARENTS

Name of Father	Year	County	Name of Mother	Year	County
1 Jas. Collins	Dead	Atoka	Eliz. Collins	Dead	Atoka
2					
3					
4					
5					
6 On 1896 roll as Joe Collins					
7					
8					
9					
10					
11					
12					
13					
14					
15				Date of Application for Enrollment.	Aug 30/99
16					
17					

Choctaw By Blood Enrollment Cards 1898-1914

RESIDENCE: Atoka COUNTY. **Choctaw Nation** **Choctaw Roll** *(Not Including Freedmen)* CARD NO.
POST OFFICE: Atoka, I.T. FIELD NO. 4206

Dawes' Roll No.	NAME		Relationship to Person First Named	AGE	SEX	BLOOD	TRIBAL ENROLLMENT Year	County	No.
11793	1 Jones, Sucky	43		40	F	Full	1896	Atoka	7287
11794	2 Moore, Fannie	21	Dau	18	"	"	1896	"	7289
11795	3 Jones, Solomon	11	Son	8	M	"	1896	"	7288
11796	4 Moore, Ida	1	Dau of No2	6mo	F	"			

ENROLLMENT
~~OF NOS.~~ ~~1, 2, 3 and 4~~ ~~HEREON~~
APPROVED BY THE SECRETARY
OF INTERIOR Mar 10, 1903

TRIBAL ENROLLMENT OF PARENTS

Name of Father	Year	County	Name of Mother	Year	County
1 Ne-tak-en-lubbee	Dead	Kiamitia	Easter	Dead	Towson
2 Harris Williams	"	Jacks Fork	No1		
3 Frank Jones			No1		
4 Willie Moore	Choctaw card #3740		No2		

No2 on 1896 roll as Fannie Jones

No4 Born May 24, 1902: enrolled Nov. 25, 1902
~~No2 is now wife of Willie Moore Choctaw card #3740~~
For child of No2 see NB (March 3, 1905) #1347

#1 to 3

Date of Application for Enrollment. Aug 30/99

Bentley Okla for Nos 1,2 & 4
Atoka " " No4

RESIDENCE: Atoka COUNTY. **Choctaw Nation** **Choctaw Roll** *(Not Including Freedmen)* CARD NO.
POST OFFICE: Oconee, I.T. FIELD NO. **4207**

Dawes' Roll No.	NAME		Relationship to Person First Named	AGE	SEX	BLOOD	TRIBAL ENROLLMENT Year	County	No.
DEAD	1 ~~Guynes, Henry~~			~~36~~	~~M~~	~~1/4~~	~~1896~~	~~Atoka~~	~~4950~~
I.W. 1011	2 Henderson, Sarah	39	Wife	36	F	I.W.	1896	"	14581
11797	3 Guynes, Thomas	18	Son	15	M	1/8	1896	Atoka	4951
11798	4 " James H	16	"	13	"	1/8	1896	"	4952
11799	5 " William J	10	"	7	"	1/8	1896	"	4953
11800	6 " Ishmael W	8	"	5	"	1/8	1896	"	4954
11801	7 " Rosa L	6	Dau	3	F	1/8	1896	"	4955
11802	8 " Lorena	5	"	1	"	1/8			
11803	9 " Dora	2	"	2mo	"	1/8			

ENROLLMENT OF NOS. 2 HEREON APPROVED BY THE SECRETARY OF INTERIOR Oct 21 1904

No.8 Affidavit of birth to be supplied:- Filed Oct 26/99

No.9 Enrolled May 23, 1901

No1 died Aug 6 1902, proof filed Nov 22, 1902

TRIBAL ENROLLMENT OF PARENTS

	Name of Father	Year	County	Name of Mother	Year	County
1	~~John Guynes~~	~~Dead~~	~~Non Citz~~	~~Manda Guynes~~	~~Dead~~	~~Choctaw~~
2	George Odgen[sic]	"	" "	Mary E Odgen	"	Non Citz
3	No1			No2		
4	No1			No2		
5	No1			No2		
6	No1			No2		
7	No1			No2		
8	No1			No2		
9	No.1			No.2		

ENROLLMENT OF NOS. 3,4,5,6,7,8 and 9 HEREON APPROVED BY THE SECRETARY OF INTERIOR Mar 10 1903

No.1 hereon dismissed under order of the Commission to the Five Civilized Tribes of March 31, 1905.

No4 on 1896 roll as Jas. H. Guynes
~~No5 " 1896 " " Wm "~~
~~No6 " 1896 " " Ishmael W "~~
No7 " 1896 " " Rosa Lee "
First four were admitted by Act of
~~Choctaw Council, approved Dec 20/89~~
~~No4 was admitted as J. H. Guynes~~
No2 on 1896 roll as Sarah Gunners

#1 to 8
Date of Application for Enrollment.
Aug 30/99

No2 goes also by the name of Sallie. See letter of No1 filed June 15 1901

RESIDENCE: Blue COUNTY. **Choctaw Nation** **Choctaw Roll** *(Not Including Freedmen)* CARD NO.
POST OFFICE: Boggy Depot, I.T. FIELD NO. **4208**

Dawes' Roll No.	NAME	Relationship to Person First Named	AGE	SEX	BLOOD	TRIBAL ENROLLMENT Year	County	No.
DEAD	~~Barnett, Melvina~~	~~Named~~	~~21~~	~~F~~	~~Full~~	~~1896~~	~~Blue~~	~~9787~~
11804	Neal Annie 16	Sister	13	"	1/2	1896	"	9788
11805	" Nancy L 12	"	9	"S	1/2	1896	"	9789

ENROLLMENT OF NOS. 2 and 3 HEREON APPROVED BY THE SECRETARY OF INTERIOR Mar 10 1903

No.1 hereon dismissed under order of the Commission to the Five Civilized Tribes of March 31, 1905.

For child of No2 see NB (Apr 26-06) Card #317

TRIBAL ENROLLMENT OF PARENTS

Name of Father	Year	County	Name of Mother	Year	County
~~Barnett~~	~~Dead~~	~~Choctaw~~	~~Molsey Neal~~	~~Dead~~	~~Blue~~
Harvey Neal		Non Citz	" "		
" "		" "	" "		

No1 Died March 25, 1900. Proof of death filed March 6 1905
No1 on 1896 roll as Melvina Neal
No3 " 1896 " " Nancy "

Guardian of Nos 2 and 3 is N.A. Perkins, Choctaw card #3437
11/17/02

No.3 died - - 1901: Enrollment cancelled by Department July 8, 1904
Name of No.3 restored to roll under Departmental authority of June 1, 1905
(I.T.D. 5562 - 1905) she being alive on Sept. 25, 1902 June 9, 1905

Date of Application for Enrollment Aug 30/99

RESIDENCE: Jacks Fork COUNTY.
POST OFFICE: Tushkahomma[sic] I.T.

Choctaw Nation **Choctaw Roll** *(Not Including Freedmen)* CARD NO. FIELD NO. **4209**

Dawes' Roll No.	NAME		Relationship to Person First Named	AGE	SEX	BLOOD	TRIBAL ENROLLMENT Year	County	No.
11806	1 Baker, Benjamin	69	First Named	66	M	Full	1896	Jacks Fork	1896
11807	2 " Selina	51	Wife	48	F	"	1896	" "	1896
11808	3 " Charles	17	G.S.	14	M	"	1896	" "	1898
11809	4 " Lena	15	G.D.	12	F	"	1896	" "	7345

ENROLLMENT OF NOS. 1,2,3 and 4 HEREON APPROVED BY THE SECRETARY OF INTERIOR Mar 10 1903

TRIBAL ENROLLMENT OF PARENTS

Name of Father	Year	County	Name of Mother	Year	County
1 Robert Baker	Dead	Blue	An-thle-tuna	Dead	Mississippi
2 Pe-he-li-chee	"	Jacks Fork	Jincy	"	Jacks Fork
3 Folsom McGee		" "	Susan Baker	"	" "
4 Willis Jones		" "	" "	"	" "

~~No3 on 1896 roll as Charles Brown~~
No4 " 1896 " " Linnie Jones

Date of Application for Enrollment. Aug 30/99

Choctaw By Blood Enrollment Cards 1898-1914

RESIDENCE: Jackson COUNTY. **Choctaw Nation** **Choctaw Roll** *(Not Including Freedmen)* CARD NO.
POST OFFICE: Mayhew, I.T. FIELD NO. 4210

Dawes' Roll No.	NAME	Relationship to Person First Named	AGE	SEX	BLOOD	TRIBAL ENROLLMENT Year	County	No.
11810	1 Hampton, Elizabeth 31		28	F	Full	1893	Jackson	352
11811	2 McCoy, Hannah 8	Dau	5	"	"			
11812	3 Carnes, Incy 7	"	3	"	"			
14900	4 Carnes, John 2	Son	2	M	"			
	5							
	6							
	7							
	8 ENROLLMENT OF NOS. 1,2 and 3 HEREON APPROVED BY THE SECRETARY							
	9 OF INTERIOR Mar 10 1903							
	10							
	11							
	12							
	13 ENROLLMENT OF NOS. 4 HEREON							
	14 APPROVED BY THE SECRETARY OF INTERIOR May 21 1903							
	15							
	16							
	17							

TRIBAL ENROLLMENT OF PARENTS

Name of Father	Year	County	Name of Mother	Year	County
1 Abel Hampton	Dead	Atoka	Ettie Hampton	Dead	Atoka
2 Price McCoy	"	"	No1		
3 Lymon Carnes		"	No1		
4 Ellis Carnes	1896	Jackson	No1		
5					
6					
7					
8					
9					
10					

11 No1 on 1893 Pay Roll, Page 39, No. 352
12 Jackson Co
13 ~~Nos 2-3 Affidavits of birth to be supplied:- Filed Oct 26/99~~
14 No.1 on 1896 Choctaw roll as Elizabeth Byington; page 45 #1834
15 No.2 " 1896 " " " Hannah " " " " #1835
~~No.3 " 1896 " " " Levinia " " " " #1836~~
16 ~~No4 Born Oct 30, 1900. Application made 2/23/01. Proof of birth filed March 7/03.~~
17 For child of No.1 see NB (Apr 26, 1906) Card No.6

#1 to 3
Date of Application for Enrollment.
Aug 30/99

RESIDENCE: Atoka COUNTY. **Choctaw Nation** **Choctaw Roll** *(Not Including Freedmen)* CARD NO.
POST OFFICE: Lehigh, I.T. FIELD NO. 4211

Dawes' Roll No.	NAME	Relationship to Person First Named	AGE	SEX	BLOOD	TRIBAL ENROLLMENT Year	County	No.
11813	1 Roberts, Sampson 48	First Named	45	M	Full	1896	Atoka	10983
	2							
	3							
	4							
	5							
	6							
	7							
	8							
	9							
	10							
	11							
	12							
	13							
	14							
	15							
	16							
	17							

ENROLLMENT
OF NOS. 1 HEREON
APPROVED BY THE SECRETARY
OF INTERIOR MAR 10 1903

TRIBAL ENROLLMENT OF PARENTS

Name of Father	Year	County	Name of Mother	Year	County
1 Jackson Roberts	Dead	Atoka	Sally Roberts	Dead	Atoka
2					
3					
4					
5					
6					
7 No.1 husband of Eliza Byington, Choctaw card #4023					
8					
9					
10					
11					
12					
13					
14					
15				Date of Application for Enrollment.	Aug 30/99
16					
17					

RESIDENCE: Chickasaw Natn COUNTY. **Choctaw Nation** **Choctaw Roll** *(Not Including Freedmen)* CARD NO.
POST OFFICE: Durwood, I.T. FIELD NO. 4212

Dawes' Roll No.		NAME	Relationship to Person First Named	AGE	SEX	BLOOD	TRIBAL ENROLLMENT Year	County	No.
✓ *	1	Swagger, Sarah	✓	37	F	1/8			
	7	Record in Choctaw #5082							

TRIBAL ENROLLMENT OF PARENTS

	Name of Father	Year	County	Name of Mother	Year	County
1	W. R. Sessums		Choctaw	Eliza A Sessums		Non Citz

5 No1 Denied in 96 Case #452
6 Admitted by U.S. Court, Central Dist,
7 Jany 20/98, Case No 10. As to residence see her testimony
8 Judgment of U.S. Ct admitting No1 vacated and set aside by Decree of Choctaw Chickasaw Citizenship Court Dec 17 '02
9 No1 now in C.C.C.C. Case #36
10 No1 denied in C.C.C.C. Case #36 March 9 '04

DENIED CITIZENSHIP BY THE CHOCTAW AND CHICKASAW CITIZENSHIP COURT

Date of Application for Enrollment. Aug 30/99

RESIDENCE: Jacks Fork COUNTY. **Choctaw Nation** **Choctaw Roll** *(Not Including Freedmen)* CARD NO.
POST OFFICE: Stringtown, I.T. FIELD NO. 4213

Dawes' Roll No.		NAME		Relationship to Person First Named	AGE	SEX	BLOOD	TRIBAL ENROLLMENT Year	County	No.
11814	1	Bond, Simeon	33		30	M	Full	1896	Jacks Fork	1909
11815	2	" Silway	50	Wife	47	F	"	1896	" "	1910
11816	3	" Eleas	6	Son	3	M	"	1896	" "	1912
11817	4	" Mila S	13	Ward	10	F	"	1896	" "	1911
11818	5	Wilson, Josiah	11	S.S.	8	M	"	1896	" "	14096
11819	6	Bond, Derias	1	Son	8mo	M	"			

ENROLLMENT OF NOS. 1,2,3,4,5 and 6 HEREON APPROVED BY THE SECRETARY OF INTERIOR Mar 10 1903

TRIBAL ENROLLMENT OF PARENTS

	Name of Father	Year	County	Name of Mother	Year	County
1	Moses Bond		Jacks Fork	Narcissa Bond	Dead	Jacks Fork
2	James Peter	Dead	" "	Mary Hampton	"	" "
3	No1			No2		
4	Loring Meshoticubby		Atoka	Susie Lolin	Dead	Atoka
5	John Wilson	Dead	Jacks Fork	No2		
6	№1			№2		

No2 on 1896 roll as Selina Bond
No3 " 1896 " " Elias S Bond
No4 " 1896 " " Millie S "
~~№6 Born Sept 12, 1901: enrolled May 13, 1902~~
For child of Nos 1&2 see NB (March 3, 1905) #1348

#1 to 5
Date of Application for Enrollment.
Aug 30/99

Choctaw By Blood Enrollment Cards 1898-1914

RESIDENCE: Atoka COUNTY. **Choctaw Nation** **Choctaw Roll** (*Not Including Freedmen*) CARD NO.
POST OFFICE: Oconee, I.T. FIELD NO. 4214

Dawes' Roll No.		NAME	Relationship to Person First Named	AGE	SEX	BLOOD	TRIBAL ENROLLMENT Year	County	No.
	1	Cantrell, Ellen C	Named	48	F	1/4			
	2	" Thomas J	Son	23	M	1/8			
	3	" Oscar	"	20	"	1/8			
	4	" Lillie J	Dau	12	F	1/8			
	5	" Susan E	Grand dau	3mo	F	1/16			
	6								
	7								
	8								
	9	DISMISSED							
	10	SEP 22 1904							
	11								
	12								
	13								
	14								
	15								
	16								
	17								

TRIBAL ENROLLMENT OF PARENTS

	Name of Father	Year	County	Name of Mother	Year	County
1	William West		Non Citz	Susan West	Dead	Choctaw
2	William Cantrell	Dead	" "	No1		
3	" "	"	" "	No1		
4	" "	"	" "	No1		
5	No.2			Edner Cantrell		nin-citizen

No1 to 4 Denied in 96 Case #968 See also 905 - 1106

Admitted by U.S. Court, Central Dist
Jany 18/98, Case No 30. As to residence, see testimony of No1

No.2 is now the husband of Edner Cantrell, a non-citizen:
evidence of marriage filed Jany 8, 1902

No.5 born Oct. 8, 1901: Enrolled Jany 8, 1902

Judgment of U.S. Ct admitting No1 to 4 incl. vacated and set aside by Decree of Choctaw Chickasaw Citizenship Court Dec 17'02

No appeal to C.C.C.C.

For child of No2 see NB #981 (Act Apr 26-1906)
" " " No4 " " #1181 " " "

Date of Application for Enrollment. Aug 31/99

RESIDENCE: Atoka COUNTY. **Choctaw Nation** **Choctaw Roll** *(Not Including Freedmen)* CARD NO. / FIELD NO. 4215

POST OFFICE: Atoka, I.T.

Dawes' Roll No.		NAME	Relationship to Person First Named	AGE	SEX	BLOOD	TRIBAL ENROLLMENT Year	County	No.
	1	~~Shockey, Louisa~~	~~Named~~	~~56~~	~~F~~	~~1/4~~			
	2	~~Crockett, Arthur~~	~~G.S.~~	~~10~~	~~M~~	~~1/16~~			

No 1&2 DISMISSED

DEC 24 1904

TRIBAL ENROLLMENT OF PARENTS

	Name of Father	Year	County	Name of Mother	Year	County
1	~~William West~~		~~Non Citz~~	~~Susan West~~	~~Dead~~	~~Choctaw~~
2	~~Jas. Crockett~~	~~Dead~~	" "	~~Ara L Crockett~~	"	"

Admitted by U.S. Court, Central Dist, Jany 18-98, Case No 30. As to residence, see testimony of No1

~~Judgment of U.S. Ct admitting No vacated and set aside by Decree of Choctaw Chickasaw Citizenship Court Dec 17'02~~

No appeal to C.C.C.C.

Date of Application for Enrollment. Aug 31/99

P.O. address is now Cumberland I.T. 6/28/01

Choctaw By Blood Enrollment Cards 1898-1914

ENCE: Chickasaw Nation ~~COUNTY.~~ **Choctaw Nation** **Choctaw Roll** *(Not Including Freedmen)* CARD NO.
OFFICE: Cumberland, I.T. FIELD NO. 4216

es' No.		NAME	Relationship to Person First Named	AGE	SEX	BLOOD	TRIBAL ENROLLMENT Year	County	No.
	1	M^c^Dowell Matilda		54	F	1/4			
	2	"	Dau	24	"	1/8			
	3	"	"	22	"	1/8			
	4	Munkus,	G.Dau	7mo	F	1/16			
	5								
	6								
Nos 1 2 3 & 4	7	DISMISSED							
	8	DEC 24 1904							
	9								
	10								
	11								
	12								
	13								
	14								
	15								
	16								
	17								

TRIBAL ENROLLMENT OF PARENTS

	Name of Father	Year	County	Name of Mother	Year	County
1	William West		Non Citz	Susan West	Dead	Choctaw
2	Robt M^c^Dowell	Dead	" "	No1		
3	" "	"	" "	No1		
4	Joseph F Munkus		non-citizen	№2		
5						
6						

Nos1,2&3 Admitted by U S. Court, Central Dist, Jany 18-98 Case No 30. As to residence, see her testimony – No1
№2 is now the wife of Joseph F Munkus- non-citizen. See affidavit of №1 relative t the marriage, also letter from I. P. Clay filed Oct. 6, 1902
№4 Born March 1, 1902, enrolled Oct. 6, 1902
Judgment of U.S. Ct admitting Nos 1, 2 & 3 vacated and set aside by Decree of Choctaw Chickasaw Citizenship Court Dec 17 '02
No appeal to C.C.C.C.

Date of Application for Enrollment.
Aug 31/99

P.O. Ara IT 7/23/04

Choctaw By Blood Enrollment Cards 1898-1914

RESIDENCE: Jacks Fork COUNTY. **Choctaw Nation** **Choctaw Roll** *(Not Including Freedmen)* CARD NO.
POST OFFICE: Stringtown, I.T. FIELD NO. 4217

Dawes' Roll No.		NAME	Relationship to Person First Named	AGE	SEX	BLOOD	TRIBAL ENROLLMENT Year	County	No.
11820	1	Baker, Benjamin F 42		39	M	Full	1896	Jacks Fork	1931
11821	2	" Annie 16	Dau	13	F	"	1896	" "	1933
11822	3	" Julia 13	"	10	"	"	1896	" "	1934
11823	4	" Alexander 10	Son	7	M	"	1896	" "	1935
DEAD.	5	~~" Esther DEAD~~	~~Dau~~	~~1½~~	~~F~~	~~"~~			
DEAD.	6	~~" Emeline DEAD~~	~~"~~	~~1½~~	~~"~~	~~"~~			

ENROLLMENT
OF NOS. 1,2,3 and 4 HEREON
APPROVED BY THE SECRETARY
OF INTERIOR MAR 10 1903

No. 5 and 6 HEREON DISMISSED UNDER ORDER OF THE COMMISSION TO THE FIVE CIVILIZED TRIBES OF MARCH 31, 1905.

See Cards 7- 3100 & 3241
also 7- 77B 1154

TRIBAL ENROLLMENT OF PARENTS

	Name of Father	Year	County	Name of Mother	Year	County
1	Benj Baker		Jacks Fork	Sukey Baker	Dead	Jacks Fork
2	No1			Betsy Baker	"	" "
3	No1			" "	"	" "
4	No1			" "	"	" "
5	~~No1~~			~~" "~~	~~"~~	~~" "~~
6	~~No1~~			~~" "~~	~~"~~	~~" "~~

No1 on 1896 roll as Bilinsie F Baker
No2 " 1896 " " Emy "
~~Nos 5-6 Affidavits of birth to be supplied:~~ Filed Oct 26/99
No6 died 29 day October, 1899
Proof of death filed Dec 30, 1902
~~No5 died October 19, 1899~~
~~Proof of death filed Dec 30, 1902~~

Date of Application for Enrollment.
Aug 31/99

Choctaw By Blood Enrollment Cards 1898-1914

RESIDENCE: Atoka COUNTY. **Choctaw Nation** **Choctaw Roll** *(Not Including Freedmen)* CARD NO.
POST OFFICE: Atoka, I.T. FIELD NO. 4218

Dawes' Roll No.	NAME		Relationship to Person First Named	AGE	SEX	BLOOD	TRIBAL ENROLLMENT Year	County	No.
11824	1 Folsom, Forbis	39	First Named	36	M	Full	1896	Atoka	4434
11825	2 " Czarina	26	Wife	23	F	"	1896	"	4435
	3								
	4								
	5								
	6								
	7								
	8								
	9								
	10								
	11								
	12								
	13								
	14								
	15								
	16								
	17								

ENROLLMENT
OF NOS. 1 and 2 HEREON
APPROVED BY THE SECRETARY
OF INTERIOR MAR 10 1903

TRIBAL ENROLLMENT OF PARENTS

	Name of Father	Year	County	Name of Mother	Year	County
1	Simon Folsom		Atoka	Vicey Folsom	Dead	Atoka
2		Dead	Jacks Fork	Siley Colbert	"	Jacks Fork
3						
4						
5						
6	No1 on 1896 roll as Forbes Folsom					
7						
8						
9						
10						
11						
12						
13						
14						
15				Date of Application for Enrollment.		Aug 31/99
16						
17						

Choctaw By Blood Enrollment Cards 1898-1914

RESIDENCE: Jackson COUNTY. **Choctaw Nation** **Choctaw Roll** *(Not Including Freedmen)* CARD NO.
POST OFFICE: Mayhew, I.T. FIELD NO. **4219**

Dawes' Roll No.		NAME	Relationship to Person First Named	AGE	SEX	BLOOD	TRIBAL ENROLLMENT Year	County	No.
~~11826~~	1	DIED PRIOR TO SEPTEMBER 25, 1902 ~~Anderson, Tina~~ 55	~~Named~~	~~52~~	~~F~~	~~Full~~	~~1896~~	~~Atoka~~	~~451~~
I.W. 1012	2	" William H 54	Husb	51	M	I.W.	1896	"	14265
	3								
	4								
	5								
	6								
	7								
	8								
	9								
	10								
	11								
	12								
	13								
	14								
	15								
	16								
	17								

ENROLLMENT
OF NOS. 1 HEREON
APPROVED BY THE SECRETARY
OF INTERIOR Mar 10 1903

ENROLLMENT
OF NOS. ~~~ 2 ~~~ HEREON
APPROVED BY THE SECRETARY
OF INTERIOR Oct 21 1904

TRIBAL ENROLLMENT OF PARENTS

	Name of Father	Year	County	Name of Mother	Year	County
1	~~Cha-fa-tubbee~~	~~Dead~~		~~Ya-key~~	~~Dead~~	~~Skullyville~~
2	Wm Anderson	"	Non Citz		"	Non Citz
3						
4						
5						
6						
7						
8						
9						
10						
11						
12						
13						
14						
15						
16						
17						

No2- As to marriage, see testimony
of Rev Joseph H Murrow

#2 on 96 Roll as W^m H Anderson
No2 now husband of Nancy Lewis on Choctaw card #1741: evidence
of marriage filed Dec. 6, 1902
~~No1 died April 10, 1901. Enrollment cancelled by Department July 8, 1904~~

Date of Application for Enrollment.
Aug 31/99

P.O. Antlers I.T. 12/1/03

Dec 15 1903 P.O. Atoka I.T

Choctaw By Blood Enrollment Cards 1898-1914

RESIDENCE: Atoka COUNTY. **Choctaw Nation** **Choctaw Roll** *(Not Including Freedmen)* CARD NO.
POST OFFICE: Legal, I.T. FIELD NO. 4220

Dawes' Roll No.	NAME	Relationship to Person First Named	AGE	SEX	BLOOD	TRIBAL ENROLLMENT Year	County	No.
11827	1 Riddle, George 34 DIED PRIOR TO SEPTEMBER 25, 1902		33	M	Full	1896	Sans Bois	10688
11828	2 " Siney 31	Wife	28	F	"	1896	" "	10689
	3							
	4							
	5							
	6							
	7							
	8							
	9							
	10							
	11							
	12							
	13							
	14							
	15							
	16							
	17							

ENROLLMENT OF NOS. 1 and 2 HEREON APPROVED BY THE SECRETARY OF INTERIOR Mar 10 1903

TRIBAL ENROLLMENT OF PARENTS

Name of Father	Year	County	Name of Mother	Year	County
1 Jerry Riddie	Dead	Sans Bois	Lucy Bohanan		Atoka
2 Anderson King		Atoka	Sophia King	Dead	"
3					
4					
5					
6 No 1 died Sept 22, 1900: Enrollment cancelled by Department July 8, 1904					
7					
8					
9					
10					
11					
12					
13					
14					
15				Date of Application for Enrollment.	Aug 31/99
16					
17					

RESIDENCE: Atoka COUNTY. **Choctaw Nation** **Choctaw Roll** *(Not Including Freedmen)* CARD NO.
POST OFFICE: Legal, I.T. FIELD NO. 4221

Dawes' Roll No.	NAME		Relationship to Person First Named	AGE	SEX	BLOOD	TRIBAL ENROLLMENT Year	County	No.
11829	1 Harkins, William	27		24	M	Full	1896	Sans Bois	5109
11830	2 " Sillen	23	Wife	20	F	"	1896	" "	5110
	3								
	4								
	5								
	6								
	7								
	8								
	9								
	10								
	11								
	12								
	13								
	14								
	15								
	16								
	17								

ENROLLMENT OF NOS. 1 and 2 HEREON APPROVED BY THE SECRETARY OF INTERIOR Mar 10 1903

TRIBAL ENROLLMENT OF PARENTS

Name of Father	Year	County	Name of Mother	Year	County
1 Nelson Harkins	Dead	Sans Bois	Eliz Harkins	Dead	Skullyville
2 Sim Bohanan	"	" "	Lucy Bohanan		Atoka
3					
4					
5					
6					
7 No1 on 1896 roll as Wm Harkins					
8					
9					
10					
11					
12					
13					
14					Date of Application for Enrollment.
15					Aug 31/99
16					
17					

RESIDENCE: Jackson COUNTY. **Choctaw Nation** **Choctaw Roll** (*Not Including Freedmen*) CARD NO.
POST OFFICE: Mayhew, I.T. FIELD NO. 4222

Dawes' Roll No.		NAME		Relationship to Person First Named	AGE	SEX	BLOOD	TRIBAL ENROLLMENT Year	County	No.
11831	1	Brown, Moses	50	First Named	47	M	Full	1896	Tobucksy	915
11832	2	" Mila	38	Wife	35	F	"	1896	"	916
11833	3	" David	16	Son	13	M	"	1896	"	917
11834	4	" Elijah	15	"	12	"	"	1896	"	918
	5									
	6									
	7									
	8									
	9									
	10									
	11									
	12									
	13									
	14									
	15									
	16									
	17									

ENROLLMENT
OF NOS. 1,2,3 and 4 HEREON
APPROVED BY THE SECRETARY
OF INTERIOR Mar. 10, 1903

TRIBAL ENROLLMENT OF PARENTS

	Name of Father	Year	County	Name of Mother	Year	County
1	John Brown	Dead	Tobucksy	Ima Brown	Dead	Sans Bois
2		"	Sans Bois	Liney Durant		Jackson
3	No.1			No.2		
4	No.1			No.2		
5						
6						
7	No.2 on 1896 roll as Minnie Brown					
8	No.4 " 1896	" "	Eliza "			
9						
10						
11						
12						
13						
14						Date of Application for Enrollment.
15						Aug 31/99
16						
17						

RESIDENCE: Atoka COUNTY. **Choctaw Nation** Choctaw Roll *(Not Including Freedmen)* CARD NO.

POST OFFICE: Atoka, I.T. FIELD NO. 4223

Dawes' Roll No.		NAME		Relationship to Person First Named	AGE	SEX	BLOOD	TRIBAL ENROLLMENT		
								Year	County	No.
~~11835~~	1	Died prior to September 25, 1902 ~~Durant, Hicks~~	61	~~First Named~~	~~58~~	~~M~~	~~Full~~	~~1896~~	~~Atoka~~	~~3588~~
11836	2	" Rhoda	46	Wife	43	F	"	1896	"	3589
	3									
	4									
	5									
	6									
	7									
	8									
	9									
	10									
	11									
	12									
	13									
	14									
	15									
	16									
	17									

ENROLLMENT
OF NOS. 1 and 2 HEREON
APPROVED BY THE SECRETARY
OF INTERIOR Mar 10, 1903

TRIBAL ENROLLMENT OF PARENTS

	Name of Father	Year	County	Name of Mother	Year	County
1	~~Ellis Durant~~	~~Dead~~	~~Eagle~~	~~Pe-sa-cha-na~~	~~dead~~	~~Eagle~~
2		"	"	Loh-ma-te-ma	"	Jackson
3						
4						
5						
6						
7	No.1 died Jan. 19, 1900: Enrollment cancelled by Department Sept. 16, 1904					
8						
9						
10						
11						
12						
13						
14						
15					Date of Application for Enrollment.	Aug 31/99
16						
17						

RESIDENCE: Jackson COUNTY. **Choctaw Nation** **Choctaw Roll** *(Not Including Freedmen)* CARD NO.
POST OFFICE: Mayhew, I.T. FIELD NO. 4224

Dawes' Roll No.	NAME		Relationship to Person First Named	AGE	SEX	BLOOD	TRIBAL ENROLLMENT Year	County	No.
11837	1 LeFlore, Abel	53	First Named	50	M	Full	1896	Jackson	8152
11838	2 " Moses	17	Son	14	"	"	1896	"	8155
	3								
	4								
	5								
	6								
	7								
	8								
	9								
	10								
	11								
	12								
	13								
	14								
	15								
	16								
	17								

ENROLLMENT
OF NOS. 1 and 2 HEREON
APPROVED BY THE SECRETARY
OF INTERIOR Mar 10 1903

TRIBAL ENROLLMENT OF PARENTS

Name of Father	Year	County	Name of Mother	Year	County
1 Simmie LeFlore	Dead	Jackson	Lo-me-tu-na	Dead	Jackson
2 No.1			Mary Tulhko		"
3					
4					
5					
6					
7					
8					
9					
10					
11					
12					
13					
14					Date of Application for Enrollment.
15					Aug 31/99
16					
17					

Choctaw By Blood Enrollment Cards 1898-1914

RESIDENCE: Jackson COUNTY. **Choctaw Nation** **Choctaw Roll** *(Not Including Freedmen)* CARD NO.
POST OFFICE: Mayhew, I.T. FIELD NO. 4225

Dawes' Roll No.	NAME		Relationship to Person First Named	AGE	SEX	BLOOD	TRIBAL ENROLLMENT Year	County	No.
11839	1 Lewis, William	23		20	M	Full	1896	Jackson	8257
11840	2 " Phoebe	21	Wife	18	F	"	1896	"	8154
	3								
	4								
	5								
	6								
	7								
	8								
	9								
	10								
	11								
	12								
	13								
	14								
	15								
	16								
	17								

ENROLLMENT OF NOS. 1 and 2 HEREON APPROVED BY THE SECRETARY OF INTERIOR Mar 10 1903

TRIBAL ENROLLMENT OF PARENTS

Name of Father	Year	County	Name of Mother	Year	County
1 Josen Lewis	Dead	Atoka	Rhoda Lewis	Dead	Atoka
2 Abel LeFlore		Jackson	Loh-ma-hema	"	Jackson
3					
4					
5					
6 No.2 on 1896 roll as Phoebe LeFlore					
7					
8					
9					
10					
11					
12					
13					
14					Date of Application for Enrollment.
15					Aug 31/99
16					
17 P.O. Atoka I.T.					

Choctaw By Blood Enrollment Cards 1898-1914

RESIDENCE: Atoka COUNTY. **Choctaw Nation** **Choctaw Roll** *(Not Including Freedmen)* CARD NO.
POST OFFICE: Atoka, I.T. FIELD NO. **4226**

Dawes' Roll No.		NAME		Relationship to Person First Named	AGE	SEX	BLOOD	TRIBAL ENROLLMENT Year	County	No.
11841	1	Roberts, Ramsey	30		27	M	Full	1896	Atoka	10963
11842	2	" Elias	10	Son	6	M	1/2	1896	"	10964
	3									
	4									
	5									
	6									
	7									
	8									
	9									
	10									
	11									
	12									
	13									
	14									
	15									
	16									
	17									

ENROLLMENT
OF NOS. 1 and 2 HEREON
APPROVED BY THE SECRETARY
OF INTERIOR Mar 10 1903

TRIBAL ENROLLMENT OF PARENTS

	Name of Father	Year	County	Name of Mother	Year	County
1	Stephen Roberts		Atoka	Molsey Roberts	Dead	Towson
2	No.1			Susan Jones	1896	Chickasaw
3						
4						
5						
6						
7						
8						
9						
10						
11						
12						
13						
14						
15						
16						
17						

On 1896 roll as Robert Ramsey
No.2 enrolled on Chickasaw Card #92: Sept. 2, 1898: transferred to this card Dec. 19, 1902
~~Mother of No.2 is Susan Jones on Chickasaw card #92~~

Date of Application for Enrollment Aug 31/99
No.2 Sept. 2, 1898

RESIDENCE: Atoka COUNTY. **Choctaw Nation** Choctaw Roll (Not Including Freedmen) CARD NO.
POST OFFICE: Lehigh, I.T. FIELD NO. 4227

Dawes' Roll No.	NAME	Relationship to Person First Named	AGE	SEX	BLOOD	TRIBAL ENROLLMENT Year	County	No.
11843	1 Peter, Davis 30	First Named	27	M	Full	1896	Atoka	10541
11844	2 " Susan 19	Wife	16	F	"	1896	"	6036

ENROLLMENT OF NOS. 1 and 2 HEREON APPROVED BY THE SECRETARY OF INTERIOR MAR 10 1903

TRIBAL ENROLLMENT OF PARENTS

	Name of Father	Year	County	Name of Mother	Year	County
1	William Peter		Atoka		Dead	Atoka
2	Holston	Dead	Blue	Edna Holston	"	Blue

No2 on 1896 roll as Susan Holston

Date of Application for Enrollment.
Aug 31/99

RESIDENCE: Atoka COUNTY. **Choctaw Nation** **Choctaw Roll** *(Not Including Freedmen)* CARD NO.
POST OFFICE: Coalgate, I.T. FIELD NO. 4228

Dawes' Roll No.	NAME		Relationship to Person First Named	AGE	SEX	BLOOD	TRIBAL ENROLLMENT Year	County	No.
11845	1 Frazier, Hudson	43	First Named	40	M	Full	1896	Blue	4419
11846	2 " Martha	53	Wife	50	F	"	1893	Atoka	795
11847	3 Washington, Ellen	19	Dau	16	"	"	1896	Blue	4342
11848	4 Frazier, Winnie	13	"	10	"	"	1896	"	4418
11849	5 Washington, Ida	1	Gr Dau	5mo	F	"			
	6								
	7								
	8								
	9 ENROLLMENT								
	OF NOS. 1,2,3,4 and 5 HEREON								
	10 APPROVED BY THE SECRETARY								
	OF INTERIOR Mar 10 1903								
	11								
	12								
	13								
	14								
	15								
	16								
	17								

TRIBAL ENROLLMENT OF PARENTS

Name of Father	Year	County	Name of Mother	Year	County
1 Jackson Frazier	Dead	Blue	Tennessee Frazier	Dead	Blue
2	"	Jacks Fork		"	Atoka
3 No 1			No 2		
4 No 1			No 2		
5 Marcus Washington	1896	Blue	№3		

No2 on 1893 Pay Roll, Page 76, No. 795, Atoka Co, as Martha M^c^Gee

No4 on 1896 roll as Wincey Frazier

~~№3 is now the wife of Marcus Washington on Choctaw card #3719. Evidence of~~ marriage filed Nov. 5, 1902

№5 Born June 18, 1902 enrolled Nov. 5, 1902

For child of No1 see NB (Apr 26, 1906) Card No. 141

~~" " " No4 " " " " 727~~

" " " No1 " " (March 3, 1905) " " 1499

#1 to 4 inc

Date of Application for Enrollment. Aug 31/99

P.O. Foster, I.T.
10/20/02

RESIDENCE: Blue COUNTY. **Choctaw Nation** Choctaw Roll (Not Including Freedmen) CARD NO.
POST OFFICE: Caddo, I.T. FIELD NO. 4229

Dawes' Roll No.	NAME	Relationship to Person First Named	AGE	SEX	BLOOD	TRIBAL ENROLLMENT Year	County	No.
11850	1 Byington, Henry 51	First Named	48	M	Full	1896	Blue	1721
11851	2 " Lorena 29	Wife	26	F	"	1896	"	1722
DEAD.	3 ~~" Joseph P F~~	~~Son~~	~~6~~	~~M~~	~~"~~	~~1896~~	~~"~~	~~1723~~
11852	4 " Philip J 3	"	6mo	"	"			
15475	5 " Richard H 16	"	16	M	1/2	1893	Blue	Page 12 129

ENROLLMENT OF NOS. 1,2 and 4 HEREON APPROVED BY THE SECRETARY OF INTERIOR MAR 10 1903

ENROLLMENT OF NOS. 5 HEREON APPROVED BY THE SECRETARY OF INTERIOR MAY 9 1904

No. 3 HEREON DISMISSED UNDER ORDER OF THE COMMISSION TO THE FIVE CIVILIZED TRIBES OF MARCH 31, 1905.

TRIBAL ENROLLMENT OF PARENTS

	Name of Father	Year	County	Name of Mother	Year	County
1	Cyrus Byington	Dead	Blue	Polly Byington	Dead	Blue
2	Morris Mosely	"	"	Mary Mosely	"	"
3	~~No1~~			~~No2~~		
4	No1			No2		
5	No.1			Mary Burke		white woman

No2 on 1896 roll as Rena Byington
No3 " 1896 " " J.P.F. "
Nº1 is father of Richard Henry Byington on Choctaw card #D727

No3 died July 31, 1901; proof of death filed Nov 25, 1902
No.5 transferred from Choctaw card #D.727: see decision of Feby. 27, 1904

For child of Nos 1&2 see NB (Mar 3-05) Card #319

Date of Application for Enrollment. For Nos 1 to 4 Incl. Aug 31/99

RESIDENCE: Jackson COUNTY. **Choctaw Nation** **Choctaw Roll** CARD NO.
POST OFFICE: Jackson, I.T. *(Not Including Freedmen)* FIELD NO. 4230

Dawes' Roll No.	NAME	Relationship to Person First Named	AGE	SEX	BLOOD	TRIBAL ENROLLMENT Year	County	No.
11853	1 Tutt, Isabelle 33	First Named	30	F	Full	1893	Blue	683
I.W. 674	2 " Richard T 39	Hus	39	M	IW			
	3							
	4							
	5							
	6							
	7							
	8							
	9							
	10							
	11							
	12							
	13							
	14							
	15							
	16							
	17							

ENROLLMENT OF NOS. 1 HEREON APPROVED BY THE SECRETARY OF INTERIOR MAR 10 1903

ENROLLMENT OF NOS. 2 HEREON APPROVED BY THE SECRETARY OF INTERIOR MAR 26 1904

TRIBAL ENROLLMENT OF PARENTS

Name of Father	Year	County	Name of Mother	Year	County
1 Ison[sic] Shontubbee	Dead	Blue	Betsy Shontubbee	Dead	Blue
2 John Tutt	Dead	noncitizen	Nancy Tutt		noncitizen
3					
4					
5					
6					
7					
8					
9					
10					
11					
12					
13					
14					
15					
16					
17					

No2 transferred from Choctaw card D651 January 25, 1904
See decision of January 7, 1904
On 1893 Pay Roll, Page 65, No 683, Blue
~~Co, as Isabelle Johnson~~
~~No1 is now the wife of Richard T. Tutt on Choctaw card #D.651~~
Aug. 20, 1901

Date of Application for Enrollment.
Aug 31/99

No.2 P.O. Antlers IT 11-21-02

Choctaw By Blood Enrollment Cards 1898-1914

RESIDENCE: Jackson COUNTY. **Choctaw Nation** **Choctaw Roll** (Not Including Freedmen) CARD NO. 4231
POST OFFICE: Jackson, I.T. FIELD NO. 4

Dawes' Roll No.	NAME	Relationship to Person First Named	AGE	SEX	BLOOD	TRIBAL ENROLLMENT Year	County	No.
11854	1 Nowabbi, Hannah 24	First Named	21	F	Full	1893	Towson	45
11855	2 Foster, Thomas 3	Son	7mo	M	"			
	3							
	4							
	5							
	6							
	7							
	8							
	9							
	10							
	11							
	12							
	13							
	14							
	15							
	16							
	17							

ENROLLMENT OF NOS. 1 and 2 HEREON APPROVED BY THE SECRETARY OF INTERIOR MAR 10 1903

TRIBAL ENROLLMENT OF PARENTS

Name of Father	Year	County	Name of Mother	Year	County
1 Forbis Meashiya	Dead	Kiamitia	Molsey	Dead	Kiamitia
2 Solomon Foster		Jackson	No.1		

For child of No.1 see NB (Mar 3 1905) card #320

On 1893 Pay Roll, Page 55, No 45, Towson Co, as Hannah Meashaya

No.2 illegitimate son of No.1 and Solomon Foster on Choctaw card #4266: Enrolled Oct 29, 1900

No1 is now wife of James Nowabbi, Choctaw Card #4154, see affidavit of Silas L. Bacon filed Dec 26, 1902

#1
Date of Application for Enrollment.
Aug 31/99

P.O. seems to be Kosoma[sic] I.T.

Choctaw By Blood Enrollment Cards 1898-1914

RESIDENCE: Atoka COUNTY. **Choctaw Nation** **Choctaw Roll** *(Not Including Freedmen)* CARD NO.
POST OFFICE: Wapanucka, I.T. FIELD NO. 4232

Dawes' Roll No.	NAME	Relationship to Person First Named	AGE	SEX	BLOOD	TRIBAL ENROLLMENT Year	County	No.
11856	1 Harkins, Nelson 37	First Named	34	M	Full	1896	Blue	5891
	2							
	3							
	4							
	5							
	6							
	7							
	8							
	9							
	10							
	11							
	12							
	13							
	14							
	15							
	16							
	17							

ENROLLMENT
OF NOS. 1 HEREON
APPROVED BY THE SECRETARY
OF INTERIOR MAR 10 1903

TRIBAL ENROLLMENT OF PARENTS

Name of Father	Year	County	Name of Mother	Year	County
1 Chas. Harkins	Dead	Blue	Jincey Harkins	Dead	Blue
2					
3					
4					
5					
6					
7					
8					
9					
10					
11					
12					
13					
14					
15					
16					
17					

Date of Application for Enrollment.
Aug 31/99

RESIDENCE: Jackson COUNTY. POST OFFICE: Mayhew, I.T.

Choctaw Nation

Choctaw Roll *(Not Including Freedmen)* CARD NO. FIELD NO. 4233

Dawes' Roll No.	NAME	Relationship to Person First Named	AGE	SEX	BLOOD	TRIBAL ENROLLMENT Year	County	No.
11857	1 Patton, Moses 24	First Named	21	M	Full	1893	Blue	961

ENROLLMENT OF NOS. 1 HEREON APPROVED BY THE SECRETARY OF INTERIOR MAR 10 1903

TRIBAL ENROLLMENT OF PARENTS

Name of Father	Year	County	Name of Mother	Year	County
1 Simon Patton	Dead	Blue	Lucy Patton	Dead	Jackson

On 1893 Pay Roll, Page 92, No 961, Blue Co, as Moses Patton

Also on 1896 roll, Page 267, No 10470 as Moses Perry, Jackson Co

No.1 is now the husband of Silvey Billis on Choctaw card #4243: April 11, 1905

See N.B. (Apr. 26,06) Card No 280 for child of No.1

Date of Application for Enrollment. Aug 31/99

P.O. Boswell, I.T.
April 11, 1905

Choctaw By Blood Enrollment Cards 1898-1914

RESIDENCE: Atoka COUNTY. **Choctaw Nation** **Choctaw Roll** *(Not Including Freedmen)* CARD NO.
POST OFFICE: Atoka, I.T. FIELD NO. 4234

Dawes' Roll No.	NAME		Relationship to Person First Named	AGE	SEX	BLOOD	TRIBAL ENROLLMENT Year	County	No.
11858	1 Steel, Thomas	42	First Named	39	M	Full	1893	Atoka	952
DEAD.	2 ~~" Lucy~~		~~Wife~~	~~57~~	~~F~~	~~"~~	~~1893~~	~~"~~	~~175~~
11859	3 " Andrew	13	Son	10	M	"	1893	"	953
11860	4 Harkins, Levi	21	S.Son	18	"	"	1893	Jackson	78
11861	5 Cooper, Mattie	13	Ward	10	F	"	1893	Kiamitia	461
11862	6 Miashaya, Rinda	12	"	9	"	"	1893	"	462
11863	7 " Adeline	10	"	7	"	"	1893	"	463

8 No2 died March 21, 1900; proof of death filed Nov 25, 1902
9 No6 on 1896 roll, Page 219, No 8746 as Rena Mishaya
10 ~~No7 on 1896 roll, Page 219,~~
11 ~~No 8747 as Adaline Mishaya~~
12 Nos 1-2-3 on 1896 roll, Page 302, Nos 11674, 11676, 11675 respectively
13 ~~under name of Still~~

ENROLLMENT OF NOS. 1,3,4,5,6 and 7 HEREON APPROVED BY THE SECRETARY OF INTERIOR MAR 10 1903

No. 2 HEREON DISMISSED UNDER ORDER OF THE COMMISSION TO THE FIVE CIVILIZED TRIBES OF MARCH 31, 1905.

TRIBAL ENROLLMENT OF PARENTS

Name of Father	Year	County	Name of Mother	Year	County
1 John Steel	Dead	Atoka	Nancy Steel	Dead	Atoka
2 ~~Jack M^c^Clure~~	~~"~~	~~"~~	~~Lixie M^c^Clure~~	~~"~~	~~"~~
3 No1			Eliz. Hampton		Jackson
4 Wallace Harkins	Dead	Jackson	No2		
5 Human Cooper	"	Kiamitia	Susan Cooper	Dead	Atoka
6 Forbis Miashaya	"	"	Susan Miashaya	"	"
7 " "	"	"	" "	"	"

No1 on 1893 Pay Roll, Page 97, No 952, Atoka Co
~~No2 " 1893 " " " 16 " 175 " "~~ as Lucy Carn
~~No3 " 1893 " " " 97 " 953 " "~~
No4 " 1893 " " " 9 " 78 Jackson Co
No5 " 1893 " " " 57 " 461 Kiamitia Co as Mandy Miashaya
~~No6 " 1893 " " " 57 " 462 " "~~
~~No7 " 1893 " " " 57 " 463 " "~~ as Edline Miashaya

Date of Application for Enrollment. Aug 31/99

Choctaw By Blood Enrollment Cards 1898-1914

RESIDENCE: Atoka COUNTY. **Choctaw Nation** **Choctaw Roll** *(Not Including Freedmen)* CARD NO.
POST OFFICE: Atoka, I.T. FIELD NO. 4235

Dawes' Roll No.		NAME		Relationship to Person First Named	AGE	SEX	BLOOD	TRIBAL ENROLLMENT Year	County	No.
11864	1	Homer, Jacob	27	First Named	24	M	Full	1896	Kiamitia	6016
11865	2	" Czarina	23	Wife	20	F	"	1896	Blue	11605
DEAD.	3	~~" Jesse~~ DEAD.		~~Son~~	~~1~~	~~M~~	"			
	4									
	5									
	6									
	7									
	8									
	9									
	10									
	11									
	12									
	13									
	14									
	15									
	16									
	17									

ENROLLMENT OF NOS. 1 and 2 HEREON APPROVED BY THE SECRETARY OF INTERIOR MAR 10 1903

No. 3 HEREON DISMISSED UNDER ORDER OF THE COMMISSION TO THE FIVE CIVILIZED TRIBES OF MARCH 31, 1905.

TRIBAL ENROLLMENT OF PARENTS

	Name of Father	Year	County	Name of Mother	Year	County
1	Wilson Homer	Dead	Kiamitia	Isabelle Homer		Jackson
2	Stephen Samuel	"	Nashoba	Sophie		Chick Natn
3	~~No1~~			~~No2~~		
4						
5						
6						
7						
8						
9						
10						
11						
12						
13						
14						
15						
16						
17						

No2 on 1896 roll as Czarina P. Samuel
No3- Affidavit of birth to be supplied: Filed Nov 2/99
~~No3 Died November 19, 1900: proof of death filed Nov 22, 1902~~

Date of Application for Enrollment. Aug 31/99

Choctaw By Blood Enrollment Cards 1898-1914

RESIDENCE: Atoka COUNTY. **Choctaw Nation** Choctaw Roll (Not Including Freedmen) CARD NO. FIELD NO. 4236

POST OFFICE: Atoka, I.T.

Dawes' Roll No.	NAME	Relationship to Person First Named	AGE	SEX	BLOOD	TRIBAL ENROLLMENT Year	County	No.
11866	1 LeFlore, Mary 48		45	F	Full	1893	Atoka	729
11867	2 " Lucy A 20	Dau	17	"	"	1893	"	731

ENROLLMENT OF NOS. 1 and 2 HEREON APPROVED BY THE SECRETARY OF INTERIOR MAR 10 1903

No.2 – Died prior to September 25, 1902; not entitled to land or money.
(See Indian Office letter September 22, 1910, D.C. #1306-1910)

TRIBAL ENROLLMENT OF PARENTS

	Name of Father	Year	County	Name of Mother	Year	County
1	Taylor Durant		Atoka	Betsy Durant	Dead	Atoka
2	William Hunter	Dead	"	No1		

No1 on 1893 Pay Roll, Page 70, No 729, Atoka Co
No2 " 1893 " " " 70 " 731 " " as
Lozeam LeFlore

Date of Application for Enrollment. Aug 31/99

RESIDENCE: Atoka COUNTY. **Choctaw Nation** **Choctaw Roll** *(Not Including Freedmen)* CARD NO.
POST OFFICE: Atoka, I.T. FIELD NO. 4237

Dawes' Roll No.	NAME	Relationship to Person First Named	AGE	SEX	BLOOD	TRIBAL ENROLLMENT Year	County	No.
11868	1 Katiotubbi, Johnson 22	First Named	19	M	Full	1896	Jacks Fork	7661

ENROLLMENT OF NOS. 1 HEREON APPROVED BY THE SECRETARY OF INTERIOR MAR 10 1903

TRIBAL ENROLLMENT OF PARENTS

Name of Father	Year	County	Name of Mother	Year	County
1 Ka-tio-tubbi	Dead	Jacks Fork	Alice Katiotubbi	Dead	Jacks Fork

No 1 is now husband of Phoebe Felma on Choctaw card #4166

Date of Application for Enrollment. Aug 31/99

Choctaw By Blood Enrollment Cards 1898-1914

RESIDENCE: Jackson COUNTY. Choctaw Nation Choctaw Roll (Not Including Freedmen) CARD NO.

POST OFFICE: Mayhew, I.T. FIELD NO. 4238

Dawes' Roll No.	NAME		Relationship to Person First Named	AGE	SEX	BLOOD	TRIBAL ENROLLMENT Year	County	No.
11869	1 Hayes, Picken	39		36	M	Full	1896	Jackson	5796
~~11870~~	~~2 " Martha~~ DIED PRIOR TO SEPTEMBER 25, 1902	38	~~Wife~~	~~35~~	~~F~~	~~"~~	~~1896~~	~~"~~	~~13830~~
11871	3 Belvin, Lizzie	21	Dau	18	"	"	1896	"	5798
11872	4 Frazier, Adeline	13	S. D	10	"	"	1896	"	13831
11873	5 Williams, Rachel	11	" "	8	"	"	1896	"	13832
11874	6 Belvin, Sallie	1	G.Dau	4mo	F	"			
	7								
	8								
	9								
	10								
	11								
	12								
	13								
	14								
	15								
	16								
	17								

ENROLLMENT OF NOS. 1,2,3,4,5 and 6 HEREON APPROVED BY THE SECRETARY OF INTERIOR MAR 10 1903

TRIBAL ENROLLMENT OF PARENTS

Name of Father	Year	County	Name of Mother	Year	County
1 Nichodemus Hayes		Jackson	Siney Hayes	Dead	Jackson
~~2 John Anderson~~	~~Dead~~	~~"~~	~~Becky Anderson~~	~~"~~	~~"~~
3 No1			Winnie Hayes	"	"
4 Thomas Frazier	Dead	Jackson	No2		
5 David Williams	"	"	No2		
6 Robinson Belvin	1896	Jackson	No3		
7					
8					

No.1 on 1896 roll as Piken Hayes

~~No2 on 1896 roll as Martha Williams~~

No4 " 1896 " " Adaline "

No3 is now the wife of Robinson Belvin on Choctaw Card #4182. See letter of Peean[sic] Hayes filed Sept 26, 1901. Evidence of marriage requested.

~~No.6 Enrolled Sept 26, 1901~~

No 2 died Jan 17 1900; Enrollment cancelled by Department July 8, 1904

#1 to 5 inc
Date of Application for Enrollment.
Aug 31/99

Choctaw By Blood Enrollment Cards 1898-1914

RESIDENCE: Blue COUNTY. **Choctaw Nation** **Choctaw Roll** *(Not Including Freedmen)* CARD NO.
POST OFFICE: Bok Chito, I.T. FIELD NO. 4239

Dawes' Roll No.	NAME		Relationship to Person First Named	AGE	SEX	BLOOD	TRIBAL ENROLLMENT Year	County	No.
11875	1 Collins, Emily	22	First Named	19	F	Full	1893	Jackson	303
	2								
	3								
	4								
	5								
	6								
	7								
	8								
	9								
	10								
	11								
	12								
	13								
	14								
	15								
	16								
	17								

ENROLLMENT
OF NOS. 1 HEREON
APPROVED BY THE SECRETARY
OF INTERIOR MAR 10 1903

TRIBAL ENROLLMENT OF PARENTS

Name of Father	Year	County	Name of Mother	Year	County
1 Sampson Collins	Dead	Blue	Sophie Collins	Dead	Blue
2					
3					
4					
5					
6					
7 On 1893 Pay Roll, Page 35, No 303, Jackson Co as Emily Collin					
8					
9					
10					
11					
12					
13					
14					Date of Application for Enrollment.
15					Aug 31/99
16					
17					

RESIDENCE: Jacks Fork COUNTY. **Choctaw Nation** **Choctaw Roll** *(Not Including Freedmen)* CARD No.
POST OFFICE: Stringtown, I.T. FIELD No. 4240

Dawes' Roll No.	NAME	Relationship to Person First Named	AGE	SEX	BLOOD	TRIBAL ENROLLMENT Year	County	No.
11876	1 Miller, Edgar P 24	First Named	21	M	1/4	1896	Kiamitia	8718
I.W. 755	2 " Maggie M (25)	Wife	20	F	IW			
11877	3 " Ruby Marie 2	Dau	3mo	F	1/8			
14901	4 " Lucretia R 1	Dau	3mo	F	1/8			
	5							
	6							
	7							
	8							
	9							
	10							
	11							
	12							
	13							
	14							
	15							
	16							
	17							

ENROLLMENT OF NOS. 1 and 3 HEREON APPROVED BY THE SECRETARY OF INTERIOR MAR 10 1903

ENROLLMENT OF NOS. 4 HEREON APPROVED BY THE SECRETARY OF INTERIOR MAY 21 1903

~~ENROLLMENT~~ OF NOS. ~~~~~ 2 ~~~~~ HEREON ~~APPROVED BY THE SECRETARY~~ OF INTERIOR MAY -7 1904

TRIBAL ENROLLMENT OF PARENTS

Name of Father	Year	County	Name of Mother	Year	County
1 J. H. Miller		Non Citz	Ella Miller		Jacks Fork
2 J. E. Roach		" "	Ada Roach		Non Citz
3 No.1			No.2		
4 №1			№2		
5					
6					
7					

8 ~~No2 See Decision of March 2 '04~~
9 No3 Enrolled January 3, 1901
10 №4 Born Sept. 19, 1902, application made Dec 22, 1902. Proof of birth filed 2/2/03.

Date of Application for Enrollment.
Aug 31/99

Choctaw By Blood Enrollment Cards 1898-1914

RESIDENCE: Jacks Fork COUNTY. **Choctaw Nation** **Choctaw Roll** *(Not Including Freedmen)* CARD NO.
POST OFFICE: Stringtown, I.T. FIELD NO. 4241

Dawes' Roll No.	NAME	Relationship to Person First Named	AGE	SEX	BLOOD	TRIBAL ENROLLMENT Year	County	No.
11878	1 Spring, Joseph B 25	First Named	22	M	1/2	1893	Kiamitia	695

ENROLLMENT OF NOS. 1 HEREON APPROVED BY THE SECRETARY OF INTERIOR MAR 10 1903

TRIBAL ENROLLMENT OF PARENTS

Name of Father	Year	County	Name of Mother	Year	County
1 Jas. Spring	Dead	Kiamitia	Mary A Crowder		Jackson

On 1893 Pay Roll, Page 84, No 695, Kiamitia Co, as Joseph Spring

No.1 is now the husband of Ida E. Kelly on Choc card #1417 Dec 4, 1901

For child of No1 see NB (Apr 26 1906) #569

Date of Application for Enrollment. Aug 31/99

P.O. Ridden I.T.

Choctaw By Blood Enrollment Cards 1898-1914

RESIDENCE: Jacks Fork COUNTY. **Choctaw Nation** **Choctaw Roll** *(Not Including Freedmen)* CARD NO.
POST OFFICE: Stringtown, I.T. FIELD NO. 4242

Dawes' Roll No.	NAME		Relationship to Person First Named	AGE	SEX	BLOOD	TRIBAL ENROLLMENT Year	County	No.
11879	1 Miller, Ella J	45	First Named	42	F	1/2	1896	Kiamitia	8717
11880	2 " Samuel G	22	Son	19	M	1/4	1896	"	8719
11881	3 Glenn, Ida B	19	Dau	16	F	1/4	1896	"	8720
11882	4 Miller, William W	17	Son	14	M	1/4	1896	"	8721
11883	5 " James H Jr	14	"	11	"	1/4	1896	"	8722
11884	6 " Ruby C	11	Dau	8	F	1/4	1896	"	8723
11885	7 " Edith R	5	"	2	"	1/4			
11886	8 " Frank Wright	1	Son	2mo	M	1/4			
11887	9 Glenn, Mary Virginia	1	Grand Dau	1mo	F	1/8			
I.W. 675	10 " William T	25	Hus of No3	25	M	I.W.			

11 No.2 is now husband of No.5 on Choc #3163 (Hattie Brown)
Evidence of marriage to be supplied
12 ~~No.3 is now the wife of W.T. Glenn~~
13 on Choctaw card #D.606 Jany 11, 1901

ENROLLMENT OF NOS. 10 HEREON APPROVED BY THE SECRETARY OF INTERIOR Mar 26 1904

No.9 Enrolled Sept 30, 1901
For child of No.2 see NB (March 3,1905) #1405

TRIBAL ENROLLMENT OF PARENTS

	Name of Father	Year	County	Name of Mother	Year	County
1	William Roebuck	Dead	Kiamitia	Anna Roebuck		Kiamitia
2	James H. Miller		Intermarried	No1		
3	" " "		"	No1		
4	" " "		"	No1		
5	" " "		"	No1		
6	" " "		"	No1		
7	" " "		"	No1		
8	" " "		"	No.1		
9	W. T. Glenn		"	No3		
10	John H Glenn		non citizen	Mary Glenn		non citizen

ENROLLMENT OF NOS. 1,2,3,4,5,6,7,8 and 9 HEREON APPROVED BY THE SECRETARY OF INTERIOR Mar 10 1903

~~No2 on 1896 roll as Samuel J Miller~~
No4 " 1896 " " William "
No5 " 1896 " " Jas H "
~~No6 " 1896 " " Reuben C "~~
~~No7- Affidavit of birth to be~~
supplied:- Filed Oct 26/99
Husband James H Miller on
Card No D.394. Transferred to Choctaw card #5752 March 17, 1904
P.O. Grant I.T.

~~No10 transferred from Choctaw card D.606~~
Jan 21,1904. See decision of Jan 4, 1904
No.8 Enrolled July 27 1901

#1 to 7
Date of Application for Enrollment.
Aug 31/99

For child of Nos 3&10 see NB (Apr 26 '06) Card #81
" " " " " " 42 " (Mar 3 '05) " #321

RESIDENCE: Jackson COUNTY. **Choctaw Nation** **Choctaw Roll** *(Not Including Freedmen)* CARD NO.
POST OFFICE: Jackson, I.T. FIELD NO. 4243

Dawes' Roll No.	NAME	Relationship to Person First Named	AGE	SEX	BLOOD	TRIBAL ENROLLMENT Year	County	No.
11888	1 Billis, Silvey 29	First Named	26	F	Full	1893	Blue	235
~~11889~~	~~2 Ramsey, Susan 4~~ DIED PRIOR TO SEPTEMBER 25, 1902	~~Dau~~	~~1~~	~~F~~	~~"~~			
15858	3 Patton, Simon 1	Son	1	M	"			

ENROLLMENT
OF NOS. 1 and 2 HEREON
APPROVED BY THE SECRETARY
OF INTERIOR MAR 10 1903

ENROLLMENT
OF NOS. ~~~~ 3 ~~~~ HEREON
APPROVED BY THE SECRETARY
OF INTERIOR JUN 12 1905

TRIBAL ENROLLMENT OF PARENTS

Name of Father	Year	County	Name of Mother	Year	County
1 Thompson Billis	Dead	Jackson	Sally Chubbee	Dead	Jackson
~~2 Leas Ramsey~~	~~Dead~~	~~Jackson~~	~~No1~~		
3 Moses Patton	1893	Blue	No.1		

No1 on 1893 Pay Roll, Page 22, No 235, Blue Co, as Sibbay Billis

~~No1 also on 1896 roll, Page 279, No 10879 as Silway Ramsey, Jackson Co~~

No2 died Oct 16, 1899: Enrollment cancelled by Department Dec 14, 1904

Application was made for enrollment of No.3, Dec 24, 1902: name placed on this card April 11th, 1905

~~No.1 is now the wife of Moses Patton on Choctaw card #4233: April 11, 1905~~

Child of No1 on NB (Apr 26-06) Card #280- D.A. of No1 on file in this case

Date of Application for Enrollment. For Nos 1&2

Aug 31/99

P.O. Boswell, I.T.

April 11, 1905

Choctaw By Blood Enrollment Cards 1898-1914

RESIDENCE: Jackson COUNTY. **Choctaw Nation** **Choctaw Roll** *(Not Including Freedmen)* CARD NO.
POST OFFICE: Mayhew, I.T. FIELD NO. 4244

Dawes' Roll No.	NAME	Relationship to Person First Named	AGE	SEX	BLOOD	TRIBAL ENROLLMENT Year	County	No.
11890	1 Chubbee, Louisa 58	First Named	55	F	Full	1893	Jackson	327
	2							
	3							
	4							
	5							
	6							
	7							
	8							
	9							
	10							
	11							
	12							
	13							
	14							
	15							
	16							
	17							

ENROLLMENT
OF NOS. 1 HEREON
APPROVED BY THE SECRETARY
OF INTERIOR MAR 10 1903

TRIBAL ENROLLMENT OF PARENTS

Name of Father	Year	County	Name of Mother	Year	County
1 Wa-ha-cha	Dead	Jackson	Becky	Dead	Jackson

On 1893 Pay Roll, Page 37, No 327, Jackson Co, as Lewiser Harrion

№1 also on 1896 Choctaw census roll #4853 as Louisa Gipson.

Date of Application for Enrollment.

Aug 31/99

Choctaw By Blood Enrollment Cards 1898-1914

RESIDENCE: Jackson COUNTY. **Choctaw Nation** **Choctaw Roll** *(Not Including Freedmen)* CARD NO.
POST OFFICE: Mayhew, I.T. FIELD NO. 4245

Dawes' Roll No.	NAME		Relationship to Person First Named	AGE	SEX	BLOOD	TRIBAL ENROLLMENT Year	County	No.
11891	1 Billy, Harlie	25	First Named	22	M	Full	1896	Jackson	1530
11892	2 Loring, Sibby	11	S.D.	8	F	"	1896	"	8161

ENROLLMENT
OF NOS. 1 and 2 HEREON
APPROVED BY THE SECRETARY
OF INTERIOR MAR 10 1903

TRIBAL ENROLLMENT OF PARENTS

Name of Father	Year	County	Name of Mother	Year	County
1 Asa Billy	Dead	Jackson	Liza A Billy	Dead	Jackson
2 Eleas Loring	"	"	Louisa Loring		"

No1 also on 1896 roll as Billy Harlie
Page 142, No 5827 Jackson Co
No2 is daughter of Louisa Hooper (Hopa)

Date of Application for Enrollment.
Aug 31/99

Choctaw By Blood Enrollment Cards 1898-1914

RESIDENCE: Jackson COUNTY. **Choctaw Nation** **Choctaw Roll** *(Not Including Freedmen)* CARD NO.
POST OFFICE: Mayhew, I.T. FIELD NO. 4246

Dawes' Roll No.	NAME	Relationship to Person First Named	AGE	SEX	BLOOD	TRIBAL ENROLLMENT Year	County	No.
11893	1 Oshter, Isham 24	First Named	21	M	Full	1896	Jackson	9992
	2							
	3							
	4							
	5							
	6							
	7							
	8							
	9							
	10							
	11							
	12							
	13							
	14							
	15							
	16							
	17							

ENROLLMENT OF NOS. 1 HEREON APPROVED BY THE SECRETARY OF INTERIOR MAR 10 1903

TRIBAL ENROLLMENT OF PARENTS

Name of Father	Year	County	Name of Mother	Year	County
1 Luke Oshter		Jackson	Sibby Oshter		Jackson
2					
3					
4					
5					
6 On 1896 roll as Isham Oushtubbee					
7					
8					
9					
10					
11					
12					
13					Date of Application for Enrollment.
14					
15					Aug 31/99
16					
17					

RESIDENCE: Jackson COUNTY. **Choctaw Nation** **Choctaw Roll** *(Not Including Freedmen)* CARD NO.
POST OFFICE: Mayhew, I.T. FIELD NO. 4247

Dawes' Roll No.	NAME	Relationship to Person First Named	AGE	SEX	BLOOD	TRIBAL ENROLLMENT Year	County	No.
11894	1 Cole, Selina 23	First Named	20	F	Full	1893	Jackson	295
16207	2 Wright, Winnie	Dau	1	F	Full			

ENROLLMENT OF NOS. 1 HEREON APPROVED BY THE SECRETARY OF INTERIOR Mar 10 1903

No2 – Granted Feb 19 1907

ENROLLMENT OF NOS. ~~~ 2 ~~~~~~ HEREON APPROVED BY THE SECRETARY OF INTERIOR Mar 4-1907

TRIBAL ENROLLMENT OF PARENTS

	Name of Father	Year	County	Name of Mother	Year	County
1						
2	Milton Wright	#7-	3834	No 1		

On 1893 Pay Roll, Page 33, No 295 Jackson Co, as Slina Gould.

Could not ascertain name of parents

No.1 is the wife of Joseph Cole on Choctaw card #1625

Application was made April 25, 1905 for the enrollment of No2 in accordance with the provisions of the Act of March 3, 1905.

Date of Application for Enrollment. Aug 31/99

RESIDENCE: Atoka COUNTY. **Choctaw Nation** **Choctaw Roll** *(Not Including Freedmen)* CARD NO.
POST OFFICE: Atoka, I.T. FIELD NO. 4248

Dawes' Roll No.	NAME		Relationship to Person First Named	AGE	SEX	BLOOD	TRIBAL ENROLLMENT Year	County	No.
11895	1 Folsom, Smallwood	29		26	M	Full	1896	Atoka	4421
11896	2 " Sina	32	Wife	29	F	"	1896	"	4422
11897	3 " Silas	7	Son	4	M	"	1896	"	4423
11898	4 " Edward	6	"	3	"	"	1896	"	4424
11899	5 " Lizzie	4	Dau	1	F	"			
11900	6 " Sarah	1	Dau	1	F	"			
	7								
	8								
	9								
	10								
	11								
	12								
	13								
	14								
	15								
	16								
	17								

ENROLLMENT
OF NOS. 1,2,3,4,5 and 6 HEREON
APPROVED BY THE SECRETARY
OF INTERIOR Mar 10 1903

TRIBAL ENROLLMENT OF PARENTS

Name of Father	Year	County	Name of Mother	Year	County
1 Simon Folsom		Atoka	Vicey Folsom	Dead	Atoka
2 Jas Jerry	Dead	"	Sally Jerry	"	"
3 No. 1			No. 2		
4 No. 1			No 2		
5 No. 1			No 2		
6 No. 1			No 2		
7					
8					
9					
10					
11					
12					
13					
14					
15					
16					
17 P.O. Lane I.T. 5/23/08					

No2 on 1896 roll as Sine Folsom

No5 affidavit of birth to be supplied:- Filed Oct 26/99

~~No.6 born August 26, 1901: enrolled Dec 15, 1902~~

For child of nos 1&2 see N.B. (Apr 26-06) Card #626

#1 to 5 inc

Date of Application for Enrollment. Aug 31/99

RESIDENCE: Atoka COUNTY. **Choctaw Nation** **Choctaw Roll** *(Not Including Freedmen)* CARD NO.
POST OFFICE: Atoka, I.T. FIELD NO. 4249

Dawes' Roll No.		NAME	Relationship to Person First Named	AGE	SEX	BLOOD	TRIBAL ENROLLMENT Year	County	No.
11901	1	Folsom, Isaac 22	First Named	19	M	Full	1896	Atoka	4442
	2								
	3								
	4								
	5	ENROLLMENT							
	6	OF NOS. ~~1~~ HEREON APPROVED BY THE SECRETARY							
	7	OF INTERIOR Mar 10 1903							
	8								
	9								
	10								
	11								
	12								
	13								
	14								
	15								
	16								
	17								

TRIBAL ENROLLMENT OF PARENTS

	Name of Father	Year	County	Name of Mother	Year	County
1	Aaron Folsom	Dead	Atoka	Molsey Folsom		Atoka
2						
3						
4						
5						
6	Nº1 is husband of Sallie Mullin Choctaw card #4118.					
7						
8						
9						
10						
11						
12						
13						
14						
15						Date of Application for Enrollment.
16						Aug 31/99
17	Caldoway[sic] I.T. 2/4/03					

RESIDENCE: Atoka COUNTY. **Choctaw Nation** **Choctaw Roll** *(Not Including Freedmen)* CARD NO.
POST OFFICE: Atoka, I.T. FIELD NO. 4250

Dawes' Roll No.		NAME	Relationship to Person First Named	AGE	SEX	BLOOD	TRIBAL ENROLLMENT Year	County	No.
DEAD	1	~~LeFlore, Jefferson~~	~~Named~~	~~26~~	~~M~~	~~Full~~	~~1896~~	~~Atoka~~	~~8352~~
11902	2	" Sina 31	Wife	28	F	"	1896	"	8353
	3								
	4								
	5								
	6								
	7								
	8								
	9								
	10								
	11								
	12								
	13								
	14								
	15								
	16								
	17								

ENROLLMENT
OF NOS. 2 HEREON
APPROVED BY THE SECRETARY
OF INTERIOR Mar 10 1903

No.1 hereon dismissed under order of the Commission to the Five Civilized Tribes of March 31, 1905.

TRIBAL ENROLLMENT OF PARENTS

	Name of Father	Year	County	Name of Mother	Year	County
1	~~Watkin LeFlore~~	~~Dead~~	~~Atoka~~	~~Sibby LeFlore~~	~~Dead~~	~~Atoka~~
2	Pe-sak-ma-kin-tuby	"	"	Becky	"	"
3						
4						
5						
6						
7						
8						
9						
10						
11						
12						
13						
14						
15						
16						
17						

No2 on 1896 roll as Sinie LeFlore

No1 died March 11, 1902: proof of death filed Nov 26 1902

Date of Application for Enrollment Aug 31/99

RESIDENCE: Atoka COUNTY. **Choctaw Nation** **Choctaw Roll** *(Not Including Freedmen)* CARD NO.
POST OFFICE: Boggy Depot, I.T. FIELD NO. 4251

Dawes' Roll No.	NAME	Relationship to Person First Named	AGE	SEX	BLOOD	TRIBAL ENROLLMENT Year	County	No.
11903	1 Underwood, Harrison C [35]	First Named	32	M	1/2	1896	Atoka	12585
I.W. 834	2 " May (27)	Wife	23	F	IW	1896	"	15131
	3							
	4							
	5							
	6							
	7							
	8							
	9							
	10							
	11							
	12							
	13							
	14							
	15							
	16							
	17							

ENROLLMENT OF NOS. 1 HEREON APPROVED BY THE SECRETARY OF INTERIOR Mar 10 1903

ENROLLMENT OF NOS. 2 HEREON APPROVED BY THE SECRETARY OF INTERIOR May 21 1904

TRIBAL ENROLLMENT OF PARENTS

Name of Father	Year	County	Name of Mother	Year	County
1 E-ma-spa-ca	Dead	Chick Roll	Isabelle	Dead	Blue
2 William Jones		Non Citz	Harriet Jones	"	Non Citz

No1 on 1896 roll as Colon Underwood
See affidavit of No2 as to residence at time of marriage to No1 filed July 22 1903

Date of Application for Enrollment. Aug 31/99

11-21-02 Lehigh I.T.

Choctaw By Blood Enrollment Cards 1898-1914

RESIDENCE: Atoka COUNTY. **Choctaw Nation** **Choctaw Roll** *(Not Including Freedmen)* CARD NO. [redacted]
POST OFFICE: Atoka, I.T. FIELD NO. 4252

Dawes' Roll No.		NAME	Relationship to Person First Named	AGE	SEX	BLOOD	TRIBAL ENROLLMENT Year	County	No.
11904	1	McKinney, William H 40	First Named	37	M	Full	1896	Nashoba	9286
11905	2	" Phoebe 43	Wife	40	F	"	1896	"	9287
DEAD.	3	~~Taylor, Narcissa~~	~~S.D~~	~~16~~	~~"~~	~~"~~	~~1896~~	~~"~~	~~12176~~
VOID	4	~~Homer, Weycia~~	~~Dau of No3~~	~~1~~	~~F~~	~~"~~			
	5								
	6								
	7								
	8								
	9								
	10								
	11								
	12								
	13								
	14								
	15								
	16								
	17								

ENROLLMENT OF NOS. 1 and 2 HEREON APPROVED BY THE SECRETARY OF INTERIOR MAR 10 1903

No. 3 HEREON DISMISSED UNDER ORDER OF THE COMMISSION TO THE FIVE CIVILIZED TRIBES OF MARCH 31, 1905.

TRIBAL ENROLLMENT OF PARENTS

	Name of Father	Year	County	Name of Mother	Year	County
1	Min-te-nubbee	Dead	Nashoba	Po-ho-na	Dead	Nasoba
2	Pe-sa-ha	"	Bok Tuklo	She-ma-hoke	"	Bok Tuklo
3	~~Calvin Taylor~~	~~"~~	~~Nashoba~~	~~No2~~		[redacted]
4	~~Byington Homer on Choctaw Card #1386~~			~~No 3~~		[redacted]
5						
6						
7						
8						
9						
10						
11						
12						
13						
14						
15						
16						
17						

No1 on 1896 roll as Wm H. McKinney

No.4 Born July 6th 1901: Enrolled July 14th 1902

No3 died June 29 1902; proof of death filed Dec 5, 1902
No4 placed on this card in error; transferred to Choc Card #2023
Dec 13, 1902

Date of Application for Enrollment. Aug 31/99

Choctaw By Blood Enrollment Cards 1898-1914

RESIDENCE: Jackson COUNTY. **Choctaw Nation** **Choctaw Roll** (*Not Including Freedmen*) CARD NO.
POST OFFICE: Mayhew, I.T. FIELD NO. 4253

Dawes' Roll No.	NAME	Relationship to Person First Named	AGE	SEX	BLOOD	TRIBAL ENROLLMENT		
						Year	County	No.
11906	1 Nail, Peter 37 ✓	First Named	34	M	Full	1896	Kiamitia	9776
11907	2 " Wilson 14 ✓	Son	11	"	"	1896	"	9778
15060	3 Hopa, Louisa 40 ✓	Wife	40	F	"	1896	Jackson	5811

ENROLLMENT OF NOS. ~~~~~3~~~~~ HEREON APPROVED BY THE SECRETARY OF INTERIOR FEB 16 1904

ENROLLMENT OF NOS. 1-2 HEREON APPROVED BY THE SECRETARY OF INTERIOR MAR 10 1903

TRIBAL ENROLLMENT OF PARENTS

	Name of Father	Year	County	Name of Mother	Year	County
1	Isom Nail	Dead	Gaines	Susan Nail	Dead	Tobucksey[sic]
2	No.1			Littie Nail		Atoka
3	Simpson Hopa	Dead	Choctaw	Rinda Hopa	Dead	Choctaw

No 5811
No3 on 1896 Choctaw Census Roll page 142, as Louisa Hooper
No3 " Leased District 1893 Payroll Cedar Co No 213 Mother of Sibbie Loring on Choctaw Card 4245
No3 Transferred from Choctaw Card D899

Aug 31, 1899

Choctaw By Blood Enrollment Cards 1898-1914

RESIDENCE: Atoka COUNTY. **Choctaw Nation** **Choctaw Roll** *(Not Including Freedmen)* CARD NO.
POST OFFICE: Atoka, I.T. FIELD NO. 4254

Dawes' Roll No.	NAME		Relationship to Person First Named	AGE	SEX	BLOOD	TRIBAL ENROLLMENT Year	County	No.
11908	1 Homer, Joseph	49	First Named	46	M	Full	1896	Atoka	6078
11909	2 " LaFayette	22	Son	19	"	"	1896	"	6080
11910	3 " Ella	17	Dau	14	F	"	1896	"	6081
11911	4 " Katie	11	"	8	"	"	1896	"	6082
11912	5 Jerry, David	26	S.S.	23	M	"	1896	"	6673
	6								
	7								
	8								
	9								
	10								
	11								
	12								
	13								
	14								
	15								
	16								
	17								

ENROLLMENT
OF NOS. 1,2,3,4 and 5 HEREON
APPROVED BY THE SECRETARY
OF INTERIOR MAR 10 1903

TRIBAL ENROLLMENT OF PARENTS

Name of Father	Year	County	Name of Mother	Year	County
1 Tush-ka-homa	Dead	Towson		Dead	Kiamitia
2 No1			Rosa A Homer	"	Atoka
3 No1			" " "	"	"
4 No1			" " "	"	"
5 Morris Jerry	Dead	Atoka	" " "	"	"
6					
7					
8					
9					
10					
11 No 2 is husband of Nicey Gardner, Choctaw #1431 11/20 '02					
12					
13					
14					
15				Date of Application for Enrollment.	Aug 31/99
16					
17					

Choctaw By Blood Enrollment Cards 1898-1914

RESIDENCE: Jacks Fork COUNTY. **Choctaw Nation** Choctaw Roll (Not Including Freedmen) CARD NO.
POST OFFICE: Antlers, I.T. FIELD NO. 4255

Dawes' Roll No.	NAME		Relationship to Person First Named	AGE	SEX	BLOOD	Tribal Enrollment Year	County	No.
11913	1 Wesley, Nelson	37	First Named	34	M	Full	1896	Jacks Fork	14129
11914	2 " Sillen	31	Wife	28	F	"	1896	" "	14130
11915	3 " Moses	11	Son	8	M	"	1896	" "	14131
11916	4 " Emma	6	Dau	3	F	"	1896	" "	14132
14902	5 " Joshua	1	Son	3mo	M	"			

ENROLLMENT OF NOS. 1,2,3 and 4 HEREON APPROVED BY THE SECRETARY OF INTERIOR MAR 10 1903

ENROLLMENT OF NOS. 5 HEREON APPROVED BY THE SECRETARY OF INTERIOR MAY 21 1903

TRIBAL ENROLLMENT OF PARENTS

	Name of Father	Year	County	Name of Mother	Year	County
1	Thompson Wesley	Dead	Jacks Fork	Ellen Wesley		Chick Dist
2	Billy Fletcher		" "	Susan Impson	Dead	Jacks Fork
3	No1			No2		
4	No1			No2		
5	№1			№2		

No2 on 1896 roll as Silliann Wesley

№5 Born Sept. 13, 1902, application made Dec 4 1902: Proof of birth filed 2/5/03

#1 to 4

Date of Application for Enrollment.

Au

Choctaw By Blood Enrollment Cards 1898-1914

RESIDENCE: Jacks Fork COUNTY. **Choctaw Nation** **Choctaw Roll** *(Not Including Freedmen)* CARD NO.
POST OFFICE: Stringtown, I.T. FIELD NO. 4256

Dawes' Roll No.		NAME	Relationship to Person First Named	AGE	SEX	BLOOD	TRIBAL ENROLLMENT Year	County	No.
DEAD	1	~~Wesley, John~~ DEAD.	~~Named~~	~~45~~	~~M~~	~~Full~~	~~1896~~	~~Jacks Fork~~	~~14118~~
11917	2	" Melissa 26	Wife	23	F	"	1896	" "	14119
DEAD.	3	~~" Emily~~ DEAD.	~~Dau~~	~~1~~	~~"~~	~~"~~			
	4								
	5								
	6								
	7								
	8								
	9								
	10								
	11								
	12								
	13								
	14								
	15								
	16								
	17								

ENROLLMENT
OF NOS. 2 HEREON
APPROVED BY THE SECRETARY
OF INTERIOR MAR 10 1903

No. 1 and 3 HEREON DISMISSED UNDER ORDER OF THE COMMISSION TO THE FIVE CIVILIZED TRIBES OF MARCH 31, 1905.

TRIBAL ENROLLMENT OF PARENTS

	Name of Father	Year	County	Name of Mother	Year	County
1	~~Mon-tubbee~~	~~Dead~~	~~Jacks Fork~~	~~Oka-ste-ma~~	~~Dead~~	~~Skullyville~~
2	She-le-chubbee	"	Tobucksy	Betsy Shelechubbee		Jacks Fork
3	~~No1~~			~~No2~~		
4						
5						
6						
7						
8						
9						
10						
11						
12						
13						
14						
15						
16						
17						

No3- Affidavit of birth to be supplied:- Red Dec 18/99. Irregular and returned for correction.

No.1 died January 21, 1901; proof of death filed Nov. 25, 1902
No.3 died September – 1900; proof of death filed Nov. 25, 1902

Date of Application for Enrollment.
Aug 31/99

RESIDENCE: Atoka COUNTY. **Choctaw Nation** **Choctaw Roll** *(Not Including Freedmen)* CARD NO.
POST OFFICE: Atoka, I.T. FIELD NO. 4257

Dawes' Roll No.		NAME		Relationship to Person First Named	AGE	SEX	BLOOD	TRIBAL ENROLLMENT Year	County	No.
11918	1	Allison, Calvin	62	First Named	59	M	Full	1896	Atoka	437
11919	2	" Sallie	33	Wife	30	F	"	1896	"	438
11920	3	" Sarah	21	Ward	18	"	3/8	1896	"	439
11921	4	" Agnes	2	"	10mo	F	3/8			

ENROLLMENT
OF NOS. 1,2,3 and 4 HEREON
APPROVED BY THE SECRETARY
OF INTERIOR MAR 10 1903

TRIBAL ENROLLMENT OF PARENTS

	Name of Father	Year	County	Name of Mother	Year	County
1	John Allison	Dead	Atoka	Elisie Allison	Dead	Atoka
2	A-non-po-chubbee	"	"	Nancy	"	"
3	James Hihkabee	"	"	Eliz. Allison	"	"
4	Unknown			No.3		

All on 1896 roll under name of Allerson
No3 on 1896 roll as Sallie Allerson
~~No.4 Born December 10, 1900 and Enrolled October 28, 1901.~~
For child of No.3 see NB (March 3, 1905) #776

Date of Application for Enrollment.
Aug 31/99

RESIDENCE: Atoka COUNTY. **Choctaw Nation** **Choctaw Roll** *(Not Including Freedmen)* CARD NO.
POST OFFICE: Atoka, Ind. Ter. FIELD NO. 4258

Dawes' Roll No.		NAME		Relationship to Person First Named	AGE	SEX	BLOOD	TRIBAL ENROLLMENT Year	County	No.
11922	1	Tumbler, Willie	31		28	M	1/2	1896	Atoka	12457
11923	2	" Maggie	32	Wife	29	F	1/2	1896	"	12458
DEAD.	3	~~" Katie~~		~~Dau~~	~~1~~	~~"~~	~~1/2~~			
	4									
	5									
	6									
	7									
	8									
	9									
	10									
	11									
	12									
	13									
	14									
	15									
	16									
	17									

ENROLLMENT
OF NOS. 1 and 2 HEREON
APPROVED BY THE SECRETARY
OF INTERIOR MAR 10 1903

No. 3 HEREON DISMISSED UNDER
ORDER OF THE COMMISSION TO THE FIVE
CIVILIZED TRIBES OF MARCH 31, 1905.

TRIBAL ENROLLMENT OF PARENTS

	Name of Father	Year	County	Name of Mother	Year	County
1	Jesse Tumbler	Dead	Atoka	Molsey Tumbler	Dead	Chick Dist
2				Elizabeth Ellis		" "
3	~~No.1~~			~~No.2~~		
4						
5						
6						
7						
8						
9						
10						
11						
12						
13						
14						
15						
16						
17						

~~No1 Transferred to Chickasaw Card #1570 March 6th 1900~~
No1 Re-transferred to this Card Novr 3rd 1902
No3 Affidavit of Birth to be supplied. Filed Oct 26" 1899
~~No.3 Died June 1900: Proof of death filed March 21, 1901~~

Date of ... for En...
Au...

Choctaw By Blood Enrollment Cards 1898-1914

RESIDENCE: Atoka COUNTY. **Choctaw Nation** **Choctaw Roll** *(Not Including Freedmen)* CARD NO.
POST OFFICE: Atoka, I.T. FIELD NO. 4259

Dawes' Roll No.	NAME	Relationship to Person First Named	AGE	SEX	BLOOD	TRIBAL ENROLLMENT Year	County	No.
11924	1 Tumbler, Annie 57	First Named	54	F	Full	1896	Atoka	12462
	2							
	3							
	4							
	5							
	6							
	7							
	8							
	9							
	10							
	11							
	12							
	13							
	14							
	15							
	16							
	17							

ENROLLMENT
OF NOS. 1 HEREON
APPROVED BY THE SECRETARY
OF INTERIOR MAR 10 1903

TRIBAL ENROLLMENT OF PARENTS

	Name of Father	Year	County	Name of Mother	Year	County
1	No-ka-a-homa	Dead			Dead	
2						
3						
4						
5						
6						
7						
8						
9						
10						
11						
12						
13						
14						Date of Application for Enrollment.
15						Aug 31/99
16						
17						

Choctaw By Blood Enrollment Cards 1898-1914

RESIDENCE: Atoka COUNTY. Citra I.T. **Choc[redacted] Roll** CARD NO.
POST OFFICE: Atoka, I.T.(~~Citra I.T.~~) *(Not Including Freedmen)* FIELD NO. 4260

Dawes' Roll No.	NAME	Relationship to Person First Named	AGE	SEX	BLOOD	TRIBAL ENROLLMENT Year	County	No.
11925	1 Lewis, Israel 41	First Named	38	M	Full	1896	Atoka	8244
11926	2 " Sarah 28	Wife	25	F	"	1896	"	8245
DEAD	3 ~~" Sexton~~	~~Son~~	~~1~~	~~M~~	~~"~~			
16117	4 Lewis, Johnson	Son	1	M	"			

ENROLLMENT OF NOS. 1 and 2 HEREON APPROVED BY THE SECRETARY OF INTERIOR MAR 10 1903

No. 3 HEREON DISMISSED UNDER ORDER OF THE COMMISSION TO THE FIVE CIVILIZED TRIBES OF MARCH 31, 1905

ENROLLMENT OF NOS. ~~~~~ 4 ~~~~~ HEREON APPROVED BY THE SECRETARY OF INTERIOR FEB 21 1907

TRIBAL ENROLLMENT OF PARENTS

	Name of Father	Year	County	Name of Mother	Year	County
1	Nashoba Noah	Dead	Tobucksy	Ho-ta-ma	Dead	Tobucksy
2	William Hall		Atoka	Sarah Lewis		Atoka
3	~~No1~~			~~No2~~		
4	No.2			No.2		

No3 Affidavit of birth to be supplied:- Filed Nov 2/99
~~No3 died in 1899: Proof of death filed Nov 18, 1902~~
~~No.4 was born April 26, 1901; application received March 4, 1905,~~
under Act of Congress approved March 3, 1905
More proof required 7/20/05

#1 to 3

Date of Application for Enrollment. Aug 31/99

Choctaw By Blood Enrollment Cards 1898-1914

RESIDENCE: Atoka COUNTY. **Choctaw Nation** **Choctaw Roll** *(Not Including Freedmen)* CARD NO.
POST OFFICE: Coalgate, I.T. FIELD NO. 4261

Dawes' Roll No.		NAME		Relationship to Person First Named	AGE	SEX	BLOOD	TRIBAL ENROLLMENT Year	County	No.
11927	1	Ward, Joseph L	40	First Named	37	M	1/16	1896	Atoka	14002
I.W. 404	2	" Letty	38	Wife	36	F	IW			
11928	3	" Coleman J	19	Son	16	M	1/32	1896	Atoka	14003
11929	4	" Lucy E	16	Dau	13	F	1/32	1896	"	14008
11930	5	" Robb D	14	Son	11	M	1/32	1896	"	14004
11931	6	" Henry J	13	"	10	"	1/32	1896	"	14005
11932	7	" Warren G	11	"	8	"	1/32	1896	"	14006
11933	8	" George H	7	"	4	"	1/32	1896	"	14007
11934	9	" Bryan G	5	"	2	"	1/32			
11935	10	" Hazle[sic] May	3	Dau	4mo	F	1/32			
	11									
	12	~~No9- Affidavit of birth to~~								
	13	be supplied:- Filed Oct 26/99								
	14	No.8 admitted as a citizen by								
		~~blood by Dawes Commission in~~								
	15	~~1896: Choctaw case #538: no appeal~~								
	16									
	17									

TRIBAL ENROLLMENT OF PARENTS

	Name of Father	Year	County	Name of Mother	Year	County
1	Joseph Ward	Dead	Non Citz	Eliz Ward	Dead	Atoka
2	Jas. Simmons	"	" "	Eliz Simmons		Non Citz
3	No1			No2		
4	No1			No2		
5	No1			No2		
6	No1			No2		
7	No1			No2		
8	No1			No2		
9	No1			No2		
10	No.1			No.2		
11	~~No1 on 1896 roll as J.L. Ward~~					
12	No6 " 1896 " " Joe H "					
13	No7 " 1896 " " Warren "					
	~~No8 " 1896 " " Geo H "~~					
14	~~No2 admitted by Dawes Com~~					
15	Case No 528					
16	No.10 Enrolled May 24, 1900					
17	~~Limestone Gap 11/19/02~~					

ENROLLMENT OF NOS. 1,3,4,5,6,7,8,9 and 10 HEREON APPROVED BY THE SECRETARY OF INTERIOR MAR 10 1903

ENROLLMENT OF NOS. 2 HEREON APPROVED BY THE SECRETARY OF INTERIOR SEP 12 1903

#1 to 9
Date of Application for Enrollment.
Aug 31/99

RESIDENCE: Jacks Fork COUNTY. **Choctaw Nation** **Choctaw Roll** *(Not Including Freedmen)* CARD NO.
POST OFFICE: Atoka, I.T. FIELD NO. 4262

Dawes' Roll No.	NAME		Relationship to Person First Named	AGE	SEX	BLOOD	TRIBAL ENROLLMENT Year	County	No.
11936	1 Shield, Nancy	39		36	F	1/2	1893	Gaines	526
11937	2 " Sarah	19	Dau	16	"	1/4	1893	"	627
11938	3 " Israel	12	Son	9	M	1/4	1893	"	528
11939	4 " Jonas	10	"	7	"	1/4	1893	"	529
11940	5 " Lurena	8	Dau	5	F	1/4			
11941	6 " Hattie	6	"	3	"	1/4			
11942	7 " Classie	2	Dau	2	F	1/4			

ENROLLMENT
OF NOS. 1,2,3,4,5,6 and 7 HEREON
APPROVED BY THE SECRETARY
OF INTERIOR MAR 10 1903

TRIBAL ENROLLMENT OF PARENTS

	Name of Father	Year	County	Name of Mother	Year	County
1	Nelson Ishcomer	Dead	Colored man	Martha Ishcomer	Dead	Blue
2	Jack Shield		" "	No1		
3	" "		" "	No1		
4	" "		" "	No1		
5	" "		" "	No1		
6	" "		" "	No1		
7	" "		" "	No1		

First four on 1893 Pay Roll, Page 56, Gaines Co

Nos 5-6 Affidavit of birth to be supplied: ~~Filed Oct 26/99~~

No7 born August 30, 1900: enrolled Dec. 5, 1902

#1 to 6 inc

Date of Application for Enrollment.

Aug 31/99

For child of No2 see N.B. 931 (Act Apr 26-06)
" " " No1 " " 1371 (Act March 3-05)
" " " No2 " " 1429 (" " " ")

Choctaw By Blood Enrollment Cards 1898-1914

RESIDENCE: Atoka   COUNTY. **Choctaw Nation**   **Choctaw Roll** *(Not Including Freedmen)*   CARD NO.
POST OFFICE: Atoka, I.T.   FIELD NO. 4263

Dawes' Roll No.	NAME		Relationship to Person First Named	AGE	SEX	BLOOD	TRIBAL ENROLLMENT Year	County	No.
11943	1 Armstrong, Murrow	30	First Named	27	M	Full	1896	Atoka	433
11944	2 " Annie	23	Wife	20	F	"	1896	"	434
11945	3 " Mary	3	Dau	4mo	F	"			
11946	4 " Sofa	1	Dau	3mo	F	"			

ENROLLMENT OF NOS. 1,2,3 and 4 HEREON APPROVED BY THE SECRETARY OF INTERIOR Mar 10 1903

TRIBAL ENROLLMENT OF PARENTS

	Name of Father	Year	County	Name of Mother	Year	County
1	Wylis Armstrong		Atoka	Nicey Armstrong		Atoka
2	Noel Jones		"	Mary Jones	Dead	Jackson
3	No1			No2		
4	No1			No2		

For child of Nos 1&2 see NB (Mar 3 1905) Card #322

No.3 Enrolled June 4, 1900

~~No.4 Born Dec 6, 1901: enrolled March 24, 1902~~

#1&2

Date of Application for Enrollment.
Aug 31/99

RESIDENCE: Atoka COUNTY. **Choctaw Nation** **Choctaw Roll** *(Not Including Freedmen)* CARD NO.
POST OFFICE: Atoka, I.T. FIELD NO. 4264

Dawes' Roll No.		NAME		Relationship to Person First Named	AGE	SEX	BLOOD	TRIBAL ENROLLMENT Year	County	No.
11947	1	Lewis, Joseph	32		29	M	Full	1896	Atoka	8249
11948	2	" Eliza	23	Wife	20	F	"	1896	"	8251
	3									
	4									
	5									
	6									
	7									
	8									
	9									
	10									
	11									
	12									
	13									
	14									
	15									
	16									
	17									

ENROLLMENT OF NOS. 1 and 2 HEREON APPROVED BY THE SECRETARY OF INTERIOR Mar 10, 1903

TRIBAL ENROLLMENT OF PARENTS

	Name of Father	Year	County	Name of Mother	Year	County
1	A-che-le-tubbee	Dead	Kiamitia	Emily	Dead	Atoka
2	Cephus Baker	"	Blue	Littie Baker	"	"
3						
4						
5						
6	No.2 on 1896 roll as Elias Leader					
7						
8						
9						
10						
11						
12						
13						
14						
15						
16				Date of Application for Enrollment.		Aug 31/99
17						

Choctaw By Blood Enrollment Cards 1898-1914

RESIDENCE: Kiamitia COUNTY. **Choctaw Nation** **Choctaw Roll** *(Not Including Freedmen)* CARD NO.
POST OFFICE: Antlers, I.T. FIELD NO. 4265

Dawes' Roll No.	NAME	Relationship to Person First Named	AGE	SEX	BLOOD	TRIBAL ENROLLMENT Year	County	No.
11940	1 Willis, Wright DIED PRIOR TO SEPTEMBER 25 1902	Named	23	M	Full	1896	Kiamitia	13762
	2							
	3							
	4							
	5							
	6							
	7							
	8							
	9							
	10							
	11							
	12							
	13							
	14							
	15							
	16							
	17							

ENROLLMENT
OF NOS. 1 HEREON
APPROVED BY THE SECRETARY
OF INTERIOR MAR 10 1903

TRIBAL ENROLLMENT OF PARENTS

	Name of Father	Year	County	Name of Mother	Year	County
1	Joel Willis	Dead	Red River	Betsy Willis	Dead	Red River
2						
3						
4						
5						
6	No.1 died in 1899: Enrollment cancelled by Department May 2, 1906					
7						
8						
9						
10						
11						
12						
13						
14						Date of Application for Enrollment.
15						Aug 31/99
16						
17						

Choctaw By Blood Enrollment Cards 1898-1914

RESIDENCE: Jackson COUNTY. Choctaw Nation Choctaw Roll (Not Including Freedmen) CARD NO.
POST OFFICE: Jackson, I.T. FIELD NO. 4266

Dawes' Roll No.	NAME	Relationship to Person First Named	AGE	SEX	BLOOD	TRIBAL ENROLLMENT Year	County	No.
11950	1 Foster, Solomon 23	First Named	20	M	Full	1896	Jackson	4271
	2							
	3							
	4							
	5							
	6							
	7							
	8							
	9							
	10							
	11							
	12							
	13							
	14							
	15							
	16							
	17							

ENROLLMENT OF NOS. 1 HEREON APPROVED BY THE SECRETARY OF INTERIOR MAR 10 1903

TRIBAL ENROLLMENT OF PARENTS

Name of Father	Year	County	Name of Mother	Year	County
1 Alixon Foster	Dead	Jackson	Silway Foster	Dead	Jackson
2					
3					
4					
5					
6					
7					
8					
9					
10					
11					
12					
13					
14					
15					
16					
17					

~~No.1 father of Thomas Foster on Choctaw card #4231~~

"Died prior to September 25, 1902 not entitled to land or money"
(See Indian Office letter of June 20, 1910 D.C. #847-1910)

Date of Application for Enrollment.
Aug 31/99

RESIDENCE: Atoka COUNTY. **Choctaw Nation** **Choctaw Roll** *(Not Including Freedmen)* CARD NO.
POST OFFICE: Atoka, I.T. FIELD NO. 4267

Dawes' Roll No.	NAME	Relationship to Person First Named	AGE	SEX	BLOOD	TRIBAL ENROLLMENT Year	County	No.
11951	1 Jones, Sam 58	First Named	50	M	Full	1896	Atoka	7284
11952	2 " Martha A 53	Wife	50	F	1/2	1896	"	7285
	3							
TIZENSHIP CERTIFICATE	4							
SUED FOR NO. 1	5 MAY 5 1903							
	6							
	7							
	8							
	9							
SHIP CERTIFICATE	10							
OR NO 2 NOV 17 1903	11							
	12							
	13							
	14							
	15							
	16							
	17							

ENROLLMENT OF NOS. 1 - 2 HEREON APPROVED BY THE SECRETARY OF INTERIOR MAR 10 1903

TRIBAL ENROLLMENT OF PARENTS

	Name of Father	Year	County	Name of Mother	Year	County
1	Solomon Jones	Dead	Jackson		Dead	Boktuklo
2	Ellis		Non Citizen	Nancy Ellis	"	Red River
3						
4						
5						
6						
7						
8						
9						
10						
11	No.2 on 1896 Roll as Malsey Jones					
12						
13						
14						
15						
16						
17						Aug 31, 1899

Choctaw By Blood Enrollment Cards 1898-1914

RESIDENCE: Jacks Fork COUNTY. **Choctaw Nation** Choctaw Roll (Not Including Freedmen) CARD NO.
POST OFFICE: Stringtown I.T. FIELD NO. 4268

Dawes' Roll No.	NAME	Relationship to Person First Named	AGE	SEX	BLOOD	TRIBAL ENROLLMENT Year	County	No.
11953	1 Cravatt, Johnson 28	First Named	25	M	Full	1896	Jacks Fork	2996
I.W. 1339	2 " Effie 21	Wife	18	F	IW			
11954	3 " Elma Pearl 2	Dau	10mo	F	1/2			

ENROLLMENT OF NOS. 1 and 3 HEREON APPROVED BY THE SECRETARY OF INTERIOR MAR 10 1903

ENROLLMENT OF NOS. 2 HEREON APPROVED BY THE SECRETARY OF INTERIOR MAR 14 1905

TRIBAL ENROLLMENT OF PARENTS

Name of Father	Year	County	Name of Mother	Year	County
1 Louis Cravatt	Dead	Kiamitia	Mary Cravatt	Dead	Kiamitia
2 Richerson		Non Citz	Sally Richerson	"	Non Citz
3 No1			No2		

No1 on 1896 roll as Johnson Cole

No1 on Page 23, No 226, 1893 Pay Roll
Jacks Fork, Co, as Johnson Cravate

No.3 born Dec 6, 1900: Enrolled Oct. 21st, 1901
No's 1 and 2 are now separated; the child being with the mother 12/12 '02

Date of Application for Enrollment.
Aug 31/99

of No2
PO Hartshorne, IT 11/12/04
PO of No2 is Coleman I.T.
2/2/04

Choctaw By Blood Enrollment Cards 1898-1914

RESIDENCE: Atoka COUNTY. **Choctaw Nation** **Choctaw Roll** *(Not Including Freedmen)* CARD NO.
POST OFFICE: Atoka, I.T. FIELD NO. 4269

Dawes' Roll No.		NAME	Relationship to Person First Named	AGE	SEX	BLOOD	TRIBAL ENROLLMENT Year	County	No.
11955	1	Wood, Harrison 27	First Named	24	M	Full	1896	Atoka	13964
11956	2	" Ella 24	Wife	21	F	"	1896	"	5946
DEAD	3	~~Homer, Hannibal~~	~~Son~~	~~1~~	~~M~~	"			
	4								
	5								
	6								
	7	ENROLLMENT							
	8	OF NOS. 1 and 2 HEREON APPROVED BY THE SECRETARY							
	9	OF INTERIOR Mar 10 1903							
	10	No. 3 hereon dismissed under order of							
	11	the Commission to the Five Civilized							
	12	Tribes of March 31, 1905.							
	13								
	14								
	15								
	16								
	17								

TRIBAL ENROLLMENT OF PARENTS

	Name of Father	Year	County	Name of Mother	Year	County
1	Abner Wood		Atoka	Sealy A. Wood	Dead	Atoka
2	Dixon Fillmore		Blue	Isabelle Fillmore		"
3	~~Davis Homer~~			~~No2~~		
4						
5						
6						
7		No1 on 1896 roll as Harrison Woods				
8		No2 " 1896 " " Ella Homma				
9		No3- Affidavit of birth to be				
10		supplied.- ~~Filed Oct 26/99~~				
11		No3 died Sept – 1900 proof of death filed Nov				
12		No.2 is known as Ella Fillmore 11/21 '02				
12	For children (twins) of No1 see NB (Apr 26-06) Card #662					
13	~~" child " No2 " " " Card #745~~					
13	~~" " " No1 " " (Mar 3 '05) " #323~~					
14	" children " No2 " " " " " " #1311					
15				Date of Application for Enrollment		Aug 31/99
16						
17	P.O. Tupelo I.T. 4/26/05					

RESIDENCE: Atoka COUNTY. **Choctaw Nation** **Choctaw Roll** *(Not Including Freedmen)* CARD NO.
POST OFFICE: Atoka, I.T. FIELD NO. 4270

Dawes' Roll No.		NAME		Relationship to Person First Named	AGE	SEX	BLOOD	TRIBAL ENROLLMENT Year	County	No.
11957	1	DIED PRIOR TO SEPTEMBER 25, 1902 Jones, Robert M	40		38	M	Full	1896	Atoka	7272
11958	2	DIED PRIOR TO SEPTEMBER 25, 1902 " Sallie	36	Wife	33	F	"	1896	"	7273
11959	3	" Andrew	17	Son	14	M	"	1896	"	7274
11960	4	" Robert M Jr	13	"	10	"	"	1896	"	7275
11961	5	" Abagail	11	Dau	8	F	"	1896	"	7278
11962	6	" Jasper	9	Son	6	M	"	1896	"	7276
11963	7	" Impson	7	"	4	"	"	1896	"	7277
11964	8	" Mary	4	Dau	1½	F	"			

ENROLLMENT
OF NOS. 1,2,3,4,5,6,7 and 8 HEREON
APPROVED BY THE SECRETARY
OF INTERIOR Mar 10 1903

No1 died Sept 22, 1901: No2 died Feb - 1901: Enrollment cancelled by Department July 8, 1904

TRIBAL ENROLLMENT OF PARENTS

	Name of Father	Year	County	Name of Mother	Year	County
1	Impson Jones	Dead	Blue	Jincy Jones		Blue
2	Silas Ward	"	Tobucksy	Edna Ward	Dead	"
3	No1			No2		
4	No1			No2		
5	No1			No2		
6	No1			No2		
7	No1			No2		
8	No1			No2		

No1 on 1896 roll as R. M. Jones
No4 " 1896 " " Robert "
No5 " 1896 " " Abbey "

Date of Application for Enrollment.
Aug 31/99

Choctaw By Blood Enrollment Cards 1898-1914

RESIDENCE: Atoka COUNTY. **Choctaw Nation** Choctaw Roll (Not Including Freedmen) CARD NO.

POST OFFICE: Atoka, I.T. FIELD NO. 4271

Dawes' Roll No.	NAME		Relationship to Person First Named	AGE	SEX	BLOOD	TRIBAL ENROLLMENT Year	County	No.
11965	1 Harkins, Stephen	45	First Named	42	M	Full	1896	Jacks Fork	6112
11966	2 " Elsie	35	Wife	32	F	"	1896	" "	6113

ENROLLMENT OF NOS. 1 and 2 HEREON APPROVED BY THE SECRETARY OF INTERIOR MAR 10 1903

TRIBAL ENROLLMENT OF PARENTS

	Name of Father	Year	County	Name of Mother	Year	County
1		Dead	Sans Bois	O-kli-o-key	Dead	Gaines
2	William James	"	Blue		"	Blue

Date of Application for Enrollment.

Aug 31/99

Choctaw By Blood Enrollment Cards 1898-1914

RESIDENCE: Atoka COUNTY. **Choctaw Nation** **Choctaw Roll** (*Not Including Freedmen*) CARD NO.
POST OFFICE: Atoka, I.T. FIELD NO. 4272

Dawes' Roll No.	NAME	Relationship to Person First Named	AGE	SEX	BLOOD	TRIBAL ENROLLMENT Year	County	No.
11967	1 Scott, Cephus 36	First Named	33	M	Full	1896	Atoka	11652
	2							
	3							
	4							
	5							
	6							
	7							
	8							
	9							
	10							
	11							
	12							
	13							
	14							
	15							
	16							
	17							

ENROLLMENT
OF NOS. 1 HEREON
APPROVED BY THE SECRETARY
OF INTERIOR M 10 1903

TRIBAL ENROLLMENT OF PARENTS

Name of Father	Year	County	Name of Mother	Year	County
1 Simon Scott	Dead	Atoka	Eliz Scott	Dead	Atoka
2					
3					
4					
5					
6					
7					
8					
9					
10					
11					
12					
13					
14					Date of Application for Enrollment.
15					Aug 31/99
16					
17					

Choctaw By Blood Enrollment Cards 1898-1914

RESIDENCE: Atoka COUNTY. **Choctaw Nation** **Choctaw Roll** *(Not Including Freedmen)* CARD NO.
POST OFFICE: Atoka, I.T. FIELD NO. 4273

Dawes' Roll No.	NAME		Relationship to Person First Named	AGE	SEX	BLOOD	TRIBAL ENROLLMENT Year	County	No.
11968	1 Willis, Siney	22	First Named	19	F	Full	1896	Atoka	13989
DEAD.	2 ~~Scott, Simon~~		~~Son~~	~~1~~	~~M~~	~~"~~			
14903	3 " George	1	"	18mo	M	"			

ENROLLMENT OF NOS. 1 HEREON APPROVED BY THE SECRETARY OF INTERIOR MAR 10 1903

No. 2 HEREON DISMISSED UNDER ORDER OF THE COMMISSION TO THE FIVE CIVILIZED TRIBES OF MARCH 31, 1905.

ENROLLMENT OF NOS. 3 HEREON APPROVED BY THE SECRETARY OF INTERIOR MAY 21 1903

TRIBAL ENROLLMENT OF PARENTS

Name of Father	Year	County	Name of Mother	Year	County
1 Simon Willis	Dead	Tobucksy	Lucy Willis	Dead	Atoka
2 ~~Cephus Scott~~		~~Atoka~~	~~No1~~		
3 " "			Nº1		

~~No2 Affidavit of birth to be supplied:- Filed Dec 14/99~~

No.1 is wife of Willie Tullihela, Choc #4927

~~No2 Died Feby – 1901 proof of death filed Nov 22 1902~~

~~Nº3 Born Sept 15, 1901 Application made Nov. 19, 1901, proof of birth filed March 17, 1903~~

For children of No1 see NB (Apr 26-06) Card #308

#1&2

Date of Application for Enrollment.

Aug 31/99

Choctaw By Blood Enrollment Cards 1898-1914

RESIDENCE: Atoka COUNTY: **Choctaw Nation** **Choctaw Roll** *(Not Including Freedmen)* CARD NO.

POST OFFICE: Atoka, I.T. FIELD NO. 4274

Dawes' Roll No.	NAME		Relationship to Person First Named	AGE	SEX	BLOOD	TRIBAL ENROLLMENT Year	TRIBAL ENROLLMENT County	TRIBAL ENROLLMENT No.
11969	1 Leader, Joel	48	First Named	45	M	Full	1896	Atoka	8253
11970	2 " Icey	37	Wife	34	F	"	1896	"	8254
11971	3 " James	6	Ward	3	M	"			

ENROLLMENT
OF NOS. 1,2 and 3 HEREON
APPROVED BY THE SECRETARY
OF INTERIOR MAR 10 1903

TRIBAL ENROLLMENT OF PARENTS

Name of Father	Year	County	Name of Mother	Year	County
1 Ish-fa-la-ma	Dead	Atoka		Dead	Jacks Fork
2	"	Jacks Fork		"	" "
3 Silas Leader		Atoka	Jennie Peter		Atoka

~~No2 on 1896 roll as Licey Leader~~

No3- Affidavit of birth to be ~~supplied:- Filed Oct 26/99~~

~~Nº1 is guardian of Nº3. See certified copy of~~ guardianship papers filed May 16, 1903.

Date of Application for Enrollment.

Aug 31/99

RESIDENCE: Atoka COUNTY. **Choctaw Nation** Choctaw Roll (Not Including Freedmen) CARD NO.
POST OFFICE: Atoka, I.T. FIELD NO. 4275

Dawes' Roll No.	NAME	Relationship to Person First Named	AGE	SEX	BLOOD	TRIBAL ENROLLMENT Year	County	No.
11972	1 Homer, Josiah 47		44	M	Full	1896	Atoka	5951
DEAD	2 ~~" Sallie~~	~~Wife~~	~~54~~	~~F~~	~~"~~	~~1896~~	~~"~~	~~5952~~
11973	3 " Sophia 12	Dau	9	"	"	1896	"	5953
11974	4 " Oceana 6	"	3	"	"	1896	"	5954
DEAD	5 ~~" Cynthia~~	~~"~~	~~6mo~~	~~"~~	~~"~~			

ENROLLMENT OF NOS. 1, 3 and 4 HEREON APPROVED BY THE SECRETARY OF INTERIOR Mar. 10, 1903

No.2 and 5 hereon dismissed under order of the Commission to the Five Civilized Tribes of March 31, 1905.

TRIBAL ENROLLMENT OF PARENTS

Name of Father	Year	County	Name of Mother	Year	County
1 Edmond Homer	Dead	Kiamitia	Lucy Homer	Dead	Kiamitia
2 ~~Joe Collins~~	~~"~~	~~"~~	~~Mary Collins~~	~~"~~	~~"~~
3 No.1			No.2		
4 No.1			No.2		
5 ~~No.1~~			~~No.2~~		

No.1 on 1896 roll as Josiah Homma
No.2 " 1896 " " Sallie "
No.3 " 1896 " " Sophy "
~~No.4 " 1896 " " Oceana "~~
No.5 Affidavit of birth to be supplied: Filed Oct. 26/99
No.2 died July 24, 1900: proof of death filed Nov 25, 1902
~~No.5 died July 28, 1901: proof of death filed Nov 25, 1902~~

Date of Application for Enrollment.
Aug 31/99

RESIDENCE: Bok Tuklo COUNTY. **Choctaw Nation** **Choctaw Roll** *(Not Including Freedmen)* CARD NO.
POST OFFICE: Lukfatah[sic], I.T. FIELD NO. 4276

Dawes' Roll No.		NAME	Relationship to Person First Named	AGE	SEX	BLOOD	TRIBAL ENROLLMENT Year	County	No.
11975	1	Watson, Adam [20]		17	M	Full	1896	Bok Tuklo	13427
	2								
	3								
	4								
	5	ENROLLMENT							
	6	OF NOS. 1 HEREON APPROVED BY THE SECRETARY							
	7	OF INTERIOR MAR 10 1903							
	8								
	9								
	10								
	11								
	12								
	13								
	14								
	15								
	16								
	17								

TRIBAL ENROLLMENT OF PARENTS

	Name of Father	Year	County	Name of Mother	Year	County
1	Ca-nan-tubbee	Dead	Bok Tuklo		Dead	Bok Tuklo
2						
3						
4						
5						
6	№1 also on 1896 Choctaw census roll page 365 #13912 as Adam Williams					
7	№1 is 23 years of age. See testimony of July 22, 1903					
8						
9						
10						
11						
12						
13						
14						Date of Application for Enrollment.
15						Aug 31/99
16						
17						

RESIDENCE: Atoka COUNTY. **Choctaw Nation** Choctaw Roll (*Not Including Freedmen*) CARD NO.
POST OFFICE: Atoka, I.T. FIELD NO. 4277

Dawes' Roll No.	NAME	Relationship to Person First Named	AGE	SEX	BLOOD	TRIBAL ENROLLMENT Year	County	No.
11976	1 Thompson, Wilburn 38	First Named	35	M	Full	1896	Atoka	12432
DEAD.	2 " ~~Lista~~	~~Wife~~	~~20~~	~~F~~	"	~~1893~~	"	~~757~~
11977	3 " Malinda 13	Dau	10	"	"	1896	"	12437
11978	4 " Philip 12	Son	9	M	"	1896	"	12434
11979	5 " Alfred 10	"	7	"	"	1896	"	12435
11980	6 " David 9	"	6	"	"	1896	"	12436
	7							
	8							
	9							
	10 ENROLLMENT							
	11 OF NOS. 1,3,4,5 and 6 HEREON APPROVED BY THE SECRETARY							
	12 OF INTERIOR MAR 10 1903							
	13 No. 2 HEREON DISMISSED UNDER							
	14 ORDER OF THE COMMISSION TO THE FIVE							
	15 CIVILIZED TRIBES OF MARCH 31, 1905.							
	16							
	17							

TRIBAL ENROLLMENT OF PARENTS

Name of Father	Year	County	Name of Mother	Year	County
1 Wallace Thompson	Dead	Atoka	Jincy Thompson	Dead	Atoka
2 ~~Abert[sic] Tom~~	"	~~Jackson~~	~~Fannie Tom~~	"	"
3 No1			Liza A Thompson	"	"
4 No1			Sally Thompson	"	Jacks Fork
5 No1			Liza A Thompson	"	Atoka
6 No1			" " "	"	"
7					
8					
9					
10					
11					
12					
13					
14					
15				Date of Application for Enrollment.	Aug 31/99
16					
17					

~~No2 on 1893 Pay Roll, Page 73, No 757 Atoka Co, as Listie Marlin~~
No3 on 1896 roll as Belindy Thompson
~~No2 " 1896 " " Lottie Mullin, Page 221, No 8813, Atoka Co.~~
No2 died January – 1901; proof of death filed Nov 25, 1902
No.4 on 1896 Roll as Phillip Thompson
For child of No.1 see NB (March 3, 1905) Card #575

RESIDENCE: Atoka COUNTY. **Choctaw Nation** **Choctaw Roll** *(Not Including Freedmen)* CARD NO.
POST OFFICE: Atoka, I.T. FIELD NO. **4278**

Dawes' Roll No.	NAME		Relationship to Person First Named	AGE	SEX	BLOOD	TRIBAL ENROLLMENT Year	County	No.
11981	1 Lewis, Sallie	43	First Named	40	F	Full	1896	Atoka	8256
11982	2 Carnes, Anderson	23	Son	20	M	"	1896	"	2972
11983	3 Lewis, Sampson	18	"	15	"	"	1896	"	8258
11984	4 " Eliza	14	Dau	11	F	"	1896	"	8261
11985	5 " John	9	Son	6	M	"	1896	"	8259
	6								
	7								
	8								
	9								
	10								
	11								
	12								
	13								
	14								
	15								
	16								
	17								

ENROLLMENT
OF NOS. 1,2,3,4 and 5 HEREON
APPROVED BY THE SECRETARY
OF INTERIOR Mar 10, 1903

TRIBAL ENROLLMENT OF PARENTS

Name of Father	Year	County	Name of Mother	Year	County
1 Wallace Thompson		Atoka	Jincy Thompson	Dead	Atoka
2 Ellis Carnes	Dead	"	No.1		
3 Josin Lewis	"	"	No.1		
4 " "	"	"	No.1		
5 " "	"	"	No.1		

No.2 on 1896 roll as Anderson Carn
No.4 " 1896 " " Liza Lewis
No.5 " 1896 " " Chan "
No.2 is now the husband of Annie Robinson on Choctaw Case #4061. See letter of A. Telle, filed Aug 13, 1902 in Choctaw Case #4061.

Date of Application for Enrollment
Aug 31/99

Choctaw By Blood Enrollment Cards 1898-1914

RESIDENCE: Atoka COUNTY. **Choctaw Nation** Choctaw Roll (Not Including Freedmen) CARD NO.
POST OFFICE: Wapanucka, I.T. FIELD NO. 4279

Dawes' Roll No.	NAME	Relationship to Person First Named	AGE	SEX	BLOOD	TRIBAL ENROLLMENT Year	County	No.
	1 Ray, Mary P		24	F	1/8			
	2 " Leroy	Son	4	M	1/16			
	3 " Ollie B	Dau	3mo	F	1/16			

All DISMISSED
SEP 20 1904

TRIBAL ENROLLMENT OF PARENTS

Name of Father	Year	County	Name of Mother	Year	County
1 William Cantrell	Dead	Non Citz	Ellen Cantrell		Choctaw
2 J. M. Ray		" "	No1		
3 " "		" "	№1		

Nos 1&2 denied in 1896: Case #1106
Nos1-3 denied in 96 Case #968
Admitted by U S. Court, Central Dist Jany 18-98, Case No 30. As to residence, see her testimony No1
№3 Born Dec 29, 1901; enrolled April 8, 1902
Judgment of U.S. Ct admitting No1-2 vacated and set aside by Decree of C.C.C.C. Dec' 17 '02
No appeal to C.C.C.C.

Date of Application for Enrollment.
Aug 31/99

P.O. Byrne 4/8/1902

Choctaw By Blood Enrollment Cards 1898-1914

RESIDENCE: Atoka COUNTY. **Choctaw Nation** **Choctaw Roll** *(Not Including Freedmen)* CARD NO.
POST OFFICE: Oconee, I T FIELD NO. 4280

Dawes' Roll No.		NAME	Relationship to Person First Named	AGE	SEX	BLOOD	TRIBAL ENROLLMENT Year	County	No.
✓	1	Buchanan Allison, Beulah L		19	F	1/8			
	2	Buchanan, William P	Son	2mo	M	1/16			
	3								
	4								
	5								
	6	DISMISSED							
	7	SEP 22	1904						
	8								
	9								
	10								
	11								
	12								
	13								
	14								
	15								
	16								
	17								

TRIBAL ENROLLMENT OF PARENTS

	Name of Father	Year	County	Name of Mother	Year	County
1	William Cantrell	Dead	Non Citz	Ellen Cantrell		Choctaw
2	J.W. Buchanan		non-citizen	No.1		
3						
4						

5 No1 Denied in 96 Case #968
Admitted by U.S. Court, Central
6 Dist, Jany 18-98, Case No 30, as
7 Beulah L. Cantrell. As to residence
see her testimony
8 No1 is now married to J.W. Buchanan a non citizen. Evidence
9 of marriage to supplied 4/27/01. Filed May 17, 1901
10 No2 Enrolled April 27, 1901
11 No1 was once married to Lee Allison but was divorced from him
February 5, 1900 Copy of the decree filed June 3, 1901
12 Judgment of U.S. Ct admitting No1 vacated and set aside by Decree of Choctaw Chickasaw Cit Ct Dec' 17 '02
13 No appeal to C.C.C.C.
14 For child of No1 see (Act Apr 26 '06) NB #1046

Date of Application for Enrollment Aug 31/99

15
16
17 Apl[sic] 21-1901 PO Byrne IT

Choctaw By Blood Enrollment Cards 1898-1914

RESIDENCE: Atoka COUNTY. **Choctaw Nation** **Choctaw Roll** (Not Including Freedmen) CARD NO.
POST OFFICE: Oconee, I.T. FIELD NO. 4281

Dawes' Roll No.		NAME	Relationship to Person First Named	AGE	SEX	BLOOD	TRIBAL ENROLLMENT Year	County	No.
✓	1	~~Winchester, Arabelle~~	~~First Named~~	~~15~~	~~F~~	~~1/8~~			
	2	~~" Lona L~~	~~Dau~~	~~1~~	~~"~~	~~1/16~~			
	3								
	4								
	5	DISMISSED							
	6	SEP 22 1904							
	7								
	8								
	9								
	10								
	11								
	12								
	13								
	14								
	15								
	16								
	17								

TRIBAL ENROLLMENT OF PARENTS

	Name of Father	Year	County	Name of Mother	Year	County
1	~~William Cantrell~~	~~Dead~~	~~Non Citz~~	~~Ellen Cantrell~~		~~Choctaw~~
2	~~Fillmore Winchester~~		~~" "~~	~~No1~~		
3						
4						

No1 denied in 96 Case #968

No1- Admitted by U.S. Court, Central Dist, Jany 18-98, Case No 30, as Arabelle Cantrell

~~As to residence and birth of No2, which occurred Nov 1/98, see her testimony~~

No2- Affidavit of birth to be supplied:- Recd Dec 18/99. Irregular and returned for correction. ~~Filed Jan 17, 1900~~

Judgements of US Court admitting No1 vacated and set aside by Decree of Choctaw Chickasaw Citizenship Court Dec 17'02

No appeal to C.C.C.C.

Aug 31/99

Date of Application for Enrollment.

Choctaw By Blood Enrollment Cards 1898-1914

RESIDENCE: Chickasaw Nation ~~COUNTY.~~ **Choctaw Nation** **Choctaw Roll** *(Not Including Freedmen)* CARD NO.
POST OFFICE: Cumberland, I.T. FIELD NO. 4282

Dawes' Roll No.	NAME	Relationship to Person First Named	AGE	SEX	BLOOD	TRIBAL ENROLLMENT Year	County	No.
✓	1 Cantrell, James W		29	M	1/8			
	2 " Fannie	Wife	29	F	IW			
✓	3 " Grover C	Son	11	M	1/16			
✓	4 " Maud L	Dau	8	F	1/16			
✓	5 " Roxie M	"	4	"	1/16			
	6 " McKinley H	Son	5m	M	1/16			
	7							
	8							
	9 DISMISSED							
	10 SEP 20 1904							
	11							
	12							
	13							
	14							
	15							
	16							
	17							

TRIBAL ENROLLMENT OF PARENTS

	Name of Father	Year	County	Name of Mother	Year	County
1	William Cantrell	Dead	Non Citz	Ellen Cantrell		Choctaw
2	William Wells	"	" "	Sally Wells	Dead	Non Citz
3	No1			No2		
4	No1			No2		
5	No1			No2		
6	No1			No2		
7						

Nos 1 to 5 incl denied in 96 Case #905
Admitted by U.S. Court, Central Dist, Jany 18-98, Case No 30. As to residence, see testimony of No1
No4 admitted as Maudie Lee Cantrell
No5 " " Roxie May "
No6 Enrolled February 7, 1901
Judgement(s) of U.S. Court admitting Nos 1 to 5 incl vacated and set aside by Decree of Choctaw Chickasaw Cit Ct Dec 17/02
No appeal to C.C.C.C.

Aug 31/99
Date of Application for Enrollment.

Byrne 7/15/1904

RESIDENCE: Atoka COUNTY. **Choctaw Nation** **Choctaw Roll** *(Not Including Freedmen)* CARD NO.
POST OFFICE: Atoka, I.T. FIELD NO. 4283

Dawes' Roll No.		NAME	Relationship to Person First Named	AGE	SEX	BLOOD	TRIBAL ENROLLMENT Year	County	No.
	1	~~Shockey, John~~	~~First Named~~	~~21~~	~~M~~	~~1/8~~			
	2								
	3								
	4								
	5	DISMISSED							
	6								
	7	DEC 24 1904							
	8								
	9								
	10								
	11								
	12								
	13								
	14								
	15								
	16								
	17								

TRIBAL ENROLLMENT OF PARENTS

	Name of Father	Year	County	Name of Mother	Year	County
1	~~George Shockey~~	~~Dead~~	~~Non Citz~~	~~Lou Shockey~~		~~Choctaw~~

Admitted by U.S. Court, Central Dist.
Jany 18-98, Case No 30. As to residence,
see his testimony

~~Judgement (sic) of U.S. Court admitting No1 vacated and set aside by Decree of Choctaw Chickasaw Cit Ct Dec 17'02~~
No appeal to C.C.C.C.

For child of No1 see NB (Apr 26 '06) No 1295

Date of Application for Enrollment.
Aug 31/99

P.O. Galo IT 12/22/03

RESIDENCE: Chickasaw Nation ~~COUNTY.~~ **Choctaw Nation** **Choctaw Roll** *(Not Including Freedmen)* CARD NO.
POST OFFICE: Cumberland, I.T. FIELD NO. 4284

Dawes' Roll No.	NAME	Relationship to Person First Named	AGE	SEX	BLOOD	TRIBAL ENROLLMENT Year	County	No.
	1 ~~Shockey, Robert~~	~~Named~~	~~28~~	~~M~~	~~1/8~~			
	2							
	3							
	4 DISMISSED							
	5							
	6 DEC 24 1904							
	7							
	8							
	9							
	10							
	11							
	12							
	13							
	14							
	15							
	16							
	17							

TRIBAL ENROLLMENT OF PARENTS

Name of Father	Year	County	Name of Mother	Year	County
1 ~~George Shockey~~	~~Dead~~	~~Non Citz~~	~~Louisa Shockey~~		~~Choctaw~~
2					
3					
4					
5					
6					
7					
8					
9					
10					
11					
12					
13					Date of Application for Enrollment.
14					
15					Aug 31/99
16					
17					

Admitted by U.S. Court, Central Dist, Jany 18-98, Case No 30. As to residence, see his testimony

~~Judgement[sic] of U.S. Court admitting No1 vacated and set aside by Decree of Choctaw Chickasaw Cit Ct Dec 17'02~~

No appeal to C.C.C.C.

Choctaw By Blood Enrollment Cards 1898-1914

RESIDENCE: Atoka COUNTY. **Choctaw Nation** **Choctaw Roll** (Not Including Freedmen) CARD NO.
POST OFFICE: Atoka, I.T FIELD NO. 4285

Dawes' Roll No.	NAME	Relationship to Person First Named	AGE	SEX	BLOOD	TRIBAL ENROLLMENT Year	County	No.
11986	1 Frazier, Noah 31	First Named	28	M	Full	1896	Atoka	4502
	2							
	3							
	4							
	5							
	6							
	7							
	8							
	9							
	10							
	11							
	12							
	13							
	14							
	15							
	16							
	17							

ENROLLMENT OF NOS. 1 HEREON APPROVED BY THE SECRETARY OF INTERIOR MAR 10 1903

TRIBAL ENROLLMENT OF PARENTS

Name of Father	Year	County	Name of Mother	Year	County
1 Davis Frazier	Dead	Atoka	Winey Frazier	Dead	Atoka
2					
3					
4					
5					
6					
7					
8					
9					
10					
11					
12					
13					
14					Date of Application for Enrollment.
15					Aug 31/99
16					
17					

On 1896 roll as Noah Fronterhouse.

For child of No1 see NB (Apr 26-06) Card #392

RESIDENCE: Jacks Fork COUNTY. **Choctaw Nation** **Choctaw Roll** *(Not Including Freedmen)* CARD NO.
POST OFFICE: Stringtown, I.T. FIELD NO. 4286

Dawes' Roll No.		NAME	Relationship to Person First Named	AGE	SEX	BLOOD	TRIBAL ENROLLMENT Year	County	No.
11987	1	Sexton, Dixon [49]	First Named	46	M	Full	1896	Jacks Fork	11713
11988	2	" Susan [45]	Wife	42	F	"	1896	" "	11714
11989	3	Jones, Nancy [29]	Dau	26	"	"	1896	" "	11715
11990	4	Neal, Minnie [20]	"	17	"	"	1896	" "	11717
11991	5	Sexton, Ella [15]	"	12	"	"	1896	" "	11719
11992	6	" Iwana [13]	"	10	"	"	1896	" "	11720
11993	7	" Alexander [10]	Son	7	M	"	1896	" "	11721
11994	8	Neal Calvin Hicks [1]	Son of No4	2mo	"	"			
	9								
	10								
	11								
	12								
	13								
	14								
	15								
	16								
	17								

ENROLLMENT
OF NOS. 1,2,3,4,5,6,7 and 8 HEREON
APPROVED BY THE SECRETARY
OF INTERIOR MAR 10 1903

TRIBAL ENROLLMENT OF PARENTS

	Name of Father	Year	County	Name of Mother	Year	County
1	Willis Sexton	Dead	Towson		Dead	Towson
2	Ta-ken-labbee	"	"	Easter	"	"
3	No1			No2		
4	No1			No2		
5	No1			No2		
6	No1			No2		
7	No1			No2		
8	Alvin Neal		non citizen	No4		

No6 on 1896 roll as Iwona Sexton

No4 is now the wife of Alvin Neal, non citizen. Evidence of marriage filed Oct 5. 1901

No8 Enrolled Oct 5, 1901

~~No3 is now wife of Sim Jones on Choctaw card #464~~

#1 to 7

Evidence of marriage filed December 15, 1902

Date of Application for Enrollment. Aug 31/99

For child of No4 see NB 940 (Act Apr 26 06)

RESIDENCE: Jacks Fork COUNTY. **Choctaw Nation** **Choctaw Roll** (*Not Including Freedmen*) CARD NO.
POST OFFICE: Stringtown, I.T. FIELD NO. 4287

Dawes' Roll No.	NAME		Relationship to Person First Named	AGE	SEX	BLOOD	TRIBAL ENROLLMENT Year	County	No.
11995	1 Sexton, Willis	23		20	M	1/2	1896	Atoka	11716
I.W. 405	2 " Maggie	22	Wife	19	F	IW			

ENROLLMENT
OF NOS. 1 HEREON
APPROVED BY THE SECRETARY
OF INTERIOR MAR 10 1903

ENROLLMENT
OF NOS. 2 HEREON
APPROVED BY THE SECRETARY
OF INTERIOR SEP 12 1903

TRIBAL ENROLLMENT OF PARENTS

Name of Father	Year	County	Name of Mother	Year	County
1 Dixon Sexton		Jacks Fork	Susan Sexton		Jacks Fork
2 Mat Good		Non Citz	Mary Good		Non Citz

Date of Application for Enrollment.
Aug 31/99

Choctaw By Blood Enrollment Cards 1898-1914

RESIDENCE: Atoka COUNTY. **Choctaw Nation** **Choctaw Roll** (Not Including Freedmen) CARD NO.
POST OFFICE: Lehigh, I.T. FIELD NO. 4288

Dawes' Roll No.	NAME		Relationship to Person First Named	AGE	SEX	BLOOD	TRIBAL ENROLLMENT Year	County	No.
11996	1 Hodges, Joseph J	45	First Named	42	M	1/4	1896	Atoka	5982
IW406	2 " Laura B	40	Wife	37	F	I.W.	1896	"	14655
11997	3 " Henry	21	Son	18	M	1/4	1896	Atoka	5983
11998	4 " Henrietta	19	Dau	16	F	1/8	1896	"	5984
11999	5 " Mary P	14	"	11	"	1/8	1896	"	5985
12000	6 " Jennie G	12	"	9	"	1/8	1896	"	5986
12001	7 " Joseph T	4	Son	2	M	1/8			

ENROLLMENT OF NOS. 1,3,4,5,6 and 7 HEREON APPROVED BY THE SECRETARY OF INTERIOR Mar 10 1903

ENROLLMENT OF NOS. 2 HEREON APPROVED BY THE SECRETARY OF INTERIOR Sep 12 1903

TRIBAL ENROLLMENT OF PARENTS

	Name of Father	Year	County	Name of Mother	Year	County
1	Jos Hodges	Dead	Non Citz	Sibble Hodges	Dead	in Mississippi
2	John Miller	"	" "	Henrietta Miller	"	Non Citz
3	No1			Rosa Hodges	"	Atoka
4	No1			No2		
5	No1			No2		
6	No1			No2		
7	No1			No2		

No1 on 1896 roll as Joe Hodges
No2 Admitted by Dawes Com,
Case No 1360
~~No7 Affidavit of birth to be supplied:-~~ Filed Oct 26/99
For child of No.4 see NB (April 26,1906) Card No 47
" " " " 4 " " (March 4,1905) " " 554
" " " " 3 " " " " " " " 729

Date of Application for Enrollment. Aug 31/99

~~No4 P.O. Midway I.T. 1/12/05~~
No3 P.O. Coalgate I.T. 4/4/05

RESIDENCE: Chickasaw Nation ~~COUNTY.~~ **Choctaw Nation** Choctaw Roll (Not Including Freedmen) CARD NO.
POST OFFICE: Linn, I.T. FIELD NO. 4289

Dawes' Roll No.	NAME	Relationship to Person First Named	AGE	SEX	BLOOD	TRIBAL ENROLLMENT Year	County	No.
12002	1 Moore, Joseph R 32		29	M	1/16	1896	Atoka	8850
	2							
	3							
	4							
	5							
	6							
	7							
	8							
	9							
	10							
	11							
	12							
	13							
	14							
	15							
	16							
	17							

ENROLLMENT
OF NOS. 1 HEREON
~~APPROVED BY THE SECRETARY~~
OF INTERIOR MAR 10 1903

TRIBAL ENROLLMENT OF PARENTS

Name of Father	Year	County	Name of Mother	Year	County
1 J. G. Moore	Dead	Choctaw Roll	Mary Moore	Dead	Non Citz
2					
3					
4					
5					
6					
7					
8					
9					
10					
11					
12					
13					
14					
15					
16					
17					

~~As to marriage of parents, see~~
testimony of Marion Tiner
No.1 also on 1896 Choctaw census roll: page 225: No 8905
~~as Joseph Moore~~

No.1 is father of Frank Moore, Choctaw #373

~~For child of No1 see NB (Mch 3-05) Card #654~~
" " " " " " (Apr 26-06) " #383

~~Date of Application for Enrollment.~~ Aug 31/99

P.O. Dixie, I.T.

RESIDENCE: Atoka COUNTY. **Choctaw Nation** **Choctaw Roll** (*Not Including Freedmen*) CARD NO.
POST OFFICE: Coalgate, I.T. FIELD NO. 4290

Dawes' Roll No.	NAME	Relationship to Person First Named	AGE	SEX	BLOOD	TRIBAL ENROLLMENT Year	County	No.
14409	1 Breedlove, Josephine 31	First Named	28	F	1/4	1896	Atoka	1790
14410	2 " Bertha 15	Dau	12	"	1/8	1896	"	1791
14411	3 " Bessie 14	"	11	"	1/8	1896	"	1792
14412	4 " Pearl 12	"	9	"	1/8	1896	"	1793
14413	5 " Myrtle 10	"	7	"	1/8	1896	"	1794
14414	6 " Wilson R 9	Son	6	M	1/8	1896	"	1795
12003	7 Summers, Joseph 19	Bro	16	"	1/16	1896	"	11670
	8							
	9							
	10							
	11							
	12							
	13							
	14							
	15							
	16							
	17							

ENROLLMENT OF NOS. 7 HEREON APPROVED BY THE SECRETARY OF INTERIOR MAR 6 1903

ENROLLMENT OF NOS. 1 2 3 4 5 and 6 HEREON APPROVED BY THE SECRETARY OF INTERIOR APR 11 1903

TRIBAL ENROLLMENT OF PARENTS

Name of Father	Year	County	Name of Mother	Year	County
1 Louis LeFlore	Dead	Atoka	Narcissa LeFlore	Dead	Atoka
2 Henry Breedlove	"	Non Citz	No1		
3 " "	"	" "	No1		
4 " "	"	" "	No1		
5 " "	"	" "	No1		
6 " "	"	" "	No1		
7 Joseph Summers	"	" "	Narcissa Summers	Dead	Atoka
8					
9					
10		No6 on 1896 roll as Roy Breedlove			
11		No7 " 1896 " " Joseph Summers			
12					
13		All but No7 were admitted by			
14		Dawes Com, Case No 885 No appeal			Date of Application for Enrollment.
15			Date of application for enrollment		Aug 31/99
16					
17					

Choctaw By Blood Enrollment Cards 1898-1914

RESIDENCE: Atoka COUNTY. **Choctaw Nation** **Choctaw Roll** *(Not Including Freedmen)* CARD NO.
POST OFFICE: Atoka, I.T. FIELD NO. 4291

Dawes' Roll No.	NAME	Relationship to Person First Named	AGE	SEX	BLOOD	TRIBAL ENROLLMENT Year	County	No.
	1 Neely, Frances C		44	M	1/4		D	
	2 " Cora A	Dau	19	F	1/8		D	
DEAD.	3 " William E	Son	17	M	1/8		D	
	4 " May E	Dau	15	F	1/8		D	
	5 " Caroline E	"	13	"	1/8		D	
	6 " Marlin O	Son	10	M	1/8		D	
	7 " Viva A	Dau	5	F	1/8		D	
	8 " Joseph R	Son	3	M	1/8		D	
	9 Hill, Neely Hadys	Granddau	1mo	F	1/16		D	
	10 #9- DISMISSED NOV 12 1904							
	11 Nos 1 to 9 incl except No3 now in C.C.C.C. Case #79							
	12 No.2 denied by C.C.C.C. as Cora A							
	13 Hill (nee Neely) or Cora A Neely							
	No.5 denied by C.C.C.C. as Caroline							
	14 E Jelks (nee Neely) or Caroline E Neely							
	15 No.6 denied by C.C.C.C. as Marlin O							
	16 Neely or Marlin C Neely							
	For child of No5 see NB #988 – (Act Apr 26 '06)							
	17							

No. 3 HEREON DISMISSED UNDER ORDER OF THE COMMISSION TO THE FIVE CIVILIZED TRIBES OF MARCH 31, 1905

TRIBAL ENROLLMENT OF PARENTS

Name of Father	Year	County	Name of Mother	Year	County
1 Allen Cryor	Dead	Non Citz	Elizabeth Cryor	Dead	Choctaw
2 Joseph W Neely		" "	No1		
3 " " "		" "	No1		
4 " " "		" "	No1		
5 " " "		" "	No1		
6 " " "		" "	No1		
7 " " "		" "	No1		
8 " " "		" "	No1		
9 Alfred Hill		non-citizen	No.2		

DENIED CITIZENSHIP BY THE CHOCTAW AND CHICKASAW CITIZENSHIP COURT

Nos 1,2,4,5,6,7&8 Case #79 in Oct 26 '04

10 No1 to 9 denied in 96 Case #1144
11 Admitted by U.S. Court, Central Dist
12 Jany 18-98, Case No 76. As to residence
see testimony of No1
13 No2 is now the wife of Alfred Hill-a noncitizen
14 Evidence of marriage filed Sept 3, 1901
15 No9 born Dec 8,1901: Enrolled Jany 21st,1902
N°5 is now the wife of Walter T Jelks on Choctaw card #D794
16 N°3 Died Jany 27, 1902; proof of death filed March 16,1903 Sept 20,1907
17 P.O. Marlow I.T. 1/5/03

No.7 denied by C.C.C.C. as Viva E Neely or Joseph R Neely
No.8 denied by C.C.C.C. James R Neely
Judgment of U.S. Ct admitting Nos 1 to 8 vacated and set aside by Decree of C.C.C.C. Dec 17 '02
name given as Cora Alva

Date of Application for Enrollment.
Aug 31/99

No9 Dismissed by C.C.C.C. for want of jurisdiction

Choctaw By Blood Enrollment Cards 1898-1914

RESIDENCE: Atoka COUNTY. **Choctaw Nation** **Choctaw Roll** *(Not Including Freedmen)* CARD NO.
POST OFFICE: Atoka, I.T. FIELD NO. 4292

Dawes' Roll No.		NAME	Relationship to Person First Named	AGE	SEX	BLOOD	TRIBAL ENROLLMENT Year	County	No.
	1	~~M^c^Gahey, Minnie A~~	~~Named~~	~~21~~	~~F~~	~~1/8~~		D	
Transferred	2	~~" " Florence L~~	~~Dau~~	~~3mo~~	~~F~~	~~1/8~~			
Transferred	3	~~" " Frances~~	~~Dau~~	~~2mo~~	~~F~~	~~1/8~~			

No.1 denied by C.C.C.C. as Minnie A McGahey (nee Neely) or Minnie A. Neely

No1 ~~DENIED CITIZENSHIP BY THE CHOCTAW AND~~ CHICKASAW CITIZENSHIP COURT

TRIBAL ENROLLMENT OF PARENTS

	Name of Father	Year	County	Name of Mother	Year	County
1	~~Joseph W Neely~~		~~Non Citz~~	~~Frances C Neely~~		~~Choctaw~~
2	~~John H. McGahey~~	~~1896~~	~~Jack[sic] Fork~~	~~No.1~~		
3	" " "	~~1896~~	" "	~~Nº1~~		

No1 denied in 96 Case #1144
Admitted by U.S. Court, Central Dist, Jany 18-98, Case No 76. As ~~to residence, see testimony of Frances C Neely.~~
No.1 is the wife of John H M^c^Gahey, on Choctaw card #1788
No2 enrolled Dec 7th 1900
Nº3 Born July 17, 1902. Enrolled Sept 27, 1902
~~Nos 2&3 transferred to card #1788: Oct 4, 1902~~
No1 now in C.C.C.C. Case #79
No.1 on Choctaw card No. 5910

Date of Application for Enrollment.
Aug 31/99

No.1 appeared 11/21'02 and attempted to apply as intermarried citizen. Her application not received

Choctaw By Blood Enrollment Cards 1898-1914

RESIDENCE: Atoka COUNTY. **Choctaw Nation** **Choctaw Roll** *(Not Including Freedmen)* CARD NO.
POST OFFICE: Atoka, I.T. FIELD NO. 4293

Dawes' Roll No.		NAME	Relationship to Person First Named	AGE	SEX	BLOOD	TRIBAL ENROLLMENT Year	County	No.
	1	~~Neely, Ora L~~	~~Named~~	~~28~~	~~F~~	~~1/8~~		D	

No.1 DENIED CITIZENSHIP BY THE CHOCTAW AND CHICKASAW CITIZENSHIP COURT

TRIBAL ENROLLMENT OF PARENTS

	Name of Father	Year	County	Name of Mother	Year	County
1	~~Joseph W Neely~~		~~Non Citz~~	~~Frances C. Neely~~		~~Choctaw~~

No1 denied in 96 Case #1144

Admitted by U.S. Court, Central Dist, Jany 18/98, Case No 76 As to residence see her testimony

Judgment of US Ct admitting No1 vacated and set aside by Decree of Choctaw Chickasaw Citizenship Court Dec 17 '02

No1 now in C.C.C.C. Case #79

Date of Application for Enrollment. Aug 31/99

Choctaw By Blood Enrollment Cards 1898-1914

RESIDENCE: Blue COUNTY. **Choctaw Nation** **Choctaw Roll** *(Not Including Freedmen)* CARD NO.

POST OFFICE: Caddo, I.T. FIELD NO. 4294

Dawes' Roll No.	NAME	Relationship to Person First Named	AGE	SEX	BLOOD	TRIBAL ENROLLMENT Year	County	No.
	1 ~~Neely, Henry A~~	~~Named~~	~~26~~	~~M~~	~~1/8~~		D	
	2 ~~" Gelia A~~	~~Wife~~	~~23~~	~~F~~	~~IW~~		D	
	3 ~~" Corda V~~	~~Dau~~	~~3~~	~~"~~	~~1/16~~		D	
DP	4 ~~" Jessie I~~	~~"~~	~~6mo~~	~~"~~	~~1/16~~		Dis	
DP	5 ~~" Homer E~~	~~Son~~	~~4mo~~	~~M~~	~~1/16~~		Dis	

DENIED CITIZENSHIP BY THE CHOCTAW AND CHICKASAW CITIZENSHIP COURT

Nos 1,2,3

Case #79 in Oct 20 '04

No.2 denied by C.C.C.C. as Gelie A Neely or Gelia A Neely

~~No3 denied by C.C.C.C. as Cordie V Neely or Corda V Neely~~

#4 – 5 – DISMISSED NOV 12 1904

TRIBAL ENROLLMENT OF PARENTS

	Name of Father	Year	County	Name of Mother	Year	County
1	~~Joseph W Neely~~		~~Non Citz~~	~~Frances C Neely~~		~~Choctaw~~
2	~~Cane~~	~~Dead~~	~~" "~~	~~Alice Smith~~		~~Non Citz~~
3	~~No1~~			~~No2~~		
4	~~No1~~			~~No2~~		
5	~~No.1~~			~~No.2~~		

Nos 1 to 3 incl denied in 96 Case #1144

First three were admitted by U.S. Court Central Dist, Jany 18-98, Case No 76.

~~As to residence and birth of No4,~~ see testimony of No2

No4- Affidavit of birth to be supplied:-

~~No5 Enrolled Sept. 17, 1901~~

Judgment of U.S. Ct admitting No1 to 3 incl vacated and set aside by Decree of C.C.C.C. Dec 17 '02

Nos 1 to 5 now in C.C.C.C. Case #79

No4&5 dismissed by C.C.C.C. for want of jurisdiction.

Date of Application for Enrollment. Aug 31/99

Choctaw By Blood Enrollment Cards 1898-1914

RESIDENCE: Atoka   COUNTY. **Choctaw Nation**   **Choctaw Roll** *(Not Including Freedmen)*   CARD NO.
POST OFFICE: Atoka, I.T.   FIELD NO. 4295

Dawes' Roll No.		NAME	Relationship to Person First Named	AGE	SEX	BLOOD	TRIBAL ENROLLMENT Year	County	No.
DEAD.	1	Adams, Almar G DEAD.		24	F	1/8			
DP	2	" Howard A	Son	2wks	M	1/16		Dis	
	3								
	4	#2- DISMISSED							
	5	NOV 12 1904							
	6								
	7								
	8								
	9								
	10								
	11								
	12								
	13								
	14								
	15								
	16								
	17								

TRIBAL ENROLLMENT OF PARENTS

	Name of Father	Year	County	Name of Mother	Year	County
1	Joseph W Neely		Non Citz	Frances C Neely		Choctaw
2	John E Adams		" "	No1		
3						
4						
5						
6						
7						

No1 denied in 96 Case #1144
No1- Admitted by U.S. Court, Central Dist Jany 18-98 Case No 76 as Almar A Neely Judgment of U.S. Ct admitting No1 vacated and set aside by Decree of C.C.C.C. Dec 17 '02
As to residence and birth of child, see her testimony
Nº1 Died Sept 27, 1901: proof of death filed March 16, 1903
No2 now in C.C.C.C. Case #79
No2 Dismissed for want of Jurisdiction by C.C.C.C. in Case #79 Oct 20 '04

Date of Application for Enrollment. Aug 31/99

Choctaw By Blood Enrollment Cards 1898-1914

RESIDENCE: Atoka COUNTY. **Choctaw Nation** **Choctaw Roll** *(Not Including Freedmen)* CARD NO.
POST OFFICE: Lehigh, I.T. FIELD NO. 4296

Dawes' Roll No.	NAME	Relationship to Person First Named	AGE	SEX	BLOOD	TRIBAL ENROLLMENT Year	County	No.
I.W. 1473	1 Rigney. Rosa E 36	First Named	33	F	IW	1885	Atoka	102
12004	2 Davis, Henry Carl 21	Son	18	M	1/8	1896	Atoka	3595
12005	3 " Etta R 15	Dau	12	F	1/8	1896	"	3596
I.W. 407	4 " Mary T 23	Dau in law	20	F	I.W.			
12006	5 " Reggie Ruth 2	Grand dau	3mo	F	1/16			

No.1 restored to roll by Departmental authority of January 19, 1909 (File 5-51)

No1- DISMISSED SEP 23 1904

Such action rescinded and

No1- GRANTED JUN 27 1905

ENROLLMENT OF NOS. 2, 3 and 5 HEREON APPROVED BY THE SECRETARY OF INTERIOR MAR 6 1903

ENROLLMENT OF NOS. 4 HEREON APPROVED BY THE SECRETARY OF INTERIOR SEP 12 1903

For child of No3 see NB (Mar 3 '05) #302
For child of No2 see NB (Mar 3 '05) #301

ENROLLMENT OF NOS. one HEREON APPROVED BY THE SECRETARY OF INTERIOR AUG 22 1905

TRIBAL ENROLLMENT OF PARENTS

Name of Father	Year	County	Name of Mother	Year	County
1 Henry C Daniel	Dead	Non Citz	Hettie Daniel	Dead	Non Citz
2 Henry W Davis	"	Atoka	No1		
3 " " "	"	"	No1		
4 Albert Tachiner		Non-citizen	Ernestine Tachiner		Non-citizen
5 No.2			No.4		

Enrollment of No1 cancelled by order of Department March 1 1907

No1 admitted in 96 Case #76

No appeal to C.C.C.C.

No1 formerly wife of Henry W Davis 1885 Atoka No 1025, and who died about 1890

No1 was admitted by U.S. Court Central Dist, Aug 26/97 Case No 178. As to residence, see her testimony

Judgment of U.S. Ct admitting No1 vacated and set aside by Decree of C.C.C.C. Dec' 17 '02

No2 on 1896 roll as H. C. Davis

No3 " 1896 " " Ella R "

See affidavit of Nº4 as to non-appearance at Atoka I.T. Nov 17 to 21,1902 filed Feby 10,1903

No.2 and No.4 married June 3d 1900

See testimony of Sterling P Collett, husband of No1, taken Oct 17 '02

No.4 Enrolled June 7, 1900

No.5 Enrolled July 6th, 1901

No.1 originally listed hereon as Rosa E Collet

Date of Application for Enrollment. Aug 31/99

INTERMARRIED STATUS. SEPTEMBER 25, 1902.

RESIDENCE: Atoka COUNTY. **Choctaw Nat**
POST OFFICE: Atoka, I.T.

Dawes' Roll No.	NAME		Relationship to Person First Named	AGE	SEX	BLOOD	TRIBAL ENROLLMENT Year	County	No.
12007	1 Cole, Ella	43	First Named	40	F	Full	1896	Atoka	8283
12008	2 Collins, Elsie	26	Dau	23	"	"	1896	"	2936
DEAD.	3 ~~" Nelson~~		~~Son~~	~~20~~	~~M~~	~~"~~	~~1896~~	~~"~~	~~2935~~
12009	4 Lawrence, Adam	18	"	15	"	"	1896	"	8284
12010	5 Collins Edmund	1	Son of ~~No 2~~	1	M	1/2			

ENROLLMENT OF NOS. 1,2,4 and 5 HEREON APPROVED BY THE SECRETARY OF INTERIOR MAR 6 1903

No. 3 HEREON DISMISSED UNDER ORDER OF THE COMMISSION TO THE FIVE ~~CIVILIZED TRIBES OF MARCH 31, 1905~~

TRIBAL ENROLLMENT OF PARENTS

Name of Father	Year	County	Name of Mother	Year	County
1 Edmund Cole	Dead	Jacks Fork	Syble Cole	Dead	Jacks Fork
2 Betipa Collins	"	" "	No1		
3 ~~" "~~	~~"~~	~~" "~~	~~No1~~		
4 Dan Lawrence		Atoka			
5 Illegitimate			No2		

~~No1 on 1896 roll as E. Lawrence~~
No2 " 1896 " " Elsey Collins
No3 died Sept, 1901; proof of death filed Nov 26, 1902
No5 born August 11, 1901: enrolled Dec 10, 1902

1 to 4 inc

Date of Application for Enrollment: Aug 31/99

~~No 2 P.O. Calloway I.T. 12/10/02~~
No2 PO Bentley Okla 11/26/10

Choctaw By Blood Enrollment Cards 1898-1914

RESIDENCE: Atoka I.T. COUNTY. **Choctaw Nation** **Choctaw Roll** *(Not Including Freedmen)*
POST OFFICE: ~~Atoka, I.~~T.

Dawes' Roll No.		NAME (Calloway, Okla)		Relationship to Person First Named	AGE	SEX	BLOOD	TRIBAL ENROLLMENT Year	County	No.
12011	1	Jackson, Willis	52		49	M	Full	1896	Atoka	7292
12012	2	" Mary	47	Wife	44	F	1/2	1896	"	7293
12013	3	M^c^Bride Winnie	24	Dau	21	"	3/4	1896	"	7298
12014	4	Jackson Sam	22	Son	19	M	3/4	1896	"	7294
12015	5	" Folsom	19	"	16	"	3/4	1896	"	7295
12016	6	" Lamar	17	"	14	"	3/4	1896	"	7296
12017	7	" Edmund	14	"	11	"	3/4	1896	"	7297
12018	8	Yarhamby, Charles	11	Ward	8	"	Full	1896	"	14245
I.W. 1340	9	Jackson Maria	30	Wife of No.4	30	F	I.W.	1896	Blue	14706

10 In 1887 No.9 married Bankston Johnson whose
11 name appears as #10488 on the lists made by this Com:
On Aug. 15, 1899 No.9 and Bankston Johnson were divorced

12–14 ENROLLMENT OF NOS. 1,2,3,4,5,6,7,8 HEREON APPROVED BY THE SECRETARY OF INTERIOR MAR 6 1903

No8 Dead Fall 1910
No8 Dead Sept 1910

15 On Aug 22, 1899 No.9 married Levi Goforth a recognized and enrolled citizen by blood
16 of the Chick Nation: identified as L.P. Goforth on the 1896 Chick Roll, Choctaw Dist,
~~page 74. They lived together until Goforth's death. In July 14, 1901 No.9 married~~
17 ~~Sam Jackson, No.4 hereon~~

TRIBAL ENROLLMENT OF PARENTS

	Name of Father	Year	County	Name of Mother	Year	County
1	Louis Jackson	Dead	in Mississippi	Sally Jackson	Dead	in Mississippi
2	John Harrison	"	Non Citz	Sukey Harrison	"	" "
3	No1			No2		
4	No1			No2		
5	No1			No2		
6	No1			No2		
7	No1			No2		
8	Willie Yarhamby	Dead	Atoka	Dixie Yarhamby	Dead	Atoka
9	Joe Casscadey	dead	Choctaw	Margaret Casscadey	dead	Choctaw

11 No.9 on 1896 roll as Maria Johnson, Page 391: No.14706
No3- See if enrolled elsewhere
12 ~~No8 On 1896 roll as Charles Yarbough~~
13 ~~No3 is now the wife of Emmette C M^c^Bride on Choctaw Card #D634 June 17,1901~~ #1 to 8 inc
14 No4 is now the Husband of Maria Goforth " " " #D518
Nos 1-6 inclusive admitted by act of Choctaw Council
15 ~~in 1889~~ ~~For child of No.3 see NB (March 3,1905) #764~~
16 ~~For child of No.5 see NB (Apr 26 '06) Card #93~~

Date of Application for Enrollment.
Aug 31/99

No.9 originally listed for enrollment on Choctaw card D-518 Nov 13/49: transferred to this card Feb 1,1905
See decision of Jan 16, 1905

RESIDENCE: Atoka COUNTY. **Choctaw Nation** **Choctaw Roll** (Not Including Freedmen) CARD NO.
POST OFFICE: Atoka, I.T. FIELD NO. 4299

Dawes' Roll No.		NAME	Relationship to Person First Named	AGE	SEX	BLOOD	TRIBAL ENROLLMENT Year	County	No.
DEAD.	1	~~Homer, Thomas~~	Named	~~50~~	~~M~~	~~Full~~	~~1896~~	~~Atoka~~	~~5970~~
12019	2	" Silvey 53	Wife	50	F	"	1896	"	5971
12020	3	LeFlore, Michael 25	S.Son	22	M	"	1896	"	8262
12021	4	M^c^Coy, Elias 6	Ward	3	"	"	1896	"	9442
	5								
	6								
	7	No. 2 HEREON DISMISSED UNDER							
	8	ORDER OF THE COMMISSION TO THE FIVE CIVILIZED TRIBES OF MARCH 31, 1905.							
	9								
	10								
	11	ENROLLMENT							
	12	OF NOS. 2, 3, 4 HEREON APPROVED BY THE SECRETARY							
	13	OF INTERIOR MAR 6 1903							
	14								
	15								
	16								
	17								

TRIBAL ENROLLMENT OF PARENTS

	Name of Father	Year	County	Name of Mother	Year	County
1	~~Edmund Homer~~	~~Dead~~	~~Towson~~	~~Lucy Homer~~	~~Dead~~	~~Kiamitia~~
2	E-me-le-chubbee	"	Atoka	Ha-ni-ye	"	Atoka
3	Nat LeFlore	"	"	No2		
4	Price M^c^Coy	"	"	Dixie M^c^Coy	"	Atoka
5						
6						
7						
8	No1 on 1896	roll as	Thomas Homma			
9	No2 " 1896	" "	Silvey "			
10	~~No1 died February 27, 1901: proof of death filed Nov 25, 1902~~					
11	For child of No.3 see N.B. (Apr 26, 1906) Card No 68					
12						
13						
14						Date of Application for Enrollment.
15						Aug 31/99
16						
17	P.O. Callaway IT 1/26/06					

Choctaw By Blood Enrollment Cards 1898-1914

RESIDENCE: Tobucksy COUNTY. **Choctaw Nation** (Not Including Freedmen) CARD NO.
POST OFFICE: M^c^Alester, I.T. FIELD NO. 4300

Dawes' Roll No.	NAME	Relationship to Person First Named	AGE	SEX	BLOOD	TRIBAL ENROLLMENT Year	County	No.
12022	1 Folsom, Lee 22	First Named	19	M	Full	1896	Tobucksy	4013
	2							
	3							
	4							
	5							
	6							
	7							
	8							
	9							
	10							
	11 P.O. address, Atoka, I.T: July 2, 1902							
	12							
	13 ENROLLMENT							
	14 OF NOS. 1 HEREON APPROVED BY THE SECRETARY							
	15 OF INTERIOR MAR 6 1903							
	16							
	17							

TRIBAL ENROLLMENT OF PARENTS

Name of Father	Year	County	Name of Mother	Year	County
1 Daniel Folsom	Dead	Atoka		Dead	Atoka
2					
3					
4					
5					
6 On 1896 roll as Lee Fulsom					
7					
8					
9					
10					
11					
12					
13					
14					
15			Date of Application for Enrollment.		Aug 31/99
16					
17					

Choctaw By Blood Enrollment Cards 1898-1914

RESIDENCE: Atoka COUNTY. **Choctaw Nation** **Choctaw Roll** *(Not Including Freedmen)* CARD NO.
POST OFFICE: Atoka, I.T. FIELD NO. 4301

Dawes' Roll No.	NAME	Relationship to Person First Named	AGE	SEX	BLOOD	TRIBAL ENROLLMENT Year	County	No.
12023	1 Wade, Joseph 21	First Named	18	M	Full	1896	Atoka	13977

ENROLLMENT
OF NOS. 1 HEREON
APPROVED BY THE SECRETARY
OF INTERIOR MAR 6 1903

TRIBAL ENROLLMENT OF PARENTS

Name of Father	Year	County	Name of Mother	Year	County
1 Dixon Wade	Dead	Atoka	Susan Wade	Dead	Atoka

On 1896 roll as Joe Wade

Date of Application for Enrollment. Aug 31/99

RESIDENCE: Atoka COUNTY. **Choctaw Nation** (Not Including Freedmen) CARD NO.

POST OFFICE: Atoka, I.T. FIELD NO. 4302

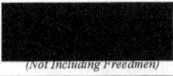

Dawes' Roll No.	NAME	Relationship to Person First Named	AGE	SEX	BLOOD	TRIBAL ENROLLMENT Year	County	No.
12024	1 Roberts, Henry 21	First Named	18	M	Full	1896	Atoka	11001
	2							
	3							
	4							
	5							
	6							
	7							
	8							
	9							
	10							
	11							
	12							
	13							
	14							
	15							
	16							
	17							

ENROLLMENT
OF NOS. 1 HEREON
APPROVED BY THE SECRETARY
OF INTERIOR MAR 6 1903

TRIBAL ENROLLMENT OF PARENTS

Name of Father	Year	County	Name of Mother	Year	County
1 Stephen Roberts		Atoka	Eliza A Harris	Dead	Atoka
2					
3					
4					
5					
6					
7 On 1896 roll as Henry Robert					
8					
9					
10					
11					
12					
13					
14					Date of Application for Enrollment.
15					Aug 31/99
16					
17					

Choctaw By Blood Enrollment Cards 1898-1914

RESIDENCE: Jacks Fork COUNTY. **Choctaw Nation** Choctaw Roll (Not Including Freedmen) CARD NO.
POST OFFICE: Stringtown, I.T. FIELD NO. 4303

Dawes' Roll No.	NAME	Relationship to Person First Named	AGE	SEX	BLOOD	TRIBAL ENROLLMENT Year	County	No.
12025	1 Jones, Jonas 47	First Named	44	M	1/4	1896	Jacks Fork	7342
12026	2 " Sophia 30	Wife	27	F	Full	1896	" "	7343
12027	3 " Joshua 13	Son	10	M	5/8	1896	" "	7335
12028	4 " Sophia Jr 11	Dau	8	F	5/8	1896	" "	7336
12029	5 " Frances 5	"	1½	"	5/8			
DEAD	6 ~~" Danil[sic]~~	~~Son~~	~~10mo~~	~~M~~	~~5/8~~			

No.6 hereon dismissed under order of the Commission to the Five Civilized Tribes of March 31, 1905.

ENROLLMENT OF NOS. 1 2 3 4 and 5 HEREON APPROVED BY THE SECRETARY OF INTERIOR Mar 6 1903

TRIBAL ENROLLMENT OF PARENTS

Name of Father	Year	County	Name of Mother	Year	County
1 Wallace Jones		Jackson	Myrah Jones	Dead	Sans Bois
2 Moses Bond		Jacks Fork	Nicey Bond	"	Jacks Fork
3 No1			Phoebe Jones	"	" "
4 No1			" "	"	" "
5 No1			No2		
6 ~~No1~~			~~No2~~		

No1 on 1896 roll as James Jones

No5- Affidavit of birth to be supplied:- Recd Oct 26/99

No.6 Enrolled July 19, 1901

For child of Nos 1&2 see NB (Mar 3 '05) #303

No.6 died March 22, 1902, evidence of death filed Nov 26, 1902

#1 to 5

Date of Application for Enrollment.

Aug 31/99

RESIDENCE: Jacks Fork COUNTY. **Choctaw Nation** **Choctaw Roll** *(Not Including Freedmen)* CARD NO.
POST OFFICE: Stringtown, I.T. FIELD NO. **4304**

Dawes' Roll No.		NAME	Relationship to Person First Named	AGE	SEX	BLOOD	TRIBAL ENROLLMENT Year	County	No.
12030	1	Tucker John E	First Named	54	M	1/4	1896	Jack's Fork	12484
12031	2	" Susan	Wife	47	F	1/4	1896	" "	12485
12032	3	" John Hampton	Son	27	M	1/4	1896	" "	12486
12033	4	" Lewis	"	24	"	1/4	1896	" "	12487
12034	5	" Earnest	"	22	"	1/4	1896	" "	12488
12035	6	Wheeler, Erna	Dau	22	F	1/4	1896	" "	12489
12036	7	Tucker, Willie	Son	19	M	1/4	1896	" "	12491
12037	8	" Mary	Dau	16	F	1/4	1896	" "	12492
12038	9	" Ethel	"	14	"	1/4	1896	" "	12493
12039	10	" Lounidas	Son	11	M	1/4	1896	" "	12494
12040	11	" Virgie	Dau	6	F	1/4	1896	" "	12495
12041	12	Wheeler Irma	Grand Dau	1mo	"	1/8			
12042	13	" Florence	Grand Dau	3wks	"	1/8			
I.W. 927	14	Tucker Ella May	Wife of No3	25	F	IW			

ENROLLMENT OF NOS. 14 HEREON APPROVED BY THE SECRETARY OF INTERIOR AUG -3 1904

ENROLLMENT 4,5,6,7,8,9,10,11,12 and 13 HEREON ED BY THE SECRETARY MAR 6 1903

No3 is now the husband of Ella May Tucker on Choctaw Card #D.789 His full given name is John Hampton 9-16-'02
No.12 Enrolled May 7, 1901
~~No.13 Born Sept 24, 1902, enrolled Oct 13, 1902~~

TRIBAL ENROLLMENT OF PARENTS

	Name of Father	Year	County	Name of Mother	Year	County
1	John Tucker	Dead	Non Citizen	Mary Tucker	Dead	Jackson
2	R. B. Willis	"	" "	Margaret Willis	"	Towson
3	No. 1			No. 2		
4	No. 1			No. 2		
5	No. 1			No. 2		
6	No. 1			No. 2		
7	No. 1			No. 2		
8	No. 1			No. 2		
9	No. 1			No. 2		
10	No. 1			No. 2		
11	No. 1			No. 2		
12	Robert J. Wheeler	1896	Tobucksy <IW>	No. 6		
13	" " "	1896	" <IW>	No. 6		
14	Edward Brown	Dead	Non Citz	Mary Brown		Non Citz

No.1 on 1896 Roll as Jno E Tucker
No.3 " 1896 " " Hamp "
~~No.4 " 1896 " " Louis "~~
No.6 " 1896 " " Erena "

No.6 is now the wife of Robert J Wheeler on Choctaw Card #4136, marriage license and certificate filed this day ~~May 7, 1901.~~

P.O. Address of No.3 is So. McAlester, I.T.

No.14 Transferred from Choctaw Card No. D.789 June 12,1904 see decision of May 27, 1904

Aug 31, 1899

Choctaw By Blood Enrollment Cards 1898-1914

RESIDENCE: Atoka COUNTY. **Choctaw Nation** **Choctaw Roll** *(Not Including Freedmen)* CARD NO.
POST OFFICE: Coalgate, I.T. FIELD NO. 4305

Dawes' Roll No.	NAME	Relationship to Person First Named	AGE	SEX	BLOOD	TRIBAL ENROLLMENT Year	County	No.
12043	1 Burris, Middleton W 23	First Named	20	M	3/4	1896	Atoka	1770
	2							
	3							
	4							
	5							
	6							
	7							
	8							
	9							
	10 ENROLLMENT							
	11 OF NOS. 1 HEREON							
	APPROVED BY THE SECRETARY							
	12 OF INTERIOR MAR 6 1903							
	13							
	14							
	15							
	16							
	17							

TRIBAL ENROLLMENT OF PARENTS

Name of Father	Year	County	Name of Mother	Year	County
1 Isaac H Burris		Atoka	Matilda Burris	Dead	Atoka
2					
3					
4					
5 On 1896 roll as M. D. Burris					
6					
7 Wife & child of No1 on Chick Card #197					
8					
9					
10					
11					
12					
13					
14					
15				Date of Application for Enrollment	Aug 31/99
16					
17					

Choctaw By Blood Enrollment Cards 1898-1914

RESIDENCE: Atoka COUNTY. **Choctaw Nation** **Choctaw Roll** *(Not Including Freedmen)* CARD NO.
POST OFFICE: Coalgate, I.T. FIELD NO. 4306

Dawes' Roll No.	NAME	Relationship to Person First Named	AGE	SEX	BLOOD	TRIBAL ENROLLMENT Year	County	No.
DEAD	1 ~~Burris, Isaac H~~	~~Named~~	~~48~~	~~M~~	~~3/4~~	~~1896~~	~~Atoka~~	~~1768~~
	2							
	3 No. 1 HEREON DISMISSED UNDER							
	4 ORDER OF THE COMMISSION TO THE FIVE							
	5 CIVILIZED TRIBES OF MARCH 31, 1905.							
	6							
	7							
	8							
	9							
	10							
	11							
	12							
	13							
	14							
	15							
	16							
	17							

CANCELLED

TRIBAL ENROLLMENT OF PARENTS

Name of Father	Year	County	Name of Mother	Year	County
1 ~~Gabriel Burris~~	~~Dead~~	~~Atoka~~		~~Dead~~	~~Atoka~~
2					
3					
4					
5					
6					
7					
8					

Died prior to September 25, 1902

9 ~~No1 Died February 10, 1901. Proof of death filed March~~
10 See testimony of Lubin Plummer of February 14
On 1896 roll as Isaac Burris
11 ~~Nº1 FATHER OF MILLY WIND, CREEK INDIAN CARD, FIELD Nº 1499 Oct 29,1902~~
12
13 See also testimony of Johnson Ott of February 15, 1905 and
14 Robert Anderson of February 13, 1905

Date of Application for Enrollment.
15 Aug 31/99
16
17

Choctaw By Blood Enrollment Cards 1898-1914

RESIDENCE: Atoka COUNTY. **Choctaw Nation** **Choctaw Roll** (Not Including Freedmen) CARD NO.
POST OFFICE: Coalgate, I.T. FIELD NO. 4307

Dawes' Roll No.	NAME	Relationship to Person First Named	AGE	SEX	BLOOD	TRIBAL ENROLLMENT Year	County	No.
12044	1 Cooper, Minnie 22		19	F	1/2	1896	Gaines	3998
DEAD.	2 ~~" Boyd~~	~~Son~~	~~1~~	~~M~~	~~1/2~~			
	3							
	4							
	5							
	6							
	7 No. 2 HEREON DISMISSED UNDER ORDER OF THE COMMISSION TO THE FIVE CIVILIZED TRIBES OF MARCH 31, 1905.							
	8							
	9							
	10							
	11 ENROLLMENT OF NOS. 1 HEREON APPROVED BY THE SECRETARY OF INTERIOR MAR 6 1903							
	12							
	13							
	14							
	15 No2 died in 1900; proof of death filed Nov. 25, 1902							
	16							
	17							

TRIBAL ENROLLMENT OF PARENTS

Name of Father	Year	County	Name of Mother	Year	County
1 Frank Freeny		Blue	Mary Freeny	Dead	Gaines
2 ~~Willis Cooper~~		~~Gaines~~	~~No1~~		
3					
4					
5					
6					
7 No1 on 1896 roll as Minnie Freeney					
8					
9 No2- Affidavit of birth to be supplied.- Filed Oct 26/99					
10					
11 Willis Cooper on Card 4856					
12 No.1 separated from Willis Cooper					
13					
14					
15				Date of Application for Enrollment.	Aug 31/99
16					
17					

RESIDENCE: Atoka COUNTY. **Choctaw Nation** **Choctaw Roll** *(Not Including Freedmen)* CARD NO.
POST OFFICE: Coalgate, I.T. FIELD NO. **4308**

Dawes' Roll No.	NAME		Relationship to Person First Named	AGE	SEX	BLOOD	TRIBAL ENROLLMENT Year	County	No.
12045	1 Ervin, William L	37	First Named	34	M	1/2	1896	Gaines	3687
12046	2 " Columbus	15	Son	12	"	1/4	1896	"	3688
12047	3 " Edward	13	"	10	"	1/4	1896	"	3689
12048	4 " Pearl	12	Dau	9	F	1/4	1896	"	3690
12049	5 " Alphonso	10	Son	7	M	1/4	1896	"	3691
12050	6 " Calvin	8	"	5	"	1/4	1896	"	3692
12051	7 " Minnie	7	Dau	4	F	1/4	1896	"	3693
12052	8 " Emma	5	"	2	"	1/4			
12053	9 " Ben	2	Son	3mo	M	1/4			
I.W. 1502	10 " Rosa	34	Wife	34	F	I.W.			
	11								
	12 ~~Nos 6 and 7 were admitted by Dawes~~								
	13 Commission in 1896: No. 1174								
	14								
	15 ENROLLMENT OF NOS. 1,2,3,4,5,6,7,8 and 9 HEREON								
	16 APPROVED BY THE SECRETARY OF INTERIOR Mar 6 1903								
	17								

TRIBAL ENROLLMENT OF PARENTS

Name of Father	Year	County	Name of Mother	Year	County
1 Calvin Ervin	Dead	Non Citz	Sally Ervin	Dead	Towson
2 No1			Rosa Ervin		Non Citz
3 No1			" "		" "
4 No1			" "		" "
5 No1			" "		" "
6 No1			" "		" "
7 No1			" "		" "
8 No1			" "		" "
9 No1			" "		" "
10 Hermon Miller	Dead	Non Citizen	Millie Hall		non-citizen

ENROLLMENT OF NOS. 10 HEREON APPROVED BY THE SECRETARY OF INTERIOR Nov 27 1905

No1 on 1896 roll as William Ervin. As to marriage to Mexican wife. Mother of ~~above children, see testimony of Allington Tille.~~

No.8: Affidavit of birth to be supplied:- Recd Dec 18/99. Irregular and returned for correction ~~Returned corrected and accepted without affidavit of at~~ tending physician and filed Feby 29th 1900

P O Ti I T

P.O. Hartshorne I.T. 8/19/05

~~No 9 Enrolled Aug 28 1900~~

No.10 placed on this card May 4, 1905 by order of Commission of that date holding ~~application was made prior to Sept. 25, 1902~~

Date of Application for Enrollment. Aug 31/99 1 to 8 inc

~~No 10 Granted~~ Oct 2-1905

RESIDENCE: Jacks Fork COUNTY. **Choctaw Nation** Choctaw Roll (Not Including Freedmen) CARD NO.
POST OFFICE: Stringtown, I.T. FIELD NO. 4309

Dawes' Roll No.	NAME		Relationship to Person First Named	AGE	SEX	BLOOD	TRIBAL ENROLLMENT Year	County	No.
I.W. 408	1 Scott, John C	40	First Named	36	M	IW			
12054	2 " Refina E	34	Wife	31	F	1/2	1896	Jacks Fork	12496
12055	3 " Gladys M	4	Dau	8mo	"	1/4			
12056	4 Thomas, Oliver G	18	S.S.	15	M	1/4	1896	Jacks Fork	12497
12057	5 " Georgia P	14	S.D.	11	F	1/4	1896	" "	12498
12058	6 Seco, Angie	13	Ward	10	"	1/4	1896	" "	11702
12059	7 Scott Johnnie C	1	Dau	2mo	F	1/4			

For child of No1 and 2 see NB (Apr 26 '06) #218

ENROLLMENT OF NOS. 2,3,4,5,6 & 7 HEREON APPROVED BY THE SECRETARY OF INTERIOR MAR 6 1903

ENROLLMENT OF NOS. 1 HEREON APPROVED BY THE SECRETARY OF INTERIOR SEP 12 1903

TRIBAL ENROLLMENT OF PARENTS

Name of Father	Year	County	Name of Mother	Year	County
1 Abe Scott	Dead	Non Citz	Angeline McBurney		Non Citz
2 Henry Seco	"	" "	Cillen Seco	Dead	" "
3 No1			No2		
4 Oliver Thomas	Dead	Non Citz	No2		
5 " "	"	" "	No2		
6 George Seco	"	Jacks Fork	Mary Seco	Dead	Jacks Fork
7 No1			No2		

No7 is a girl. Change made under Departmental instructions of November 28, 1904 (I.T.D. 12034-1904) D.C. #46323-1904

~~No2 on 1896 roll as Reafina E Thomas~~
~~No4 " 1896 " " Oliver "~~
No5 " 1896 " " Pearl P "
No6 " 1896 " " Eugene Secor
~~No3- Affidavit of birth to be supplied:- Filed Oct 26/99~~
No.7 Enrolled Sept 28, 1901

Date of Application for Enrollment. Aug 31/99

RESIDENCE: Atoka COUNTY. **Choctaw Nation** **Choctaw Roll** *(Not Including Freedmen)* CARD NO.

POST OFFICE: Atoka, I.T. FIELD NO. 4310

Dawes' Roll No.	NAME	Relationship to Person First Named	AGE	SEX	BLOOD	TRIBAL ENROLLMENT Year	County	No.
12060	1 Hodges, John M 53	First Named	50	M	1/8	1896	Atoka	5957
DEAD.	2 ~~" Martha~~	~~Wife~~	~~38~~	~~F~~	~~1/4~~	~~1896~~	~~"~~	~~5958~~
12061	3 " Ozie T 21	Son	18	M	3/16	1896	"	5959
12062	4 " Joseph M 18	Son	15	M	3/16	1896	"	6084

No. 2 HEREON DISMISSED UNDER ORDER OF THE COMMISSION TO THE FIVE CIVILIZED TRIBES OF MARCH 31, 1905.

ENROLLMENT OF NOS. 1 3 and 4 HEREON APPROVED BY THE SECRETARY OF INTERIOR MAR 6 1903

TRIBAL ENROLLMENT OF PARENTS

	Name of Father	Year	County	Name of Mother	Year	County
1	Joseph Hodges	Dead	Non Citz	Cebelle Hodges	Dead	Towson
2	~~Thompson McKinney~~	~~"~~	~~Skullyville~~	~~Manda McKinney~~		~~Atoka~~
3	No1			No2		
4	No1			No2		

No1 on 1896 roll as Jno. M. Hodges

No4 " 1896 " " Joe M "

N°2 died Sept 14, 1902, proof of death filed Nov 22, 1902

4/30/37 ~~N°3 is a male. See his testimony of May 22, 1903~~

JDF Sex of N°3 changed. Departmental Authy. D-14040-37 April 24-1937

Date of Application for Enrollment. Aug 31/99

RESIDENCE: Atoka COUNTY. **Choctaw Nation** **Choctaw Roll** *(Not Including Freedmen)* CARD NO. FIELD NO. 4311

POST OFFICE: Coalgate, I.T.

Dawes' Roll No.	NAME	Relationship to Person First Named	AGE	SEX	BLOOD	TRIBAL ENROLLMENT Year	County	No.
12063	1 Hampton, Jackson 21	First Named	18	M	3/4	1896	Gaines	5278
	2							
	3							
	4							
	5							
	6							
	7							
	8							
	9							
	10							
	11							
	12							
	13							
	14							
	15							
	16							
	17							

ENROLLMENT
OF NOS. 1 HEREON
APPROVED BY THE SECRETARY
OF INTERIOR MAR 6 1903

TRIBAL ENROLLMENT OF PARENTS

Name of Father	Year	County	Name of Mother	Year	County
1 Wade Hampton	Dead	Gaines	Nancy Hampton		Gaines
2					
3					
4					
5					
6 On 1896 roll as U. J. E. Hampton					
7					
8					
9					
10					
11					
12					
13					
14					
15					
16					
17					

Date of Application for Enrollment. Aug 31/99

Choctaw By Blood Enrollment Cards 1898-1914

RESIDENCE: Atoka COUNTY. **Choctaw Nation** **Choctaw Roll** *(Not Including Freedmen)* CARD NO.
POST OFFICE: Coalgate, I.T. FIELD NO. 4312

Dawes' Roll No.		NAME	Relationship to Person First Named	AGE	SEX	BLOOD	TRIBAL ENROLLMENT Year	County	No.
12064	1	Robert, James 25		22	M	Full	1893	Atoka	424
12065	2	" Malinda 38	Wife	35	F	"	1893	Blue	171
	3								
	4								
	5								
	6								
	7								
	8								
	9								
	10								
	11								
	12								
	13								
	14								
	15								
	16								
	17								

ENROLLMENT OF NOS. 1 and 2 HEREON APPROVED BY THE SECRETARY OF INTERIOR Mar 6 1903

TRIBAL ENROLLMENT OF PARENTS

	Name of Father	Year	County	Name of Mother	Year	County
1	Stephen Robert		Atoka	Eliza A Harris	Dead	Atoka
2	Sam Bond	Dead	Blue	Wisey Bond	"	Blue

No.1 also on 1896 Choctaw roll page 180, #7331 as Robert James

No1 on 1893 Pay Roll, Page 41, No 424, Atoka Co.
No2 " 1893 " " " 15, " 171 Blue Co.,
as Bolinda Bond

Date of Application for Enrollment.
Aug 31/99

RESIDENCE: Atoka COUNTY. **Choctaw Nation** **Choctaw Roll** (Not Including Freedmen) CARD NO.
POST OFFICE: Coalgate, I.T. FIELD NO. 4313

Dawes' Roll No.	NAME		Relationship to Person First Named	AGE	SEX	BLOOD	TRIBAL ENROLLMENT Year	County	No.
I.W. 409	1 Gills, Emmet K	43		40	M	IW	1896	Atoka	14582
12066	2 " Lillie B	39	Wife	36	F	1/16	1896	"	4956
12067	3 White, Rosa M	14	S.D.	11	"	1/32	1896	"	13927
12068	4 " Lillie O	13	" "	10	"	1/32	1896	"	13928
12069	5 " Oliver E	10	S.S.	7	M	1/32	1896	"	13929
	6								
	7								
	8								
	9								
	10								
	11								
	12								
	13								
	14								
	15								
	16								
	17								

ENROLLMENT
OF NOS. 1 HEREON
APPROVED BY THE SECRETARY
OF INTERIOR SEP 12 1903

ENROLLMENT
OF NOS. 2 3 4 and 5 HEREON
APPROVED BY THE SECRETARY
OF INTERIOR MAR 6 1903

TRIBAL ENROLLMENT OF PARENTS

Name of Father	Year	County	Name of Mother	Year	County
1 Jas. A Gills	Dead	Non Citz	Lutitia M Gills		Non Citz
2 W. M. Dunn	"	" "	Salena Dunn		Atoka
3 O. E. White	"	" "	No2		
4 " " "	"	" "	No2		
5 " " "	"	" "	No2		
6					
7 No1 on 1896 roll as E. K. Gill					
8 No3 " 1896 " " Rosa May White					
9 No4 " 1896 " " Lilly Ora "					
10					
11					
12					
13					Date of Application for Enrollment.
14					
15					Aug 31/99
16					
17					

RESIDENCE: Jacks Fork COUNTY. **Choctaw Nation** Choctaw Roll (Not Including Freedmen) CARD NO.
POST OFFICE: Stringtown, I.T. FIELD NO. 4314

Dawes' Roll No.	NAME	Relationship to Person First Named	AGE	SEX	BLOOD	TRIBAL ENROLLMENT Year	County	No.
I.W. 410	1 Self, John H (30)		27	M	IW	1896	Jacks Fork	15072
12070	2 " Leona 26	Wife	23	F	1/8	1896	" "	11722
12071	3 " William 6	Son	3	M	1/16	1896	" "	11723
12072	4 Pulcher, Ella B 11	Ward	8	F	1/16	1896	" "	10592
DEAD.	5 ~~Self, Benjamin F~~	~~Son~~	~~2mo~~	~~M~~	~~1/16~~			
12073	6 " Viva Lulu 1	Dau	2wks	F	1/16			

ENROLLMENT OF NOS. 1 HEREON APPROVED BY THE SECRETARY OF INTERIOR SEP 12 1903

ENROLLMENT OF NOS. 2 3 4 and 6 HEREON APPROVED BY THE SECRETARY OF INTERIOR MAR 6 1903

No. 5 HEREON DISMISSED UNDER ORDER OF THE COMMISSION TO THE FIVE CIVILIZED TRIBES OF MARCH 31, 1905

No.6 Born Oct. 25,1901: Enrolled Nov. 7, 1901

No[sic]

TRIBAL ENROLLMENT OF PARENTS

Name of Father	Year	County	Name of Mother	Year	County
1 W. A. Self		Non Citz	Rinda Self		Non Citz
2 Albert Pulcher	Dead	Jacks Fork	Isabelle Pulcher	Dead	Jacks Fork
3 No1			No2		
4 Stephen Pulcher	Dead	Jacks Fork	Flora Pulcher	Dead	Non Citz
5 ~~No.1~~			~~No.2~~		
6 No.1			No.2		

No1 on 1896 roll as Jno H Self

For child of Nos 1&2 see NB (Mar 3 '05) #453

No3 " 1896 " " Billy "

No4 " 1896 " " Albert Pulcher –As to ~~marriage of parents, see testimony of John E. Tucker~~

#1 to 4 inc — Date of Application for Enrollment. Aug 31/99

No1 admitted as an intermarried citizen by Dawes ~~Commission Choctaw Case #788. No appeals~~

~~No.5 Enrolled May 24, 1900~~

N°5 Died Nov 6, 1900, proof of death filed Nov 20 190[?]

Choctaw By Blood Enrollment Cards 1898-1914

RESIDENCE: Atoka COUNTY. **Choctaw Nation** **Choctaw Roll** *(Not Including Freedmen)* CARD No.
POST OFFICE: Wapanucka, I.T. FIELD No. 4315

Dawes' Roll No.	NAME	Relationship to Person First Named	AGE	SEX	BLOOD	TRIBAL ENROLLMENT Year	County	No.
12074	1 Dick, Martin 56	First Named	53	M	1/2	1896	Atoka	3614

ENROLLMENT OF NOS. 1 HEREON APPROVED BY THE SECRETARY OF INTERIOR MAR 6 1903

TRIBAL ENROLLMENT OF PARENTS

Name of Father	Year	County	Name of Mother	Year	County
1 Sampson Dick	Dead	Atoka	Lucy Dick		Creek

No1 is father of children on Chickasaw card #824 (Choc 5506)
No.1 father of Thomas Dick on Chickasaw card #819 (Choc 5406)

Date of Application for Enrollment. Aug 31/99

RESIDENCE: Atoka COUNTY. **Choctaw Nation** **Choctaw Roll** CARD NO. 4316
POST OFFICE: Atoka, I.T. *(Not Including Freedmen)* FIELD NO. 4

Dawes' Roll No.	NAME	Relationship to Person First Named	AGE	SEX	BLOOD	TRIBAL ENROLLMENT Year	County	No.
12075	1 Brown, Jack 25	First Named	22	M	1/2	1896	Atoka	1849

ENROLLMENT
OF NOS. 1 HEREON
APPROVED BY THE SECRETARY
OF INTERIOR MAR 6 1903

TRIBAL ENROLLMENT OF PARENTS

Name of Father	Year	County	Name of Mother	Year	County
1 Tom Brown		Non Cit.	Rose S Brown		Atoka

For child of No1 see NB (Apr 26 '06) #1281

DATE OF APPLICATION FOR ENROLLMENT
[illegible]

RESIDENCE: Atoka COUNTY. **Choctaw Nation** **Choctaw Roll** *(Not Including Freedmen)* CARD NO.
POST OFFICE: Atoka, I.T. FIELD NO. 4317

Dawes' Roll No.		NAME	Relationship to Person First Named	AGE	SEX	BLOOD	TRIBAL ENROLLMENT Year	County	No.
I.W. 835	1	Cline, Arthur J (37)	First Named	34	M	I.W.	1896	Atoka	14423
12076	2	" Lizzie 30	Wife	27	F	1/16	1896	Atoka	2919
12077	3	" John T 10	Son	7	M	1/32	"	"	2920
12078	4	" Joseph V. 6	"	3	M	1/32	"	"	2939
12079	5	" Edward Milton 1	"	1mo	M	1/32			

Decision Prepared No.1 11/13/03

ENROLLMENT OF NOS. 1 HEREON APPROVED BY THE SECRETARY OF INTERIOR May 21 1904

ENROLLMENT OF NOS. 2,3,4 & 5 HEREON APPROVED BY THE SECRETARY OF INTERIOR Mar 6 1903

TRIBAL ENROLLMENT OF PARENTS

	Name of Father	Year	County	Name of Mother	Year	County
1	William T. Cline			Fanny Rogers		
2	Joseph Hodges		Atoka	L.A.A. Hodges		Atoka
3	No.1			No.2		
4	" 1			" 2		
5	No.1			No.2		

No.1 Admitted by Dawes Com #721 as A. J. Cline
" 3 on roll as Jno. Tillman Cline No appeal.
No1 on 1896 roll as John Cline
~~No.5 Born Feby 7, 1902: enrolled March 25, 1901~~

Date of Application for Enrollment.
8/31/99

Choctaw By Blood Enrollment Cards 1898-1914

RESIDENCE: Atoka COUNTY. **Choctaw Nati[redacted]** **Choctaw Roll** *(Not Including Freedmen)* CARD No.

POST OFFICE: Atoka, I.T. FIELD No. 4318

Dawes' Roll No.		NAME	Relationship to Person First Named	AGE	SEX	BLOOD	TRIBAL ENROLLMENT Year	County	No.
DEAD.	1	~~Hodges, Letha A. A.~~	~~Named~~	~~68~~	~~F~~	~~1/8~~	~~1896~~	~~Atoka~~	~~5955~~
	2								
	3								
	4	No. 1 HEREON DISMISSED UNDER ORDER OF THE COMMISSION TO THE FIVE CIVILIZED TRIBES OF MARCH 31, 1905.							
	5								
	6								
	7								
	8								
	9								
	10								
	11								
	12								
	13								
	14								
	15								
	16								
	17								

CANCELLED

Applicant died prior to ratification of Choctaw Chickasaw agreement Sept 25, 1902

TRIBAL ENROLLMENT OF PARENTS

	Name of Father	Year	County	Name of Mother	Year	County
1	[Illegible] Malone		Non Cit.	Susan P. Parks		Skullyville
2						
3						
4						
5						
6						
7	No1 died Oct [illegible] Nov, 1901; proof of death filed Nov 26, 1902					
8						
9			on roll as L. A. A. Hodges			
10						
11						
12						
13						
14						
15						
16						Date of Application for Enrollment.
17						8/31/99

Choctaw By Blood Enrollment Cards 1898-1914

RESIDENCE: Atoka COUNTY. **Choctaw Nation** **Choctaw Roll** *(Not Including Freedmen)* CARD NO.

POST OFFICE: Atoka, I.T. FIELD NO. 4319

Dawes' Roll No.	NAME	Relationship to Person First Named	AGE	SEX	BLOOD	TRIBAL ENROLLMENT Year	County	No.
I.W. 756	1 Hilseweck, W^m E (28)		25	M	I.W.			
12080	2 " Alice E 27	Wife	24	F	1/16	1896	Atoka	5956
12081	3 " Lethia E 4	Dau	1	F	1/32			
12082	4 " Dorothy Jane 2	Dau	3wk	F	1/32			
12083	5 " Lewis Hodges 1	Son	2mo	M	1/32			

ENROLLMENT OF NOS. 1 HEREON APPROVED BY THE SECRETARY OF INTERIOR MAY -7 1904

ENROLLMENT OF NOS. 2 3 4 and 5 HEREON APPROVED BY THE SECRETARY OF INTERIOR MAR 6 1903

TRIBAL ENROLLMENT OF PARENTS

	Name of Father	Year	County	Name of Mother	Year	County
1	Chas L. Hilsewick[sic]	Dead	Non Citz	Esther Hilsewick		Non Citz
2	Joseph Hodges		Atoka	Letha Hodges		Atoka
3	No. 1			No. 2		
4	No. 1			No. 2		
5	No 1			No 2		

Sworn statement of №2 as to her residence at time of her marriage to №1 filed May 7,1903

No1 See Decision of March 2 '04

No2 on roll as Alice ~~Hilseweck~~ Hodges

~~Affidavit as to birth of child to be supplied. Filed Oct 26/99~~

No.4 Enrolled July 20, 1900

No.5 Enrolled June 17th 1902: Born April 26th 1902

#1 to 3

Date of Application for Enrollment. 8/31/99

RESIDENCE: Jackson COUNTY. **Choctaw Nation** **Choctaw Roll** *(Not Including Freedmen)* CARD NO.
POST OFFICE: Mayhew, I T FIELD NO. 4320

Dawes' Roll No.		NAME	Relationship to Person First Named	AGE	SEX	BLOOD	TRIBAL ENROLLMENT Year	County	No.
DEAD	1	~~Fisher, Charles~~		~~39~~	~~M~~	~~Full~~	~~1896~~	~~Jackson~~	~~4296~~
12084	2	" Lyda [36]	Wife	33	F	"	1896	"	4297
12085	3	" Daniel [23]	Son	20	M	"	1896	"	4298
12086	4	" Sallie [21]	Dau	18	F	"	1893	"	234
12087	5	" Absolam [14]	Son	11	M	"	1896	"	4301
12088	6	" John [10]	"	7	"	"	1896	"	4302
12089	7	" Joanna [11]	Dau	8	F	"	1896	"	4299
12090	8	" Mary [6]	"	3	"	"	1896	"	4300
	9								
	10	No.1 hereon dismissed under order of							
	11	the Commission to the Five Civilized							
	12	Tribes of March 31, 1905.							
	13								
	14								
	15	ENROLLMENT							
	16	OF NOS. HEREON APPROVED BY THE SECRETARY							
	17	OF INTERIOR							

TRIBAL ENROLLMENT OF PARENTS

	Name of Father	Year	County	Name of Mother	Year	County
1	~~John Fisher~~	~~Dead~~	~~Kiamitia~~		~~Dead~~	~~Kiamitia~~
2	Feh-nubbee	"	Atoka		"	Atoka
3	No1			Cillen Fisher	"	Jackson
4	No1			" "	"	"
5	No1			" "	"	"
6	No1			" "	"	"
7	No1			" "	"	"
8	No1			" "	"	"
9						
10	No3 on 1896 roll as Dollie Fisher					
11	No7 " 1896 " " Jane "					
12	No4- Affidavit of birth to be supplied					
13						
14					Date of application for enrollment	
15	No1 died July 6,1901: proof of death filed Nov. 25, 1902				Aug 31/99	
16	No.4 P.O. Bently[sic] Okla 5-17-11				Date of Application for Enrollment.	
17	No3 P.O. Burse I.T 2/13/06					

RESIDENCE: Atoka COUNTY. **Choctaw Nation** **Choctaw Roll** *(Not Including Freedmen)* CARD NO.
POST OFFICE: Atoka, I.T. FIELD NO. 4321

Dawes' Roll No.		NAME	Relationship to Person First Named	AGE	SEX	BLOOD	TRIBAL ENROLLMENT Year	County	No.
12091	1	Colbert, Allison 31	First Named	28	M	Full	1896	Atoka	2968
15859	2	" Salina 20	Wife	17	F	"	1896	"	3577
void	3	~~" Sam~~	~~Son~~	~~1½~~	~~M~~	~~"~~			
16063	4	Colbert, Susan	Dau	1	F	"			

ENROLLMENT OF NOS. 2 HEREON APPROVED BY THE SECRETARY OF INTERIOR Jun 12 1905

ENROLLMENT OF NOS. 4 HEREON APPROVED BY THE SECRETARY OF INTERIOR Nov 23 1906

ENROLLMENT OF NOS. 1 HEREON APPROVED BY THE SECRETARY OF INTERIOR Mar 6 1903

TRIBAL ENROLLMENT OF PARENTS

	Name of Father	Year	County	Name of Mother	Year	County
1	Calvin Colbert	Dead	Kiamitia	Liney Colbert		Atoka
2	Joslin Durant		Atoka	Nellie Durant	Dead	"
3	~~No1~~			~~Adeline Frazier~~		~~Blue~~
4	No.1			No.2		

No.4 was born Dec 25,1901: Application received and No4 placed on this card March 4, 1905, under Act of Congress approved March 3, 1905

~~No2 on 1896 roll as Salina Durant also on 1896 roll Page 86, No 3577, as Czarina Durant, Atoka Co,~~

No3- Affidavit of birth to be supplied:-

~~No3 transferred to Choctaw card #5336 with its mother Adline[sic] Frazier, June 8, 1900~~

correct name of No.2 is Salina Colbert. See testimony taken February 28, 1905.

No.2 originally listed on this card as Serena Colbert

No2 P.O. Calloway 2/28/05

#1&2

Date of Application for Enrollment. Aug 31/99

Choctaw By Blood Enrollment Cards 1898-1914

RESIDENCE: COUNTY. **Choctaw Nation** **Choctaw Roll** (Not Including Freedmen) CARD NO.
POST OFFICE: Coalgate, I.T. FIELD NO. 4322

Dawes' Roll No.		NAME	Relationship to Person First Named	AGE	SEX	BLOOD	TRIBAL ENROLLMENT Year	County	No.
12092	1	Lankford, Bertha M 13	First Named	10	F	1/8	1896	Atoka	8350
12093	2	" Oliver H 11	Bro	8	M	1/8	1896	"	8351
	3								
	4								
	5								
	6								
	7								
	8								
	9								
	10								
	11								
	12								
	13								
	14								
	15								
	16								
	17								

ENROLLMENT
OF NOS. 1 and 2 HEREON
APPROVED BY THE SECRETARY
OF INTERIOR MAR 6 1903

TRIBAL ENROLLMENT OF PARENTS

	Name of Father	Year	County	Name of Mother	Year	County
1	W. R. Lankford		non cit	Ella Lankford	Dd	Atoka
2	"		" "	" "	"	
3						
4						
5						
6						
7						
8						
9						
10						
11						
12						
13						
14						
15						
16						
17						

No.1 on roll as Bertha Lankford
" 2 " " " Oliver "

Date of Application for Enrollment 8/31/99

RESIDENCE: Atoka COUNTY. **Choctaw Nation** Choctaw Roll (Not Including Freedmen) CARD NO.
POST OFFICE: Coalgate, I.T. FIELD NO. 4323

Dawes' Roll No.	NAME	Relationship to Person First Named	AGE	SEX	BLOOD	TRIBAL ENROLLMENT Year	County	No.
I.W. 411	1 Roark, William 47	First Named	44	M	IW			
12094	2 " Lucy A 50	Wife	47	F	1/4	1896	Atoka	8315

ENROLLMENT OF NOS. 1 HEREON APPROVED BY THE SECRETARY OF INTERIOR SEP 12 1903

ENROLLMENT OF NOS. ~~ 2 ~~ HEREON APPROVED BY THE SECRETARY OF INTERIOR MAR 6 1903

TRIBAL ENROLLMENT OF PARENTS

Name of Father	Year	County	Name of Mother	Year	County
1 William Roark	Dead	Non Citz	Millie A Roark	Dead	Non Citz
2 George Perkins	"	Atoka	Jane Perkins	"	Atoka

No2 on 1896 roll as Lucy A Lankford

Evidence of marriage to be supplied:- Filed Oct 26/99

Date of Application for Enrollment. Sept 1/99

RESIDENCE: Jacks Fork COUNTY. **Choctaw Nation** **Choctaw Roll** *(Not Including Freedmen)* CARD NO.
POST OFFICE: Stringtown, IT FIELD NO. 4324

Dawes' Roll No.	NAME		Relationship to Person First Named	AGE	SEX	BLOOD	TRIBAL ENROLLMENT Year	County	No.
[illegible]95	1 Watson, Robinson	44	First Named	41	M	Full	1896	Jacks Fork	14092
12096	2 " Narcissa	33	Wife	30	F	"	1896	" "	14093
[illegible]097	3 " Willis	8	Son	5	M	"	1896	" "	14094
12098	4 " Richardson	2	Son	1	M	"			

ENROLLMENT OF NOS. 1 2 3 and 4 HEREON APPROVED BY THE SECRETARY OF INTERIOR MAR 6 1903

TRIBAL ENROLLMENT OF PARENTS

	Name of Father	Year	County	Name of Mother	Year	County
1	Willis Watson	Dead	Skullyville	A-le-ha-ma	Dead	Tobucksy
2	Johnson Hampton	"	Blue	Sukey Baker		Jacks Fork
3	No1			No2		
4	No1			No2		

No.4 born July 26, 1900: Enrolled Dec. 10, 1901

Date of Application for Enrollment. Sept 1/99

RESIDENCE: Atoka COUNTY. **Choctaw Nation** Choctaw Roll (Not Including Freedmen) CARD NO.
POST OFFICE: Coalgate, I.T. FIELD NO. 4325

Dawes' Roll No.	NAME	Relationship to Person First Named	AGE	SEX	BLOOD	TRIBAL ENROLLMENT Year	County	No.
12099	1 Mowdy, Viola 27	First Named	24	F	1/8	1896	Atoka	8835
12100	2 " John E 10	Son	7	M	1/16	1896	"	8836
12101	3 " Ollie L 8	Dau	5	F	1/16	1896	"	8837
12102	4 " Claude 5	Son	2	M	1/16			
12103	5 Ellis Gracie 15	Ward	12	F	3/4	1896	Atoka	3817
12104	6 Mowdy, Clide 3	Son	6mo	M	1/16			
12105	7 " Lesley Lenton 1	Son	4mo	M	1/16			

No5 also on 1896 Choctaw roll as Gracie Carn: page 69: #2938
June 6, 1900

ENROLLMENT OF NOS. 1,2,3,4,5,6 & 7 HEREON APPROVED BY THE SECRETARY OF INTERIOR Mar 6 1903

TRIBAL ENROLLMENT OF PARENTS

Name of Father	Year	County	Name of Mother	Year	County
1 Chas Alexander	Dead	Non Citz	Sarah Woods		Blue
2 F. M. Mowdy		" "	No1		
3 " " "		" "	No1		
4 " " "		" "	No1		
5 Wilson Fisk	Dead	Atoka	Margaret Ellis		Atoka
6 F. M. Mowdy		-------	No.1		
7 " " "		-----	No.1		

No1 on 1896 roll as Viola Mondy
~~No2 " 1896 " " Jno E "~~
~~No3 " 1896 " " Ollie L "~~
No4- Affidavit of birth to be supplied:- Filed Oct 26/99
For child of No.1 see NB (Mar 3 '05) #480
~~F.M. Mowdy on Choctaw R #512~~
~~No.7 born March 17, 1902: Enrolled July 8, 1902~~
For Nos 1 to 5 incl
Date of Application for Enrollment. Sept 1/99
For child of No5 see NB (Apr 26-06) Card #428
No.6 Enrolled May 24, 1900

Choctaw By Blood Enrollment Cards 1898-1914

RESIDENCE: Atoka COUNTY: Choctaw Nation Choctaw Roll (Not Including Freedmen) CARD NO.
POST OFFICE: Atoka, I.T. FIELD NO. 4326

Dawes' Roll No.	NAME	Relationship to Person First Named	AGE	SEX	BLOOD	TRIBAL ENROLLMENT Year	County	No.
12106	1 Allison, Lee [37]	First Named	34	M	Full	1896	Atoka	420
DEAD.	2 ~~" Susan~~	~~Dau~~	~~9~~	~~F~~	~~"~~	~~1896~~	~~"~~	~~423~~
12107	3 Aaron, Emma [10]	Ward	7	"	"	1896	"	424

No. 2 HEREON DISMISSED UNDER ORDER OF THE COMMISSION TO THE FIVE CIVILIZED TRIBES OF MARCH 31, 1905.

ENROLLMENT OF NOS. 1 and 3 HEREON APPROVED BY THE SECRETARY OF INTERIOR MAR 6 1903

TRIBAL ENROLLMENT OF PARENTS

Name of Father	Year	County	Name of Mother	Year	County
1 John Allison	Dead	Atoka	Alissie Allison	Dead	Atoka
2 ~~No1~~			~~Sophia Allison~~	~~"~~	~~"~~
3 Pickman Aaron	Dead	Atoka	Lucy Aaron	"	"

No1 on 1896 roll as Lee Allerson
No2 " 1896 " " Susan "
No3 " 1896 " " Emma Alern

No2 died January 10, 1900; proof of death filed Nov 25, 1902
No.1 Husband of No.2 on Choc 3848

Date of Application for Enrollment.
Sept 1/99

RESIDENCE: Atoka COUNTY. **Choctaw Nation** **Choctaw Roll** (Not Including Freedmen) CARD NO.
POST OFFICE: Atoka, I.T. FIELD NO. 4327

Dawes' Roll No.		NAME	Relationship to Person	AGE	SEX	BLOOD	Tribal Enrollment Year	Tribal Enrollment County	Tribal Enrollment No.
12108	1	Jones, Elsie 27 ✓	First Named	24	F	Full	1893	Jackson	514
12109	2	McClure, Elizabeth 10 ✓	Dau	7	"	"	1896	Atoka	9440
14818	3	Lawrence, Joseph 2 ✓	Son	2	M	[blank]			
	4								
	5								
	6								
	7								
	8								
	9								
	10								
	11								
	12	ENROLLMENT OF NOS. 3 HEREON APPROVED BY THE SECRETARY OF INTERIOR MAY 20 1903							
	13								
	14								
	15	ENROLLMENT OF NOS. 1 and 2 HEREON APPROVED BY THE SECRETARY OF INTERIOR MAR 6 1903							
	16								
	17								

TRIBAL ENROLLMENT OF PARENTS

	Name of Father	Year	County	Name of Mother	Year	County
1	John Allison	Dead	Atoka	Alissie Allison	Dead	Atoka
2	Stewart McClure	"	Jackson	No.1		
3	Henry Lawrence	1896	Atoka	No.1		
4						
5						
6						
7						
8						
9						
10						
11						
12						
13	~~No.1 on 1893 Pay Roll, Page 58, No. 514, Jackson Co, as Elcie McClure~~					
14	~~No1 is the wife of Henry Lawrence Choctaw card #3322~~					
15	No3 Born Dec 29, 1900: enrolled Dec. 24, 1902					
16						
17						Sept 1, 1899

RESIDENCE: Atoka COUNTY. **Choctaw Nation** **Choctaw Roll** *(Not Including Freedmen)* CARD NO.
POST OFFICE: Coalgate, I.T. FIELD NO. 4328

Dawes' Roll No.	NAME	Relationship to Person First Named	AGE	SEX	BLOOD	TRIBAL ENROLLMENT Year	County	No.
*	1 ~~M^c^Carty, Mary L~~	~~Named~~	~~19~~	~~F~~	~~1/16~~			

DENIED CITIZENSHIP BY THE CHOCTAW AND CHICKASAW CITIZENSHIP COURT Jan 20 04

TRIBAL ENROLLMENT OF PARENTS

Name of Father	Year	County	Name of Mother	Year	County
1 ~~E. R. Poole~~		~~Non Citz~~	~~Georgiann Poole~~		~~Choctaw~~

No1 Denied by Dawes Com in 1896 [Illegible] Case #789
* Admitted by U.S. Court, Central Dist.
Sept 9/97 Case No 63 as Mary L Poole
As to residence, see testimony of husband
John M^c^Carty

1/2 o,[sic] 1900. Duplicate of Choc Card #4965.
* Decision of U.S. Court Central District vacated and set aside by Decree of Choctaw Chickasaw Citizenship Court Decr 17 1902 : The Citizenship Court on Jan 20 1904 denied [illegible] for admission of No1 as citizen of the Choctaw Nation and [illegible...] Case #43
For child of No1 see NB #1009 (Act Apr 26 '06)

Date of Application for Enrollment. Sept 1/99

P.O. Lone Grove 11/22 '02

RESIDENCE: Jacks Fork COUNTY. **Choctaw Nation** **Choctaw Roll** (Not Including Freedmen) CARD NO.
POST OFFICE: Stringtown, I.T. FIELD NO. 4329

Dawes' Roll No.	NAME	Relationship to Person First Named	AGE	SEX	BLOOD	TRIBAL ENROLLMENT Year	County	No.
12110	1 Williams, Willy S 25	First Named	22	M	Full	1896	Jacks Fork	14095
	2							
	3							
	4							
	5							
	6							
	7							
	8							
	9							
	10							
	11							
	12							
	13							
	14							
	15							
	16							
	17							

ENROLLMENT OF NOS. 1 HEREON APPROVED BY THE SECRETARY OF INTERIOR MAR 6 1903

TRIBAL ENROLLMENT OF PARENTS

Name of Father	Year	County	Name of Mother	Year	County
1 Sampson Williams	Dead	Atoka	Sally Williams	Dead	Jacks Fork
2					
3					
4					
5					
6					
7					
8					
9					
10					
11					
12					
13					
14					Date of Application for Enrollment.
15					Sept 1/99
16					
17					

No 1 "Died prior to September 25, 1902; not entitled to land or money."
See Copy of Indian Office Letter of November 7, 1907 (I.T. 82860 – 1907)

Choctaw By Blood Enrollment Cards 1898-1914

RESIDENCE: Jackson COUNTY. **Choctaw Nation** **Choctaw Roll** *(Not Including Freedmen)* CARD NO.
POST OFFICE: Mayhew, I.T. FIELD NO. 4330

Dawes' Roll No.	NAME	Relationship to Person First Named	AGE	SEX	BLOOD	TRIBAL ENROLLMENT Year	County	No.
12111	1 Harris, Nathan 26	First Named	23	M	3/8	1893	Jackson	322
15957	2 " Millie	Dau	5	F	3/16			
15958	3 " Maria	Dau	3	F	"			
15959	4 " Paul	Son	1	M	"			

ENROLLMENT ~~OF NOS. 2 3 and 4 HEREON~~ APPROVED BY THE SECRETARY OF INTERIOR NOV 27 1905

ENROLLMENT OF NOS. ~~~ 1 ~~~ HEREON APPROVED BY THE SECRETARY OF INTERIOR MAR 6 1903

TRIBAL ENROLLMENT OF PARENTS

	Name of Father	Year	County	Name of Mother	Year	County
1	Nelson Harris		Colored man	Jincy Harris		Jackson
2	No.1			Paralee Harris		
3	No.1			" "		
4	No.1			" "		

~~On 1893 Pay Roll, Page 37, No 322~~
Jackson o.
Wife of No.1 is Paralee Harris, Choctaw freedmen card #930

~~For child of No.1 see NB (Apr 26-06) No 540~~
Nos 2 to 4 inclusive transferred from Choctaw freedman card #940 October 14, 1905
See decision of September 28, 1905

Date of Application for Enrollment.
Sept 1/99

RESIDENCE: Atoka COUNTY. **Choctaw Nation** Choctaw Roll (Not Including Freedmen) CARD NO.
POST OFFICE: Wapanucka, I.T. FIELD NO. 4331

Dawes' Roll No.	NAME	Relationship to Person First Named	AGE	SEX	BLOOD	TRIBAL ENROLLMENT Year	County	No.
12112	1 Billis, William 25	First Named	22	M	Full	1893	Atoka	132
	2							
	3							
	4							
	5							
	6							
	7							
	8							
	9							
	10							
	11							
	12							
	13							
	14							
	15							
	16							
	17							

ENROLLMENT
OF NOS. ~ 1 ~ HEREON
APPROVED BY THE SECRETARY
OF INTERIOR MAR 6 1903

TRIBAL ENROLLMENT OF PARENTS

Name of Father	Year	County	Name of Mother	Year	County
1 Jackson Billis		Atoka	Polly Billis	Dead	Chick Dist

On 1893 Pay roll, Page 12, No 132, Atoka Co
No.1 is the husband of Melissa Kececiry[sic] on Chickasaw Card #783. Evidence of marriage requested, June 18, 1901

Date of Application for Enrollment.
Sept 1/99

Choctaw By Blood Enrollment Cards 1898-1914

RESIDENCE: Jackson COUNTY. **Choctaw Nation** **Choctaw Roll** (*Not Including Freedmen*) CARD NO.
POST OFFICE: Mayhew, I.T. FIELD NO. 4332

Dawes' Roll No.	NAME	Relationship to Person First Named	AGE	SEX	BLOOD	TRIBAL ENROLLMENT Year	County	No.
12113	1 Robinson, Peter 30	First Named	27	M	1/2	1896	Jackson	10883
	2							
	3							
	4							
	5							
	6							
	7							
	8							
	9							
	10							
	11							
	12							
	13							
	14							
	15							
	16							
	17							

ENROLLMENT
OF NOS. 1 HEREON
APPROVED BY THE SECRETARY
OF INTERIOR MAR 6 1903

TRIBAL ENROLLMENT OF PARENTS

Name of Father	Year	County	Name of Mother	Year	County
1 Solomon Robinson	Dead	Eagle	Eliz. Robinson		Nashoba
2					
3					
4					
5					
6					
7					
8					
9					
10					
11					
12					
13					
14					
15					
16					
17					

Date of Application for Enrollment.
Sept 1/99

Choctaw By Blood Enrollment Cards 1898-1914

RESIDENCE: Atoka COUNTY. **Choctaw Nation** **Choctaw Roll** (*Not Including Freedmen*) CARD NO.
POST OFFICE: Atoka, I.T. FIELD NO. 4333

Dawes' Roll No.	NAME		Relationship to Person First Named	AGE	SEX	BLOOD	TRIBAL ENROLLMENT Year	County	No.
12114	1 Homer Davis A	38	First Named	35	M	Full	1896	Atoka	5942
12115	2 " Annie	27	Wife	24	F	3/4	1896	Blue	2858
12116	3 " Mary	19	Dau	16	"	Full	1896	Atoka	5944
DEAD	4 ~~" Sincy~~		~~"~~	~~13~~	~~"~~	~~"~~	~~1896~~	~~"~~	~~5945~~
12117	5 " Aaron	13	Son	10	M	"	1896	"	5943
12118	6 " Ida	4	Dau	5mo	F	7/8			
12119	7 Carnes, John	6	S.Son	3	M	7/8	1896	Blue	2859

No.4 hereon dismissed under order of the Commission to the Five Civilized Tribes of March 31, 1905.

ENROLLMENT
OF NOS. 1,2,3,5,6 & 7 HEREON
APPROVED BY THE SECRETARY
OF INTERIOR Mar 6 1903

TRIBAL ENROLLMENT OF PARENTS

	Name of Father	Year	County	Name of Mother	Year	County
1	Aaron Homer	Dead	Kiamitia	Siney Homer	Dead	Kiamitia
2	Stephen Samuels	"	Nashoba	Sophie Watson		Chick Dist
3	No1			Selina Homer	Dead	Kiamitia
4	~~No1~~			~~" "~~	~~"~~	~~"~~
5	No1			" "	"	"
6	No1			No2		
7	John Carnes	Dead	Blue	No2		

~~No1 on 1896 roll as Davis A Homma~~
No2 " 1896 " " Annie Carnes
Surnames of first six on 1896 roll as Homma
~~No7 on 1896 roll as Johnnie Carnes~~
No6- Affidavit of birth to be supplied:- Filed Dec 16/99
~~No.4 Died Mch 24, 1900. Proof of death filed Nov 22 1902~~
~~Nos 6&7 P.O. Atoka Okla R.F.D. 2~~

Date of Application for Enrollment.
Sept 1/99

RESIDENCE: Atoka COUNTY. **Choctaw Nation** **Choctaw Roll** *(Not Including Freedmen)* CARD NO.
POST OFFICE: Kiowa, I.T. FIELD NO. 4334

Dawes' Roll No.	NAME	Relationship to Person First Named	AGE	SEX	BLOOD	TRIBAL ENROLLMENT Year	County	No.
I.W. 412	1 Culbertson, Charles E 40		36	M	I.W.	1896	Atoka	14424
12120	2 " Sophia A 30	Wife	27	F	1/4	1896	"	2930
12121	3 " Charles E Jr 9	Son	6	M	1/8	1896	"	2931
12122	4 " Chloe 8	D	5	F	1/8	1896	"	2932
12123	5 " Lois 7	"	3	"	1/8	1896	"	2933
12124	6 " Mary B 6	"	2	"	1/8			
12125	7 " Zelma 4	"	1	"	1/8			
12126	8 " Lucile 2	"	3w	F	1/8			
12127	9 " William F 1	Son	3wks	M	1/8			
	10							
	11							
	12							
	13							
	14							
	15							
	16							
	17							

ENROLLMENT OF NOS. 1 HEREON APPROVED BY THE SECRETARY OF INTERIOR Sep 12 1903

ENROLLMENT OF NOS. 2,3,4,5,6,7,8&9 HEREON APPROVED BY THE SECRETARY OF INTERIOR Mar 6 1903

TRIBAL ENROLLMENT OF PARENTS

	Name of Father	Year	County	Name of Mother	Year	County
1	E. H Culbertson		Non Citz	Helen H Culbertson		Non Citz
2	J. C. Flint	Dead	" "	Mary A Rogers		Atoka
3	No1			No2		
4	No1			No2		
5	No1			No2		
6	No1			No2		
7	No1			No2		
8	No1			No2		
9	№1			№2		
10						

~~No1 on 1896 roll as Chas E Culberson[sic]~~
No2 " 1896 " " Sophie Culbertson
No3 " 1896 " " Chas. E. " Jr.
~~No6-7- Affidavits of birth to be supplied:- Filed Oct 26/99~~

~~No 2 was admitted by~~ act of Choctaw Council of Nov 1, 1881 as Sophie A. Flint.

~~#1 to 7~~

Date of Application for Enrollment. Sept 1/99

No1 admitted by Dawes Commission in 1896 as and intermarried citizen: Choctaw case #723: no appeal
~~No.8 Enrolled February 4, 1901~~
~~№9 Born Feby 5, 1902: enrolled Feby 20, 1902~~

For children of Nos 1&2 see NB (March 3, 1905) #795

Choctaw By Blood Enrollment Cards 1898-1914

No.10 Record forwarded Department March 12, 1909 with report

RESIDENCE: Atoka COUNTY. **Choctaw Nation** **Choctaw Roll** (Not Including Freedmen) CARD NO.
POST OFFICE: Lehigh, I.T. FIELD NO. 4335

Dawes' Roll No.	NAME	Relationship to Person First Named	AGE	SEX	BLOOD	TRIBAL ENROLLMENT Year	County	No.
12128	1 Marshal, Alwilda H 42	First Named	39	F	1/4	1896	Atoka	8826
12129	2 Coon, Rhoda 22	Dau	19	"	5/32	1896	"	5960
12130	3 Hodges, Myrtle 16	"	13	"	5/32	1896	"	5961
12131	4 Marshal, Gracie 15	"	12	"	1/8	1896	"	8829
12132	5 " Richard L 12	Son	9	M	1/8	1896	"	8827
12133	6 " Delilah M 9	Dau	6	F	1/8	1896	"	8830
12134	7 " Joseph E 8	Son	5	M	1/8	1896	"	8828
12135	8 " Chock 3	Dau	1mo	F	1/8	No.9 hereon dismissed under order of the Commission to the Five Civilized Tribes of March 31, 1905		
DEAD	9 ~~" Chuck~~	~~Dau~~	~~1mo~~	~~F~~	~~1/8~~			
I.W. 1341	10 " Josiah T 53	Husband	53	M	I.W.			
	11 ~~No.10 dismissed by C.C.C.C. Case #3 May 4-1903 on~~							
	12 general demurrer							
	13 No.10 was rejected by United States							
	14 Court Central Dist, Ind Ter Aug 25, 1897							
	15 ~~Court case #142~~							
	16 ENROLLMENT OF NOS. 1,2,3,4,5,6,7&8 HEREON APPROVED BY THE SECRETARY OF INTERIOR Mar 6 1903							

No 10 restored to roll by Department authority of June 1 1909 (File 5-51)

TRIBAL ENROLLMENT OF PARENTS

Name of Father	Year	County	Name of Mother	Year	County
1 James Davis	Dead	Non Citz	Selina Davis	Dead	Atoka
2 Mudge Hodges	"	Atoka	No1		
3 " "	"	"	No1		
4 Joe Marshal		Non Citz	No1		
5 " "		" "	No1		
6 " "		" "	No1		
7 " "		" "	No1		
8 " "		" "	No1		
9 ~~" "~~		~~" "~~	~~No1~~		
10 Edwin Marshal	dead	" "	Eliz. Marshal	dead	non citz

ENROLLMENT OF NOS. 10 HEREON APPROVED BY THE SECRETARY OF INTERIOR Mar 14 1905

For child of No2 see NB (Mar 3 '05) #456

11 No1 on 1896 roll as Mrs. A. H. Marshall
12 No6 " 1896 " " May

No9 Died April 6, 1902. Proof of death filed March 6, 1905

13 No.2 is now the wife of Alvy Coon on Choctaw card #D728. Evidence of marriage filed Dec 29, 1902.
~~Chock & Chuck Marshall[sic] born Dec 19/99~~
14 on Card No D-549. No10 admitted in 1896 Case No 372
15 Nos 8 and 9 born December 19, 1899: transferred to this card May 24, 1902
Joe Marshall on Card No D-421
16 ~~No10 originally listed for enrollment on Choc card D-421 Sept 2/99: transferred to this card Feb 1, 1905~~
17 See decision of Jan 16.1905. ~~Enrollment of No.10 cancelled under order of Department March 4, 1902.~~

Date of Application for Enrollment. Sept 1/99

RESIDENCE: Atoka COUNTY. **Choctaw Nation** **Choctaw Roll** (Not Including Freedmen) CARD NO.
POST OFFICE: Lehigh, I.T. FIELD NO. 4336

Dawes' Roll No.		NAME	Relationship to Person First Named	AGE	SEX	BLOOD	Tribal Enrollment Year	County	No.
14415	1	Caldwell, Maria 43	First Named	40	F	1/4			
14416	2	" Thomas 15	Son	12	M	1/8			
14417	3	" Marion L 13	Son	10	M	1/8			
14418	4	" Margaret 11	Dau	8	F	1/8			

ENROLLMENT OF NOS. 1 2 3 and 4 HEREON APPROVED BY THE SECRETARY OF INTERIOR Apr 11 1903

TRIBAL ENROLLMENT OF PARENTS

	Name of Father	Year	County	Name of Mother	Year	County
1	Reuben Marlow	Dead	Non Citz	Margaret Marlow		Choctaw
2	William Caldwell	"	" "	No1		
3	" "	"	" "	No1		
4	" "	"	" "	No1		

Further action in connection with allotment of Nos 1,2,3 and 4 suspended under protest of attorneys for Choctaw and Chickasaw Nations Jan 23 1904. Protest over-ruled by Dept No appeal. March 31-04

~~Admitted by Dawes Com. Case No 709.~~
~~No1 admitted as Miria Caldwell~~
No3 " " Marion Lee "
As to residence see testimony of No1.

No3 is a boy. Change made under Departmental instructions of July 2, 1904 (D.C. #22419-1904)

Date of Application for Enrollment. Sept 1/99

Choctaw By Blood Enrollment Cards 1898-1914

RESIDENCE: Atoka COUNTY. **Choctaw Nation** **Choctaw Roll** *(Not Including Freedmen)* CARD NO.
POST OFFICE: Lehigh, I.T. FIELD NO. 4337

Dawes' Roll No.	NAME		Relationship to Person First Named	AGE	SEX	BLOOD	TRIBAL ENROLLMENT Year	County	No.
15685	1 Marlow, Crawford	59	First Named	56	M	1/4			
I.W. 1196	2 " Etta J	41	Wife	38	F	IW			
15686	3 " Reuben F	21	Son	19	M	1/8			
15687	4 " William J	19	"	16	"	1/8			
15688	5 " George	16	"	13	"	1/8			
15689	6 " Ola	13	Dau	10	F	1/8			
	7								
	8								
	9								
	10								
	11								
	12								
	13								
	14								
	15								
	16								
	17								

ENROLLMENT
OF NOS. 1,3,4 5 and 6 HEREON
APPROVED BY THE SECRETARY
OF INTERIOR DEC -2 1904

ENROLLMENT
OF NOS. ~~~ 2 ~~~~~~ HEREON
APPROVED BY THE SECRETARY
OF INTERIOR NOV 16 1904

TRIBAL ENROLLMENT OF PARENTS

	Name of Father	Year	County	Name of Mother	Year	County
1	Reuben Marlow	Dead	Non Citz	Margaret Marlow		Choctaw
2	Finis Anthony	"	" "	Mary Anthony	Dead	Non Citz
3	No1			No2		
4	No1			No2		
5	No1			No2		
6	No1			No2		

All admitted by Dawes Com., Case No 1274: No appeal.
No4 admitted as Willie J Marlow
~~No5 " " Geo "~~
~~As to residence, see testimony of No1~~

For child of No.3 see NB (Mar 3 '05) #306

Date of Application for Enrollment. Sept 1/99

RESIDENCE: Atoka COUNTY. **Choctaw Nation** **Choctaw Roll** *(Not Including Freedmen)* CARD NO.
POST OFFICE: Lehigh, I.T. FIELD NO. 4338

Dawes' Roll No.	NAME	Relationship to Person First Named	AGE	SEX	BLOOD	TRIBAL ENROLLMENT Year	County	No.
	1 M^c^Nellis, James		60	M	IW			
	2							
	3							
	4 No. 1 HEREON DISMISSED UNDER ORDER OF THE COMMISSION TO THE FIVE CIVILIZED TRIBES OF MARCH 31, 1905.							
	5							
	6							
	7							
	8							
	9							
	10							
	11							
	12							
	13							
	14							
	15							
	16							
	17							

CANCELLED

Died prior to September 25, 1902

TRIBAL ENROLLMENT OF PARENTS

	Name of Father	Year	County	Name of Mother	Year	County
1	Michael M^c^Nelis[sic]	Dead	Non Citz	Nancy M^c^Nelis	Dead	Non Citz

Admitted by Dawes Com, Case No 399

As to marriage and separation, see his testimony

No1 died March, 1900. Proof of death filed March 9 1902

Date of Application for Enrollment.
Sept 1/99

Choctaw By Blood Enrollment Cards 1898-1914

RESIDENCE: Jacks Fork COUNTY. **Choctaw Nation** **Choctaw Roll** *(Not Including Freedmen)* CARD NO.
POST OFFICE: Stringtown, I.T. FIELD NO. 4339

Dawes' Roll No.	NAME	Relationship to Person First Named	AGE	SEX	BLOOD	TRIBAL ENROLLMENT Year	County	No.
12136	1 Moore, Samuel 23	First Named	20	M	Full	1896	Jacks Fork	8864
	2							
	3							
	4							
	5							
	6							
	7							
	8							
	9							
	10							
	11							
	12							
	13							
	14							
	15							
	16							
	17							

ENROLLMENT
OF NOS. 1 HEREON
APPROVED BY THE SECRETARY
OF INTERIOR MAR 6 1903

TRIBAL ENROLLMENT OF PARENTS

	Name of Father	Year	County	Name of Mother	Year	County
1	Joe Moore	Dead	Jacks Fork	Susan Moore	Dead	Jacks Fork
2						
3						
4						
5						
6						
7	On 1896 roll as Samuel More					
8						
9						
10						
11						
12						
13						
14						Date of Application for Enrollment.
15						Sept 1/99
16						
17						

Choctaw By Blood Enrollment Cards 1898-1914

RESIDENCE: Atoka COUNTY. **Choctaw Nation** **Choctaw Roll** *(Not Including Freedmen)* CARD NO.
POST OFFICE: Lehigh, I.T. FIELD NO. 4340

Dawes' Roll No.	NAME		Relationship to Person First Named	AGE	SEX	BLOOD	TRIBAL ENROLLMENT Year	County	No.
12137	1 Kemp, Joanna	37	First Named	34	F	5/8	1896	Atoka	7322
12138	2 James, Silas	13	Son	10	M	5/16	1896	"	7323
12139	3 " Crecy I	10	Dau	7	F	5/16	1896	"	7324
12140	4 " Doll	10	"	7	"	5/16	1896	"	7325
14819	5 Brown, Kitty Pearl	6	"	3	"	5/16			

See statement of A. Telle as to reason why name of No5 is not on 1896 Choc. Census Roll Jany 12 – 1903

No.5 appears on No.2 1896 Roll, P. 306 as ~~Kitty James, 1 year. See affidavit of No.1 filed Dec. 20, 1902~~

ENROLLMENT ~~OF NOS. 1,2, 3, 4 HEREON~~ APPROVED BY THE SECRETARY OF INTERIOR MAR 6 1903

TRIBAL ENROLLMENT OF PARENTS

	Name of Father	Year	County	Name of Mother	Year	County
1	Dixon James	Dead	Atoka	Crecy James	Dead	Atoka
2	John James		Non Citz Col.	No1		
3	" "		" " "	No1		
4	" "		" " "	No1		
5	Thomas Brown		" " "	No1		

ENROLLMENT ~~OF NOS. 5 HEREON~~ APPROVED BY THE SECRETARY ~~OF INTERIOR MAY 20 1903~~

No1 on 1896 roll as Joamia James
No2 " 1896 " " Sy "
~~No3 " 1896 " " Bella "~~

See enrollment of Martin Dick

~~No5- Affidavit of birth to be supplied:- Filed Jany 17, 1900~~

Father of N^o^2 is John Davis colored.

Father of N^os^3 and 4 is Willis McCoy Chickasaw freedman See testimony of N^o^1 taken July 29, 1903

Date of Application for Enrollment. Sept 1/99

Choctaw By Blood Enrollment Cards 1898-1914

RESIDENCE: Atoka COUNTY. **Choctaw Nation** **Choctaw Roll** *(Not Including Freedmen)*

POST OFFICE: Lehigh, I.T.

CARD NO.
FIELD NO. 1341

Dawes' Roll No.	NAME	Relationship to Person First Named	AGE	SEX	BLOOD	TRIBAL ENROLLMENT Year	County	No.
12141	1 ~~James, Elias~~ DIED PRIOR TO SEPTEMBER 25, 1902	~~Named~~	~~30~~	~~M~~	~~5/8~~	~~1896~~	~~Atoka~~	~~7326~~

ENROLLMENT
OF NOS. 1 HEREON
APPROVED BY THE SECRETARY
OF INTERIOR MAR 6 1903

TRIBAL ENROLLMENT OF PARENTS

	Name of Father	Year	County	Name of Mother	Year	County
1	~~Dixon James~~	~~Dead~~	~~Atoka~~	~~Crecy James~~	~~Dead~~	~~Atoka~~

No1 died March 9, 1902: Enrollment cancelled by Department May 2, 1906
See enrollment of Martin Dick Why?

Date of Application for Enrollment.
Sept 1/99

RESIDENCE: Atoka COUNTY. **Choctaw Nation** **Choctaw Roll** *(Not Including Freedmen)* CARD NO.
POST OFFICE: Lehigh, I.T. FIELD NO. 4342

Dawes' Roll No.	NAME	Relationship to Person First Named	AGE	SEX	BLOOD	TRIBAL ENROLLMENT Year	County	No.
12142	1 Flint, Robert 23	First Named	20	M	Full	1896	Atoka	4385
	2							
	3							
	4							
	5							
	6							
	7							
	8							
	9							
	10							
	11							
	12							
	13							
	14							
	15							
	16							
	17							

ENROLLMENT
OF NOS. 1 HEREON
APPROVED BY THE SECRETARY
OF INTERIOR MAR 6 1903

TRIBAL ENROLLMENT OF PARENTS

Name of Father	Year	County	Name of Mother	Year	County
1 Johnson Flint	Dead	Atoka	Lila Flint	Dead	Atoka
2					
3					
4					
5					
6					
7					
8					
9					
10					
11					
12					
13					
14					Date of Application for Enrollment.
15					Sept 1/99
16					
17					

Choctaw By Blood Enrollment Cards 1898-1914

RESIDENCE: Atoka COUNTY. **Choctaw Nation** **Choctaw Roll** CARD NO.
POST OFFICE: Atoka, I.T. *(Not Including Freedmen)* FIELD NO. 4343

Dawes' Roll No.		NAME		Relationship to Person First Named	AGE	SEX	BLOOD	TRIBAL ENROLLMENT Year	County	No.
I.W. 413	1	Rose, Christopher C	37	First Named	35	M	IW	1896	Atoka	14992
12143	2	" Nettie	29	Wife	26	F	1/8	1896	"	10971
12144	3	" Charles C	13	Son	10	M	1/16	1896	"	10972
12145	4	" Della	12	Dau	9	F	1/16	1896	"	10975
12146	5	" Otto	8	Son	5	M	1/16	1896	"	10973
12147	6	" Osceola	7	"	4	"	1/16	1896	"	10974
12148	7	" Robert F	4	"	5mo	"	1/16			
12149	8	" Earnest	1	Son	1mo	M	1/16			
	9									
	10									
	11									
	12									
	13									
	14									
	15									
	16									
	17									

ENROLLMENT OF NOS. 1 HEREON APPROVED BY THE SECRETARY OF INTERIOR SEP 12 1903

ENROLLMENT OF NOS. 2 3 4 5 6 7 & 8 HEREON APPROVED BY THE SECRETARY OF INTERIOR MAR 6 1903

TRIBAL ENROLLMENT OF PARENTS

	Name of Father	Year	County	Name of Mother	Year	County
1	William Rose	Dead	Non Citz	Elsie Rose		Non Citz
2	Sam Monds		" "	Jane Monds	Dead	Atoka
3	No1			No2		
4	No1			No2		
5	No1			No2		
6	No1			No2		
7	No1			No2		
8	№1			№2		
9						
10						
11						
12						
13						
14						
15						
16						
17						

No1 was admitted by Dawes Com
Case No 656 on C. C. Rose
No1 on 1896 roll as C. C. Rose
No2 " 1896 " " Nellie "
No3 " 1896 " " Chas C "
No7- Affidavit of birth to be supplied"- Recd Oct 26/99
№8 Born May 6, 1902: enrolled June 10, 1902
For child of Nos 1 and 2 see NB (Mar 3-'05) #307

Date of Application for Enrollment. Sept 1/99

RESIDENCE: Atoka COUNTY. **Choctaw Nation** Choctaw Roll (Not Including Freedmen) CARD NO.
POST OFFICE: Coalgate, I.T. FIELD NO. 4344

Dawes' Roll No.		NAME		Relationship to Person First Named	AGE	SEX	BLOOD	TRIBAL ENROLLMENT Year	County	No.
I.W. 414	1	Zanola, John	52	First Named	49	M	IW			
12150	2	" Mildred	25	Wife	22	F	1/8	1896	Atoka	14246
12151	3	" Augestine	8	Son	5	M	1/16	1896	"	14247
12152	4	" Annie	7	Dau	4	F	1/16	1896	"	14248
12153	5	" Hester	5	"	2	"	1/16			
12154	6	" Noah	3	Son	3mo	M	1/16			
12155	7	" Wavely	1	Dau	1mo	F	1/16			
	8									
	9									
	10									
	11									
	12									
	13									
	14									
	15									
	16									
	17									

ENROLLMENT OF NOS. 1 HEREON APPROVED BY THE SECRETARY OF INTERIOR SEP 12 1903

ENROLLMENT OF NOS. 2 3 4 5 6 & 7 HEREON APPROVED BY THE SECRETARY OF INTERIOR MAR 6 1903

TRIBAL ENROLLMENT OF PARENTS

	Name of Father	Year	County	Name of Mother	Year	County
1	Joe Zanolo[sic]	Dead	Non Citz	Byetrice[sic] Zanola	Dead	Non Citz
2	Sam Monds		" "	Mary J Monds	"	Atoka
3	No1			No2		
4	No1			No2		
5	No1			No2		
6	No1			No2		
7	No.1			No.2		
8						
9						
10						
11						

No1 admitted by Dawes Com, Case No 242

~~No5-6 Affidavits of birth to be supplied:- Filed Oct 26/99~~

No.7 Enrolled July 6, 1901

No.2 on 1896 Roll as Mildred Zonola[sic]

~~No.3 on 1896 Roll as Augustine Zonola~~

~~No.4 on 1896 Roll as Annie Zonola~~

#1 to 6 inc

Date of Application for Enrollment. Sept 1/99

For child of Nos 1&2 see NB (Apr 26 '06) Card #1190

Choctaw By Blood Enrollment Cards 1898-1914

RESIDENCE: Atoka COUNTY. **Choctaw Nation** **Choctaw Roll** *(Not Including Freedmen)* CARD NO.
POST OFFICE: Coalgate, I.T. FIELD NO. 4345

Dawes' Roll No.		NAME	Relationship to Person First Named	AGE	SEX	BLOOD	TRIBAL ENROLLMENT Year	County	No.
12156	1	Hampton, Ben V 32	First Named	29	M	3/4	1896	Blue	5923
I.W. 836	2	" Mattie (42)	Wife	39	F	IW	1896	"	14648
	3								
	4								
	5								
	6	ENROLLMENT							
	7	OF NOS. 2 HEREON APPROVED BY THE SECRETARY							
	8	OF INTERIOR MAY 21 1904							
	9								
	10								
	11								
	12								
	13								
	14								
	15	ENROLLMENT							
	16	OF NOS. 1 HEREON APPROVED BY THE SECRETARY							
	17	OF INTERIOR MAR 6 1903							

TRIBAL ENROLLMENT OF PARENTS

	Name of Father	Year	County	Name of Mother	Year	County
1	Collins Hampton	Dead	Gaines	Louisa Hampton	Dead	Gaines
2	Sam'l Thompson	"	Non Citz	Mary Thompson	"	Non Citz
3						
4						
5						
6						
7	~~No2 Evidence of marriage to be~~					
8	supplied Filed Nov 2/99					
9	Copy of divorce proceedings between №1 and his					
10	~~former wife received and filed March 31, 1903~~					
11						
12						
13						
14						
15					Date of Application for Enrollment.	Sept 1/99
16						
17						

RESIDENCE: Atoka COUNTY. **Choctaw Nation** Choctaw Roll (Not Including Freedmen) CARD NO.
POST OFFICE: Atoka, I.T. FIELD NO. 4346

Dawes' Roll No.	NAME	Relationship to Person First Named	AGE	SEX	BLOOD	TRIBAL ENROLLMENT Year	County	No.
12157	1 Tomlinson, Harriet 49	First Named	46	F	3/4	1896	Atoka	12440
12158	2 Jackson, Rebecca 26	Dau	23	"	3/4	1896	"	7314
12159	3 Tomlinson, Melvina 13	"	10	"	3/8	1896	"	7317
12160	4 " Sarah 8	"	5	"	3/8	1896	"	7315
I.W. 415	5 " Benjamin F 40	Hus	36	M	IW	1896	"	15115
14940	6 Jackson, Virgil[sic] 6	Dau of ~~No2~~	1	F	3/4			
	7							
	8							
	9 ENROLLMENT OF NOS. 5 HEREON APPROVED BY THE SECRETARY OF INTERIOR SEP 12 1903							
	12 ENROLLMENT OF NOS. 1 2 3 & 4 HEREON APPROVED BY THE SECRETARY OF INTERIOR MAR 6 1903							
	15 ENROLLMENT OF NOS. ~~~ 6 ~~~ HEREON APPROVED BY THE SECRETARY OF INTERIOR OCT 15 1903							

TRIBAL ENROLLMENT OF PARENTS

Name of Father	Year	County	Name of Mother	Year	County
1 Jackson Gardner	Dead	Blue	Mary Gardner	Dead	Blue
2 Drew Jackson	"	"	No1		
3 Frank Tomlinson		Non Citz	No1		
4 " "		" "	No1		
5 Peter Tomlinson		" "	Sarah Tomlinson		Non Citz
6 Peter Maytubby		Chickasaw	N°2		

No3 on 1896 roll as Lovina Jackson
No4 " 1896 " " Sarah "
No5 admitted by Dawes Com, Case No 1178,
~~as B. F. Tomlinson~~
No5 on 1896 roll as Frank Tomlinson
Father of Nos 3-4 is No.5
No.4 admitted by Dawes Commission in 1896 Case No 1178
~~N°6 Born Dec 28, 1901 Enrolled Dec 24, 1902 Proof of birth~~
defective and new affidavits requested, corrected affidavits
received and filed May 6, 1903

Date of Application for Enrollment.
Sept 1/99
No5 enrolled Sept 2/99

RESIDENCE: Atoka COUNTY. **Choctaw Nation** Choctaw Roll (Not Including Freedmen) CARD NO.
POST OFFICE: Atoka, I.T. FIELD NO. 4347

Dawes' Roll No.		NAME	Relationship to Person First Named	AGE	SEX	BLOOD	TRIBAL ENROLLMENT Year	County	No.
12162	1	Slinker, Lizzie 23	First Named	20	F	3/4	1896	Atoka	7316
12163	2	" Thomas Dewey 4	Son	1	M	3/8			
12164	3	" Hellen 1	Dau	3mo	F	3/8			

ENROLLMENT
OF NOS. 1 2 & 3 HEREON
APPROVED BY THE SECRETARY
OF INTERIOR MAR 6 1903

TRIBAL ENROLLMENT OF PARENTS

	Name of Father	Year	County	Name of Mother	Year	County
1	Drew Jackson	Dead	Atoka	Harriet Tomlinson		Atoka
2	James Slinker		Non Citz	No1		
3	" "		" "	No.1		

No1 on 1896 roll as Lizzie Jackson

~~No2- Affidavit of birth to be supplied:- Filed~~ Dec 16/99

No3 Enrolled July 10, 1901.

For child of No1 see NB (Apr 26-06) Card #774
" " " " " " (Mar 3 '05) " #308

#1&2

Date of Application for Enrollment. Sept 1/99

RESIDENCE: Atoka COUNTY. **Choctaw Nation** **Choctaw Roll** (Not Including Freedmen) CARD NO.
POST OFFICE: Atoka, I.T. FIELD NO. 4348

Dawes' Roll No.	NAME	Relationship to Person First Named	AGE	SEX	BLOOD	TRIBAL ENROLLMENT Year	County	No.
~~12165~~	1 ~~Moore, Willie~~ 24		~~21~~	~~M~~	~~Full~~	~~1893~~	~~Atoka~~	~~405~~
	2							
	3							
	4							
	5							
	6 No.1 cancelled Sept 15, 1903: See							
	7 Departmental letter of that date:							
	8 D.C. No. 25850-1903							
	9							
	10							
	11							
	12							
	13							
	14 ENROLLMENT							
	15 OF NOS. 1 HEREON							
	16 APPROVED BY THE SECRETARY OF INTERIOR MAR 6 1903							
	17							

TRIBAL ENROLLMENT OF PARENTS

	Name of Father	Year	County	Name of Mother	Year	County
1	~~Thos. Moore~~	~~Dead~~	~~Atoka~~		~~Dead~~	~~Atoka~~
2						
3						
4						
5						
6						
7	On 1893 Pay Roll, Page 29, No 405, Atoka Co.					
8						
9	No1 is now husband of Fannie Williams No2 on Choctaw card No 4206					
10	No.1 is a duplicate of No.1 on Choctaw card 3740.					
11						
12						
13						
14						Date of Application for Enrollment.
15						Sept 1/99
16						
17						

CANCELLED

Choctaw By Blood Enrollment Cards 1898-1914

RESIDENCE: Atoka COUNTY. **Choctaw Nation** Choctaw Roll CARD NO.
POST OFFICE: Atoka, I.T. (Not Including Freedmen) FIELD NO. 4349

Dawes' Roll No.	NAME	Relationship to Person First Named	AGE	SEX	BLOOD	TRIBAL ENROLLMENT Year	County	No.
I.W. 416	1 Adams, Hugh W 65	First Named	62	M	IW	1896	Atoka	14266
12166	2 " Edward B 28	Son	25	"	1/8	1896	"	444
	3							
	4							
	5							
	6							
	7							
	8							
	9							
	10							
	11							
	12							
	13							
	14							
	15							
	16							
	17							

ENROLLMENT
OF NOS. 1 HEREON
APPROVED BY THE SECRETARY
OF INTERIOR SEP 12 1903

ENROLLMENT
OF NOS. 2 HEREON
APPROVED BY THE SECRETARY
OF INTERIOR MAR 6 1903

TRIBAL ENROLLMENT OF PARENTS

Name of Father	Year	County	Name of Mother	Year	County
1 John Adams	Dead	Non Citz	Margaret Adams	Dead	Non Citz
2 No1			Lina Adams	"	Skullyville
3					
4					
5					
6 No1 on 1896 roll as H. W. Adams					
7 No2 " 1896 " " Ed. B. "					
8					
9					
10					
11					
12					
13					Date of Application for Enrollment.
14					
15					Sept 1/99
16					
17					

RESIDENCE: Atoka COUNTY. **Choctaw Nation** **Choctaw Roll** *(Not Including Freedmen)* CARD NO.
POST OFFICE: Atoka, I.T. FIELD NO. 4350

Dawes' Roll No.	NAME	Relationship to Person First Named	AGE	SEX	BLOOD	TRIBAL ENROLLMENT Year	County	No.
12167	1 Dunn, William M 40	First Named	37	M	1/8	1896	Atoka	3571
	2							
	3							
	4							
	5							
	6							
	7							
	8							
	9							
	10							
	11							
	12							
	13							
	14							
	15							
	16							
	17							

ENROLLMENT
OF NOS. 1 HEREON
~~APPROVED BY THE SECRETARY~~
OF INTERIOR MAR 6 1903

TRIBAL ENROLLMENT OF PARENTS

	Name of Father	Year	County	Name of Mother	Year	County
1	W. M. Dunn	Dead	Non Citz	Salina Dunn		Chick Dist
2						
3						
4						
5						
6	On 1896 roll as W. M. Dunn					
7						
8	~~Admitted by Act of Choctaw Council,~~					
9	No 15- approved October 20/77[sic]					
10						
11	Wife and family on Card No. 5658					
12						
13						
14						Date of Application for Enrollment.
15						Sept 1/99
16						
17						

Choctaw By Blood Enrollment Cards 1898-1914

RESIDENCE: Atoka COUNTY. **Choctaw Nation** **Choctaw Roll** (*Not Including Freedmen*) CARD NO.
POST OFFICE: Atoka, I.T. FIELD NO. 4351

Dawes' Roll No.	NAME	Relationship to Person First Named	AGE	SEX	BLOOD	TRIBAL ENROLLMENT Year	County	No.
I.W. 417	1 Dulaney, Osias L 53	First Named	50	M	IW	1896	Atoka	14483
12168	2 " Belle 51	Wife	48	F	1/8	1896	Atoka	3580

ENROLLMENT OF NOS. 1 HEREON APPROVED BY THE SECRETARY OF INTERIOR SEP 12 1903

ENROLLMENT OF NOS. 2 HEREON APPROVED BY THE SECRETARY OF INTERIOR MAR 6 1903

TRIBAL ENROLLMENT OF PARENTS

Name of Father	Year	County	Name of Mother	Year	County
1 John Dulaney	Dead	Non Citz	Cynthia Dulaney	Dead	Non Citz
2 Chas Flint		" "	Delilah J. Flint		Chick Dist

~~No1 admitted by Dawes Com.,~~
Case No 313

~~No1 on 1896 Roll as O. L. Dulaney~~

Date of Application for Enrollment.
Sept 1/99

RESIDENCE: Jacks Fork COUNTY. **Choctaw Nation** **Choctaw Roll** *(Not Including Freedmen)* CARD NO.
POST OFFICE: Stringtown, I.T FIELD NO. 4352

Dawes' Roll No.	NAME	Relationship to Person First Named	AGE	SEX	BLOOD	TRIBAL ENROLLMENT Year	County	No.
12169	1 Carnes, Benjamin B 27	First Named	24	M	Full	1896	Jacks Fork	2979
	2							
	3							
	4							
	5							
	6							
	7							
	8							
	9							
	10							
	11							
	12							
	13							
	14							
	15							
	16							
	17							

ENROLLMENT OF NOS. 1 HEREON APPROVED BY THE SECRETARY OF INTERIOR MAR 6 1903

TRIBAL ENROLLMENT OF PARENTS

Name of Father	Year	County	Name of Mother	Year	County
1 Jimpson Carnes	Dead	Jacks Fork	Ellen Carnes	Dead	Jacks Fork
2					
3					
4					
5					
6					
7 On 1896 roll as Ben Butler Carnes					
8					
9					
10					
11					
12					
13					
14					Date of Application for Enrollment
15					Sept 1/99
16					
17					

Choctaw By Blood Enrollment Cards 1898-1914

RESIDENCE: Atoka — COUNTY. **Choctaw Nation** — **Choctaw Roll** *(Not Including Freedmen)* — CARD NO.

POST OFFICE: Atoka, I.T. — FIELD NO. 4353

Dawes' Roll No.	NAME	Relationship to Person First Named	AGE	SEX	BLOOD	TRIBAL ENROLLMENT Year	County	No.
DEAD	1 ~~Standley, Mattie E~~ DEAD	~~First Named~~	~~49~~	~~F~~	~~IW~~	~~1896~~	~~Atoka~~	~~11686~~
15331	2 Standley, Eugene [31]	Son	29	M	1/16	1896	"	11677
15332	3 " Clarence [30]	"	27	"	1/16	1896	"	11678
I.W. 1342	4 " Etna [19]	Dau in law	17	F	I.W.			
15333	5 " Mattie Etna [2]	Dau of No4	4mo	F	1/32			
15334	6 " Frederick Washington [1]	Son of No4	3mo	M	1/32			

ENROLLMENT OF NOS. 2-3-5-6 HEREON APPROVED BY THE SECRETARY OF INTERIOR MAY 9 1904

Nos 2 &3 admitted by C.C.C.C. March 28 '04

No. ~~ 1 ~~ HEREON DISMISSED UNDER ORDER OF THE COMMISSION TO THE FIVE CIVILIZED TRIBES OF MARCH 31, 1905.

No5 Enrolled July 15, 1901.

No6 born Aug 18 1902: enrolled Nov 25, 1902

ENROLLMENT OF NOS. 4 HEREON APPROVED BY THE SECRETARY OF INTERIOR MAR 14 1905

TRIBAL ENROLLMENT OF PARENTS

	Name of Father	Year	County	Name of Mother	Year	County
1	~~G. L. Heggie~~	~~Dead~~	~~Non Citz~~		~~Dead~~	~~Non Citz~~
2	G. W. Standley	"	Tobucksy	No1		
3	" " "	"	"	No1		
4	Fred Sorrells		Non-citizen	Jane Sorrells		Non-citizen
5	No 3			No.4		
6	No 3			No 4		

No.3 and No.4 Married June 3rd, 1900

No1, 2 and 3 denied in 96 Case #1069

Nos 2 and 3 now in C.C.C.C. Case #85

~~All admitted by U.S. Court, Central Dist, July 13/97, Case No 34.~~ As to residence, see testimony of No3.

Judgment of U.S. Ct admitting Nos 1,2 &3 incl vacated and set aside by Decree of Choctaw Chickasaw

No.2 in House of Correction in Detroit Mich.

For child of Nos 3 and 4 see NB (Mar3'05) #457

~~No1 also on 1896 roll Page 400, No 15064 Atoka Co, as Mattie Standley~~

No.4 Enrolled June 8, 1900.

No.1 died April 21st, 1900. See testimony of No.3

P.O. Dawson, I.T. 12/20 '02

Date of Application for Enrollment: Sept 1/99

Choctaw By Blood Enrollment Cards 1898-1914

RESIDENCE: Atoka COUNTY. **Choctaw Nation** **Choctaw Roll** *(Not Including Freedmen)* CARD NO.
POST OFFICE: Atoka, I.T. FIELD NO. 4354

Dawes' Roll No.	NAME	Relationship to Person First Named	AGE	SEX	BLOOD	TRIBAL ENROLLMENT Year	County	No.
DEAD.	1 ~~Standley, Nora B. C.~~	DEAD ~~First Named~~	~~25~~	~~F~~	~~1/16~~	~~1896~~	~~Atoka~~	~~13933~~
15335	2 Wheeler, George W 9	Son	6	M	1/32	1896	"	13934
	3							
	4							
	5							
	6							
	7							
	8							
	9							
	10							
	11							
	12							
	13							
	14							
	15							
	16							
	17							

ENROLLMENT OF NOS. ~2~ HEREON APPROVED BY THE SECRETARY OF INTERIOR MAY 9 1904

No. 1 HEREON DISMISSED UNDER ORDER OF THE COMMISSION TO THE FIVE CIVILIZED TRIBES OF MARCH 31, 1905.

TRIBAL ENROLLMENT OF PARENTS

Name of Father	Year	County	Name of Mother	Year	County
1 ~~G. W. Standley~~	~~Dead~~	~~Tobucksy~~	~~Mattie Standley~~		~~white woman~~
2 Judson Wheeler		Non Citz	No1		

~~No2 Admitted by C.C.C.C. March 28 '04~~

No1&2 denied in 96 Case #1069

Admitted by U.S. Court, Central Dist
July 13/97, Case No 34.

No1 admitted as Nora Standley
No2 " " George Washington Wheeler
As to residence, see testimony of No1
No1 on 1896 roll as Nora S. Wheeler
No2 " 1896 " " Geo. W. "
No.1 died April 9, 1900. See testimony of Clarence Standley, June 8, 1900

Judgment of U.S. Ct admitting No1&2 vacated and set aside by Decree of C.C.C.C. Dec' 17 '02
No2 now in C.C.C.C. Case #85

Date of Application for Enrollment.
Sept 1/99

Date of application for enrollment

RESIDENCE: Chickasaw Nation ~~COUNTY.~~ **Choctaw Nation** Choctaw Roll *(Not Including Freedmen)* CARD NO.
POST OFFICE: Peola[sic], I.T. FIELD NO. 4355

Dawes' Roll No.	NAME	Relationship to Person First Named	AGE	SEX	BLOOD	TRIBAL ENROLLMENT Year	County	No.
12170	1 Williams, Sophia 41	First Named	38	F	1/2	1893	Blue	1152
12171	2 " Mack 11	Son	8	M	1/4	1893	"	1153
I.W. 1343	3 " William F 54	Husband	54	M	I.W.			

ENROLLMENT OF NOS. 3 HEREON APPROVED BY THE SECRETARY OF INTERIOR MAR 14 1905

ENROLLMENT OF NOS. 1 and 2 HEREON APPROVED BY THE SECRETARY OF INTERIOR MAR 6 1903

TRIBAL ENROLLMENT OF PARENTS

Name of Father	Year	County	Name of Mother	Year	County
1 Isaac Watson	Dead	Nashoba	Louvina Watson	Dead	Nashoba
2 Frank Williams		Non Citz	No1		

~~On 1893 Pay Roll, Page 113, Blue Co~~
Nos 1 and 3 were married May 12, 1892. They are separated but not divorced.
No.3 originally listed on Choctaw card R. 344
~~and transferred to this card Dec. 31, 1904. See decision of Dec. 15, 1904.~~

Date of Application for Enrollment.
Sept 1/99

No.3 P.O. Pauls Valley, I.T. 7/21/04

Choctaw By Blood Enrollment Cards 1898-1914

RESIDENCE: Atoka COUNTY. **Choctaw Nation** **Choctaw Roll** *(Not Including Freedmen)* CARD NO.
POST OFFICE: Boggy Depot, I.T. FIELD NO. 4356

Dawes' Roll No.	NAME		Relationship to Person First Named	AGE	SEX	BLOOD	TRIBAL ENROLLMENT Year	County	No.
I.W. 981	1 Perry, Dixie	28	First Named	25	F	IW			

No1 See Decision of July 19 '04

Take no further action relating to re-enrollment of No 1
Protest of Attys for Choctaw and Chickasaw Nations Jan 25 '04

ENROLLMENT OF NOS. ~1~ HEREON APPROVED BY THE SECRETARY OF INTERIOR SEP 22 1904

TRIBAL ENROLLMENT OF PARENTS

Name of Father	Year	County	Name of Mother	Year	County
1 John Morgan	Dead	Non Citz	Susan Morgan		Non Citz

Admitted by Dawes Com,
Case No 588
Nº1 is wife of Benjamin Perry on Choctaw card #3290.
Evidence of marriage received and filed Nov. 13, 1902
For child of No1 see NB (Apr 26-06) #1118

Date of Application for Enrollment.
Sept 1/99

RESIDENCE: Atoka COUNTY. **Choctaw Nation** **Choctaw Roll** *(Not Including Freedmen)* CARD NO.
POST OFFICE: Lehigh, I.T. FIELD NO. 4357

Dawes' Roll No.		NAME		Relationship to Person First Named	AGE	SEX	BLOOD	TRIBAL ENROLLMENT Year	County	No.
12172	1	Harrison, Robert	36	First Named	33	M	1/2	1896	Atoka	5998
I.W. 418	2	" Bessie	23	Wife	20	D	IW			
12173	3	" Zadoc	15	Son	12	M	1/4	1896	Atoka	5999
12174	4	" Claude	10	"	7	"	1/4	1896	"	6000
12175	5	" Robert Jr	6	"	3	"	1/4	1896	"	6001
12176	6	" Theodore R	1	Son	7mo	M	1/4			

ENROLLMENT
OF NOS. 2 HEREON
APPROVED BY THE SECRETARY
OF INTERIOR SEP 12 1903

ENROLLMENT
OF NOS. 1 3 4 5 & 6 HEREON
APPROVED BY THE SECRETARY
OF INTERIOR MAR 6 1903

TRIBAL ENROLLMENT OF PARENTS

	Name of Father	Year	County	Name of Mother	Year	County
1	Zadoc Harrison	Dead	Kiamitia	Eliz Harrison		Atoka
2	John Windrove	"	Non Citz	Nancy Windrove	Dead	Non Citz
3	No1			Sally Harrison	"	" "
4	No1			" "	"	" "
5	No1			" "	"	" "
6	Nº1			Nº2		

No1 on 1896 roll as Robt. Harrison
No5 " 1896 " " " " Jr
Evidence as to marriage of parents ~~of above children to be supplied:-~~ Filed Oct 26/99
Nº6 Born Oct 12, 1901: enrolled May 23, 1902

#1 to 5 inc
Date of Application for Enrollment.

PO Atoka, I.T. 7/27/07

RESIDENCE: Atoka COUNTY. **Choctaw Nation** **Choctaw Roll** *(Not Including Freedmen)* CARD NO.
POST OFFICE: Atoka, I.T. FIELD NO. 4358

Dawes' Roll No.	NAME	Relationship to Person First Named	AGE	SEX	BLOOD	TRIBAL ENROLLMENT Year	County	No.
12177	1 Marshall, Belle 21	First Named	18	F	1/2	1896	Atoka	8838
	2							
	3							
	4							
	5							
	6							
	7							
	8							
	9							
	10							
	11							
	12							
	13							
	14							
	15							
	16							
	17							

ENROLLMENT
OF NOS. 1 HEREON
APPROVED BY THE SECRETARY
OF INTERIOR MAR 6 1903

TRIBAL ENROLLMENT OF PARENTS

Name of Father	Year	County	Name of Mother	Year	County
1 Philip Marshall	Dead	Creek	Elzira Marshall	Dead	Tobucksy

No.1 on 1896 Roll as Belle Marshal

For children of No1 see NB (Mar 3rd 1905) Card #309

Date of Application for Enrollment.

Sept 1/99

Choctaw By Blood Enrollment Cards 1898-1914

RESIDENCE: Chickasaw Nation ~~COUNTY.~~ **Choctaw Nation** **Choctaw Roll** *(Not Including Freedmen)* CARD NO.
POST OFFICE: Elmore, I.T. FIELD NO. 4359

Dawes' Roll No.	NAME	Relationship to Person First Named	AGE	SEX	BLOOD	TRIBAL ENROLLMENT Year	County	No.
~~DP~~	1 ~~Carroll, Mary C~~ *	~~First Named~~	~~19~~	~~F~~	~~IW~~			
✓ ~~DP~~	2 ~~" Joseph W~~	~~Son~~	~~1mo~~	~~M~~	~~1/16~~			
✓ ~~DP~~	3 ~~" Hattie Elizabeth~~	~~Dau~~	~~1mo~~	~~F~~	~~1/16~~			
	4							
No1 is not mentioned in Judg[t] of C.C.C.C.	5							
This notation applies to Mary Carroll #D8	6							
	7							
Nos 2&3	8 MAY 27 1904 DISMISSED							
	9							
	10							
	11 No.1 DISMISSED							
	12 SEP 15 1904							
	13							
	14							
	15							
	16							
	17							

TRIBAL ENROLLMENT OF PARENTS

	Name of Father	Year	County	Name of Mother	Year	County
1	~~David Hinchey~~	~~Dead~~	~~Non Citz~~	~~Frances Hinchey~~	~~Dead~~	~~Non Citz~~
2	~~Thomas R Carroll~~			~~No.1~~		
3	~~" "~~			~~Nº1~~		
4						
5						
6						
7						

No1 ~~DENIED CITIZENSHIP BY THE CHOCTAW AND CHICKASAW CITIZENSHIP COURT~~ [illegible]

No1 denied in 96 Case #983
Admitted by U.S. Court Central
~~Dist. Aug 26/97- Case No 23. As to residence, see her testimony~~
Judgment of U.S. Ct admitting [illegible] by Decree of Choctaw Chickasaw Citizenship Court Dec' 17 '02
No.2 Enrolled June 27, 1900
No appeal to C.C.C.C. [remainder illegible]
~~Thomas R. Carroll, husband of No.1 on Choctaw card #D.10~~
Nº3 Born Sept. 19, 1902, enrolled Oct. 28, 1902

Date of Application for Enrollment. Sept 1/99

Choctaw By Blood Enrollment Cards 1898-1914

RESIDENCE: Chickasaw Natn ~~COUNTY.~~ **Choctaw Nation** **Choctaw Roll** *(Not Including Freedmen)* CARD NO.
POST OFFICE: Elmore, I.T. FIELD NO. 4360

Dawes' Roll No.		NAME	Relationship to Person First Named	AGE	SEX	BLOOD	TRIBAL ENROLLMENT Year	County	No.
√ √	1	~~Carroll, Elizabeth~~ *		~~46~~	~~F~~	~~IW~~			

DENIED CITIZENSHIP BY THE CHOCTAW AND CHICKASAW CITIZENSHIP COURT

TRIBAL ENROLLMENT OF PARENTS

	Name of Father	Year	County	Name of Mother	Year	County
1	~~Eli Adams~~		~~Non Citz~~	~~Margaret Adams~~	~~Dead~~	~~Non Citz~~

No1 denied in 96 Case #983
Admitted by U.S. Court, Central Dist, Aug 26/97, Case No 23. As to re-~~sidence, see her testimony~~
Judgement as of U.S. Court admitting No1 vacated and set aside by Decree of Choctaw Chickasaw Citizenship Court Dec 17 '02
No1 now in C.C.C.C. Case #98

Date of Application for Enrollment.
Sept 1/99

Choctaw By Blood Enrollment Cards 1898-1914

RESIDENCE: Atoka COUNTY. **Choctaw Nation** **Choctaw Roll** *(Not Including Freedmen)* CARD NO.
POST OFFICE: Lehigh, I.T. FIELD NO. 4361

Dawes' Roll No.	NAME	Relationship to Person First Named	AGE	SEX	BLOOD	TRIBAL ENROLLMENT Year	County	No.
I.W. 1013	1 Littlepage, Patrick H 48	First Named	45	M	IW	1896	Atoka	14781
15629	2 " Lucy E 41	Wife	38	F	Adopt White	1896	"	8321
	3							
	4							
	5							
	6							
	7							
	8							
	9							
	10							
	11							
	12							
	13							
	14							
	15							
	16							
	17							

ENROLLMENT
OF NOS. ~~~ 1 ~~~ HEREON
APPROVED BY THE SECRETARY
OF INTERIOR OCT 21 1904

ENROLLMENT
OF NOS. ~~~ 2 ~~~ HEREON
APPROVED BY THE SECRETARY
OF INTERIOR OCT 21 1904

TRIBAL ENROLLMENT OF PARENTS

Name of Father	Year	County	Name of Mother	Year	County
1 R. A. Littlepage	Dead	Non Citz	Mary Littlepage	Dead	Non Citz
2 J. P. Kingsberry	"	" "	Mariah Kingsberry	"	" "

No1 was admitted by Dawes Com. Case No 1245, as P. H. Littlepage. No appeal.
No1 on 1896 roll as P. H. Littlepage
No2 was admitted by Dawes Com, Case No 856. No appeal.
No.1 was also admitted by an Act of the Choctaw Council approved Oct. 20, 1877 (Copy of Act in 7-434)
Parents of No.2 were admitted by Act of Choctaw counsil[sic] approved Nov. 15, 1854.

Sept 1/99
Date of Application for Enrollment.

Choctaw By Blood Enrollment Cards 1898-1914

RESIDENCE: Atoka COUNTY. **Choctaw Nation** **Choctaw Roll** *(Not Including Freedmen)* CARD NO.
POST OFFICE: Atoka, I.T. FIELD NO. 4362

Dawes' Roll No.	NAME	Relationship to Person First Named	AGE	SEX	BLOOD	TRIBAL ENROLLMENT Year	County	No.
12178	1 Moses, Charles 51	First Named	48	M	1/4	1893	Atoka	811
	2							
	3							
	4							
	5							
	6							
	7							
	8							
	9							
	10							
	11							
	12							
	13							
	14							
	15							
	16							
	17							

ENROLLMENT
OF NOS. 1 HEREON
APPROVED BY THE SECRETARY
OF INTERIOR MAR 6 1903

TRIBAL ENROLLMENT OF PARENTS

Name of Father	Year	County	Name of Mother	Year	County
1 Benj. Moses	Dead	Non Citz	Louvica Moses	Dead	Skullyville
2					
3					
4					
5 On 1893 Pay Roll, Page 78, No 811, Atoka Co					
6					
7					
8 8/11/42 Wife Vicie Moses [illegible] # 3301-CC794 IDF					
9					
10					
11					
12					
13					
14					Date of Application for Enrollment.
15					Sept 1/99
16					
17					

Choctaw By Blood Enrollment Cards 1898-1914

RESIDENCE: Atoka COUNTY. **Choctaw Nation** Choctaw Roll (*Not Including Freedmen*) CARD NO.
POST OFFICE: Atoka, I.T FIELD NO. 43

Dawes' Roll No.	NAME	Relationship to Person First Named	AGE	SEX	BLOOD	TRIBAL ENROLLMENT Year	County	No.
12179	1 Armstrong, Lewis 18	First Named	15	M	Full	1896	Atoka	432
	2							
	3							
	4							
	5							
	6							
	7							
	8							
	9							
	10							
	11							
	12							
	13							
	14							
	15							
	16							
	17							

ENROLLMENT OF NOS. 1 HEREON APPROVED BY THE SECRETARY OF INTERIOR MAR 6 1903

TRIBAL ENROLLMENT OF PARENTS

Name of Father	Year	County	Name of Mother	Year	County
1 Bond Armstrong	Dead	Atoka	Eseann Armstrong	Dead	Atoka

On 1896 roll as Louisa Armstrong

No1 is now the husband of Eliza Jacob on Choctaw card #4081, April 2, 1902
For child of No1 see NB (Mar 3 '05) Card #282

Date of Application for Enrollment. Sept 1/99

RESIDENCE: Atoka COUNTY. **Choctaw Nation** **Choctaw Roll** *(Not Including Freedmen)* CARD NO.
POST OFFICE: Atoka, I.T. FIELD NO. 4364

Dawes' Roll No.		NAME		Relationship to Person First Named	AGE	SEX	BLOOD	TRIBAL ENROLLMENT Year	County	No.
I.W. 419	1	Ralls, Joseph G	38		35	M	IW	1896	Atoka	14991
12180	2	" Eva A	27	Wife	24	F	1/32	1896	"	10967
12181	3	" Sarah	8	Dau	5	"	1/64	1896	"	10968
12182	4	" Eva Claude	7	"	4	"	1/64	1896	"	10969
12183	5	" Joseph G Jr	6	Son	3	M	1/64	1896	"	10970
12184	6	" Thomas S	3	"	5mo	"	1/64			
12185	7	" Lewis Henry	2	Son	3wks	M	1/64			
	8									
	9									
	10	No2- As to marriage of								
	11	parents see enrollment of								
		Maggie Standley and others								
	12	~~No4 on 1896 roll as~~								
	13	~~Eva C. Ralls~~								
	14	No.7 Enrolled December 15, 1900								
	15	ENROLLMENT OF NOS. 2 3 4 5 6 & 7 HEREON								
	16	APPROVED BY THE SECRETARY								
	17	OF INTERIOR MAR 6 1903								

TRIBAL ENROLLMENT OF PARENTS

	Name of Father	Year	County	Name of Mother	Year	County
1	Henry Ralls	Dead	Non Citz	Sarah Ralls		Non Citz
2	Jas. S. Standley		Atoka	Alice R Standley	Dead	" "
3	No1			No2		
4	No1			No2		
5	No1			No2		
6	No1			No2		
7	No.1			No.2		
8						
9						

10 ~~No2 admitted by act of Choctaw Council of Oct 1874~~
11 No1 on 1896 roll as J. G. Ralls
12 No5 " 1896 " " J. G. Ralls Jr
~~No1 admitted by Dawes Com.,~~
13 ~~Case No 676 as J. G. Ralls~~
14 No6- Affidavit of birth to be
15 supplied:- Filed Oct 26/99
~~Certified copy of Act of Council~~
16 ~~admiting[sic] parents of No2 to be~~
17 supplied:

ENROLLMENT OF NOS. 1 HEREON APPROVED BY THE SECRETARY OF INTERIOR SEP 12 1903

#1 to 6
Date of Application for Enrollment.
Sept 1/99

For child of No[s] see NB (Apr 26, 1906) Card No 45

Choctaw By Blood Enrollment Cards 1898-1914

RESIDENCE: Atoka COUNTY. **Choctaw Nation** Choctaw Roll (Not Including Freedmen) CARD NO.
POST OFFICE: Atoka, I.T. FIELD NO. 4365

Dawes' Roll No.		NAME	Relationship to Person First Named	AGE	SEX	BLOOD	TRIBAL ENROLLMENT Year	County	No.
I.W. 837	1	Catlin, James D (30)	First Named	27	M	IW			
12186	2	" Claude M 24	Wife	21	F	1/32	1896	Atoka	11633
12187	3	" Charles W 2	Son	3 wks	M	1/64			
	4								
	5								
	6								
	7								
	8								
	9								
	10								
	11								
	12								
	13								
	14								
	15								
	16								
	17								

ENROLLMENT
OF NOS. 1 HEREON
APPROVED BY THE SECRETARY
OF INTERIOR MAY 21 1904

ENROLLMENT
OF NOS. 2&3 HEREON
APPROVED BY THE SECRETARY
OF INTERIOR MAR 6 1903

TRIBAL ENROLLMENT OF PARENTS

	Name of Father	Year	County	Name of Mother	Year	County
1	Chas. W. Catlin	Dead	Non Citz	Robert[sic] Catlin		Non Citz
2	Jas S Standley		Atoka	Alice R Standley	Dead	" "
3	No.1			No.2		

No.2 daughter of J. S. Standley who was admitted by act of Choctaw Council of October, 1874

NOV 17 1903 DECISION PREPARED

No2 on 1896 roll as Claude Standley. As to marriage of parents see enrollment of Maggie Standley and others. Also Card ~~of J. G. Ralls No 4364~~

No.3 Enrolled July 20, 1900

For child of Nos 1 and 2 see NB (Mar 3- '05) Card #310

Date of Application for Enrollment.
Sept 1/99

RESIDENCE: Atoka COUNTY. **Choctaw Nation** **Choctaw Roll** *(Not Including Freedmen)* CARD NO.
POST OFFICE: Limestone, I.T. FIELD NO. 4366

Dawes' Roll No.	NAME	Relationship to Person First Named	AGE	SEX	BLOOD	TRIBAL ENROLLMENT Year	County	No.
	P.O. Elmore IT 10/20/02							
12188	1 Kelly, John 22	First Named	19	M	1/32	1896	Atoka	7654
12189	2 " Henry 22	Bro	19	M	1/32	1896	"	7655

ENROLLMENT OF NOS. 1 & 2 HEREON APPROVED BY THE SECRETARY OF INTERIOR MAR 6 1903

TRIBAL ENROLLMENT OF PARENTS

	Name of Father	Year	County	Name of Mother	Year	County
1	W. W. Kelly	Dead	Non Citz	Sarah A Kelly		Atoka
2	" " "	"	" "	" " "		"

For child of No1 see NB (Apr 26-06) Card #491

Date of Application for Enrollment.
Sept 1/99

Choctaw By Blood Enrollment Cards 1898-1914

RESIDENCE: Atoka COUNTY. **Choctaw Nation** **Choctaw Roll** (Not Including Freedmen) CARD No.
POST OFFICE: Limestone, I.T. FIELD No. 4367

Dawes' Roll No.	NAME	Relationship to Person First Named	AGE	SEX	BLOOD	TRIBAL ENROLLMENT Year	County	No.
12190	1 Ingram, Leona 24	First Named	21	F	1/32	1896	Tobucksy	10766
DEAD.	2 ~~Russell, James F~~	~~Son~~	~~3~~	~~M~~	~~1/64~~	~~1896~~	"	~~10767~~
DEAD.	3 ~~" Edward V~~	"	~~8mo~~	"	~~1/64~~			
	4							
	5							
	6 No. 2 and 3 HEREON DISMISSED UNDER ORDER OF THE COMMISSION TO THE FIVE							
	7 CIVILIZED TRIBES OF MARCH 31, 1905.							
	8							
	9							
	10							
	11							
	12 ENROLLMENT OF NOS. 1 HEREON							
	13 APPROVED BY THE SECRETARY							
	14 OF INTERIOR MAR 6 1903							
	15 See Choctaw card D.507 for							
	16 J. R. Russell, husband of No.1							
	17	Sept 15, 1899						

TRIBAL ENROLLMENT OF PARENTS

Name of Father	Year	County	Name of Mother	Year	County
1 W. W. Kelly	Dead	Non Citz	Sarah A Kelly		Atoka
2 ~~J. R. Russell~~		" "	~~No1~~		
3 " " "		" "	~~No1~~		
4					
5					
6					
7					
8					

~~No1 on 1896 roll as Lena Russell~~

No.2 admitted as a citizen by blood in 1896: Choctaw case #1112

No3- Affidavit of birth to be supplied:- Filed Oct 26/99

~~No.1 is now the wife of John R. Ingram on Choctaw card #D.763: July 22, 1902~~

No2 died Feb, 1901; proof of death filed Nov. 26, 1902

No3 " Sept, 1901; " " " " " " "

Date of Application for Enrollment.

Sept 1/99

Choctaw By Blood Enrollment Cards 1898-1914

RESIDENCE: Atoka COUNTY. **Choctaw Nation** Choctaw Roll (Not Including Freedmen) CARD NO.
POST OFFICE: Atoka, I.T. FIELD NO. 4368

Dawes' Roll No.	NAME		Relationship to Person First Named	AGE	SEX	BLOOD	TRIBAL ENROLLMENT Year	County	No.
12191	1 Betts, Ramsey D	61	First Named	58	M	1/2	1896	Blue	1583
12192	2 " Emeline	55	Wife	52	F	1/2	1896	"	1584
12193	3 " Charlie A	29	Son	26	M	1/2	1896	"	1585
12194	4 Medell, Lula	15	Dau	13	F	1/2	1896	"	1587
I.W. 757	5 " Albert	(31)	Hus of №4	31	M	I.W.			

ENROLLMENT OF NOS. 5 HEREON APPROVED BY THE SECRETARY OF INTERIOR MAY 7 1904

ENROLLMENT OF NOS. 1 2 3 & 4 HEREON APPROVED BY THE SECRETARY OF INTERIOR MAR 6 1903

TRIBAL ENROLLMENT OF PARENTS

Name of Father	Year	County	Name of Mother	Year	County
1 David C Betts	Dead	Non Citz	Nancy Betts	Dead	Kiamitia
2 Andrew Lattin	"	" "	Liza Lattin	"	in Mississippi
3 No1			No2		
4 No1			No2		
5 Medell	dead	City of Sweden	B. Carson		City of Sweden

No.1 on 1896 Roll as Ramsy[sic] D. Betts

No.4 is now the wife of Albert Medell on Choctaw card #D.768 Aug. 1st, 1902

~~№5 transferred from Choctaw Card #D789. See decision of Feby 27, 1904~~

For child of Nos 4&5 see NB (Apr. 26, 1906) Card No 253

" " " No 3 " " " " " 707

~~" " " No 3 " " (Mar. 3, 1905) " " 311~~

~~" " " Nos4&5 " " " " " " " 707~~

Date of Application for Enrollment. Sept 1/99

No4 PO Bennington IT 4/4/05

Choctaw By Blood Enrollment Cards 1898-1914

RESIDENCE: Atoka COUNTY. **Choctaw Nation** **Choctaw Roll** *(Not Including Freedmen)* CARD NO.
POST OFFICE: Coalgate, I.T. FIELD NO. 4369

Dawes' Roll No.	NAME	Relationship to Person First Named	AGE	SEX	BLOOD	TRIBAL ENROLLMENT Year	County	No.
12195	1 Harkins, LaFayette C 38		35	M	1/2	1896	Atoka	5965
I.W. 420	2 " Lillie 31	Wife	28	F	IW	1896	"	14651
12196	3 " Annie A 9	Dau	6	"	1/4	1896	"	5966

ENROLLMENT OF NOS. 2 HEREON APPROVED BY THE SECRETARY OF INTERIOR SEP 12 1903

ENROLLMENT OF NOS. 1 & 3 HEREON APPROVED BY THE SECRETARY OF INTERIOR MAR 6 1903

TRIBAL ENROLLMENT OF PARENTS

Name of Father	Year	County	Name of Mother	Year	County
1 Clay Harkins	Dead	Atoka	Melvina Harkins	Dead	Atoka
2 J. J. Carroll		Non Citz		"	Non Citz
3 No1			No2		

No1 on 1896 roll as L. C. Harkins
No3 " 1896 " " Annie D "
No2 admitted by Dawes Com
Case No 1412 as Lillie Harkin

Date of Application for Enrollment.

Sept 1/99

RESIDENCE: Jackson COUNTY. **Choctaw Nation** Choctaw Roll (Not Including Freedmen) CARD No.
POST OFFICE: Mayhew I.T. FIELD No. 4370

Dawes' Roll No.	NAME		Relationship to Person First Named	AGE	SEX	BLOOD	TRIBAL ENROLLMENT Year	County	No.
12197	1 Carnes Ellis	28	First Named	25	M	Full	1896	Jackson	2784
12198	2 " Serena	33	Wife	30	F	"	1896	"	2785
12199	3 " Nicey	6	Dau	3	"	"	1896	"	2787
12200	4 Robinson, William	9	S.S.	6	M	"	1893	"	132
12201	5 Carnes, Louis	15	Bro	12	"	"	1896	"	2792
	6								
	7								
	8								
	9								
	10								
	11								
	12								
	13								
	14								
	15								
	16								
	17								

ENROLLMENT OF NOS. 1,2,3,4 & 5 HEREON APPROVED BY THE SECRETARY OF INTERIOR Mar 6 1903

TRIBAL ENROLLMENT OF PARENTS

Name of Father	Year	County	Name of Mother	Year	County
1 Lyman Carnes	Dead	Jackson	Mollie Carnes	Dead	Jackson
2 Nephus Moore		Blue	Katy Moore	"	Blue
3 No1			No2		
4 Loring Robinson		Blue	No2		
5 Ben Barnes	Dead	Jackson	Mollie Carnes	Dead	Jackson
6					

7 No1 on 1896 roll as Ellis Carns
8 No2 " 1896 " " Czarina "
9 No3 " 1896 " " Nicey "
No5 " 1896 " " Louis "
10 No4 on 1893 Pay Roll, Page 15, No 132
11 Jackson Co
12 No4 also on 1896 Choctaw roll as William Moore Page 219, No 8749 Jackson County
No.1 and No.2 have separated
13 For child of No1 see NB (Act Mar 3 '05) Card #285
14 " " " "2 " " " " " " #458
15 Date of Application for Enrollment. Sept 1/99
16
17 No.2 P.O. Boswell I.T.

Choctaw By Blood Enrollment Cards 1898-1914

RESIDENCE: Atoka COUNTY. **Choctaw Nation** **Choctaw Roll** *(Not Including Freedmen)* CARD No.
POST OFFICE: Kiowa, I.T. FIELD No. 4371

Dawes' Roll No.	NAME		Relationship to Person First Named	AGE	SEX	BLOOD	TRIBAL ENROLLMENT Year	County	No.
I.W. 793	1 Rowley, H. B.	42	First Named	39	M	IW			
12202	2 " Harry G	17	Son	14	"	1/32	1896	Atoka	10995

ENROLLMENT OF NOS. 1 HEREON APPROVED BY THE SECRETARY OF INTERIOR MAY 9 1904

ENROLLMENT OF NOS. 2 HEREON APPROVED BY THE SECRETARY OF INTERIOR MAR 6 1903

TRIBAL ENROLLMENT OF PARENTS

Name of Father	Year	County	Name of Mother	Year	County
1 Russell Rowley	Dead	Non Citz	Lucy B Tuttle		Non Citz
2 No1			Czarina M Rowley	Dead	Atoka

No1 admitted in 96 Case #1110
No1 admitted by U.S. Court Central Dist, Aug 4/97- Case No 26. As to residence, see his testimony
No2 on 1896 roll as Harry Rowley
Judgment of U.S. Ct admitting No1 vacated and set aside by Decree of Choctaw Chickasaw Citizenship Court Dec' 17'02
Now in C.C.C.C. Case #94 (?)
No1 Admitted by C.C.C.C. Case #94 March 28th 04
For children of No1 see NB (Apr 26-06) #1250

Date of Application for Enrollment.
Sept 1/99

See Petition No W-36

RESIDENCE: Atoka COUNTY. **Choctaw Nation** **Choctaw Roll** *(Not Including Freedmen)* CARD NO.
POST OFFICE: Atoka, I.T. FIELD NO. 4372

Dawes' Roll No.	NAME	Relationship to Person First Named	AGE	SEX	BLOOD	TRIBAL ENROLLMENT Year	County	No.
12203	1 Ward, Henry 21	First Named	18	M	1/16	1896	Atoka	13982
	2							
	3							
	4							
	5							
	6							
	7							
	8							
	9							
	10							
	11							
	12							
	13							
	14							
	15							
	16							
	17							

ENROLLMENT OF NOS. 1 HEREON APPROVED BY THE SECRETARY OF INTERIOR MAR 6 1903

TRIBAL ENROLLMENT OF PARENTS

Name of Father	Year	County	Name of Mother	Year	County
1 Edw. Ward	Dead	Atoka	Missouri Ward	Dead	Non Citz
2					
3					
4					
5					
6					
7					
8					
9					
10					
11					
12					
13					
14					Date of Application for Enrollment.
15					Sept 1/99
16					
17					

As to marriage of parents, see enrollment of sister, Nora M. Hopkins
For child of No1 see NB (March 3 1905) #1095

RESIDENCE: Atoka COUNTY. **Choctaw Nation** **Choctaw Roll** (*Not Including Freedmen*) CARD NO.
POST OFFICE: Lehigh, I.T. FIELD NO. 4373

Dawes' Roll No.	NAME		Relationship to Person First Named	AGE	SEX	BLOOD	TRIBAL ENROLLMENT Year	County	No.
12204	1 Moore, Alice M	46	First Named	43	F	1/2	1896	Atoka	5987
12205	2 Hodges, David W	21	Son	18	M	3/8	1896	"	5988
12206	3 " Claud A	19	"	16	"	3/8	1896	"	5989
12207	4 " John W	14	"	11	"	3/8	1896	"	5990
I.W. 758	5 Moore, William C	(44)	Husb	44	M	I.W.			

ENROLLMENT OF NOS. 5 HEREON APPROVED BY THE SECRETARY OF INTERIOR MAY -7 1904

ENROLLMENT OF NOS. 1 2 3 and 4 HEREON APPROVED BY THE SECRETARY OF INTERIOR MAR 6 1903

TRIBAL ENROLLMENT OF PARENTS

Name of Father	Year	County	Name of Mother	Year	County
1 Clay Harkins	Dead	Atoka	Melvina Harkins	Dead	Atoka
2 D. W. Hodges	"	"	No1		
3 " " "	"	"	No1		
4 " " "	"	"	No1		
5 Salomon Moore	Dead	non-city	Narcissa Moore	Dead	non-citz

No1 on 1896 roll as Alice M. Hodges
No4 " 1896 " " Jno W. "

Husband, W. C. Moore, on Card D402
№5 transferred from Choctaw Card #D402. See decision of Feby 29, 1904

Date of Application for Enrollment.
Sept 1/99

Choctaw By Blood Enrollment Cards 1898-1914

RESIDENCE: Atoka COUNTY. **Choctaw Nation** **Choctaw Roll** *(Not Including Freedmen)* CARD NO.
POST OFFICE: Atoka, I.T. FIELD NO. 4374

Dawes' Roll No.	NAME	Relationship to Person First Named	AGE	SEX	BLOOD	TRIBAL ENROLLMENT Year	County	No.
12208	1 Wesley, Green 35	First Named	32	M	Full	1896	Atoka	13961
	2							
	3							
	4							
	5							
	6							
	7							
	8							
	9							
	10							
	11							
	12							
	13							
	14							
	15							
	16							
	17							

ENROLLMENT OF NOS. 1 HEREON APPROVED BY THE SECRETARY OF INTERIOR MAR 6 1903

TRIBAL ENROLLMENT OF PARENTS

	Name of Father	Year	County	Name of Mother	Year	County
1	Jackson Wesley	Dead	Atoka	Betsy Wesley		Atoka
2						
3						
4						
5						
6						
7						
8						
9						
10						
11						
12						
13						
14						Date of Application for Enrollment.
15						Sept 1/99
16						
17						

RESIDENCE: Jacks Fork COUNTY. **Choctaw Nation** **Choctaw Roll** *(Not Including Freedmen)* CARD NO.
POST OFFICE: Stringtown, I.T. FIELD NO. 4375

Dawes' Roll No.		NAME	Relationship to Person First Named	AGE	SEX	BLOOD	TRIBAL ENROLLMENT Year	County	No.
■	1	~~Grant, Elizabeth~~	~~Named~~	~~59~~	~~F~~	~~IW~~			
	2								
	3								
	4	No. 1 HEREON DISMISSED UNDER							
	5	ORDER OF THE COMMISSION TO THE FIVE ~~CIVILIZED TRIBES OF MARCH 31, 1905.~~							
	6								
	7								
	8								
	9								
	10								
	11								
	12								
	13								
	14								
	15								
	16								
	17								

CANCELLED

TRIBAL ENROLLMENT OF PARENTS

	Name of Father	Year	County	Name of Mother	Year	County
1	J. C. Griffith	Dead	Non Citz	Jane Griffith	Dead	Non Citz
2						
3						
4						
5						
6						
7	Admitted by Act of Choctaw Council					
8	No [?] Approved Nov 6-1884					
9						
10	See her testimony					
11	No1 died on July 17, 1902: proof filed March 17, 1903					
12						
13						
14						Date of Application for Enrollment.
15						Sept 1/99
16						
17						

Applicant died prior to Sept 25, 1902

Choctaw By Blood Enrollment Cards 1898-1914

RESIDENCE: Atoka COUNTY. **Choctaw Nation** Choctaw Roll (Not Including Freedmen) CARD NO.
POST OFFICE: Atoka, I.T. FIELD NO. 4376

Dawes' Roll No.	NAME		Relationship to Person First Named	AGE	SEX	BLOOD	TRIBAL ENROLLMENT Year	County	No.
12209	1 Gipson, Cephus	34	First Named	31	M	Full	1896	Atoka	4963
12210	2 " Caroline	33	Wife	30	F	"	1896	"	4987
12211	3 " James	10	S.S.	7	M	"	1896	"	356
12212	4 " Sibbie	9	S.D.	6	F	"	1896	"	4988
12213	5 " Eunice	1	Dau	7mo	F	"			
	6								
	7								
	8								
	9								
	10								
	11								
	12								
	13								
	14								
	15								
	16								
	17								

ENROLLMENT OF NOS. 1,2,3,4 & 5 HEREON APPROVED BY THE SECRETARY OF INTERIOR Mar 6 1903

TRIBAL ENROLLMENT OF PARENTS

Name of Father	Year	County	Name of Mother	Year	County
1 Henry Gipson	Dead	Atoka	Mary Gibson[sic]	Dead	Atoka
2 Jackson Wesley	"	"	Betsey Wesley		"
3 Allen Gibson	"	"	No2		
4 " "	"	"	No2		
5 Nº1			Nº2		

No3 also on 1896 Choctaw roll page 180, #7333 as Gibson James

No2 on 1896 roll as Caroline Gibson
No4 " 1896 " " Sibby "
No3 on 1893 Pay Roll, Page 34, No 356

Atoka Co
Nº5 Born Aug 1, 1901: enrolled March 18, 1902

For Nos 1 to 4 incl
Date of Application for Enrollment. Sept 1/99

Choctaw By Blood Enrollment Cards 1898-1914

RESIDENCE: Atoka COUNTY. **Choctaw Nation** **Choctaw Roll** CARD NO.
POST OFFICE: Atoka, I.T. *(Not Including Freedmen)* FIELD NO. 4377

Dawes' Roll No.		NAME		Relationship to Person First Named	AGE	SEX	BLOOD	TRIBAL ENROLLMENT Year	County	No.
12214	1	Carnes, Lyon	31	First Named	28	M	Full	1896	Atoka	2913
12215	2	" Phillis	33	Wife	30	F	"	1896	"	2914
	3									
	4									
	5									
	6									
	7									
	8									
	9									
	10									
	11									
	12									
	13									
	14									
	15									
	16									
	17									

ENROLLMENT
OF NOS. 1 and 2 HEREON
APPROVED BY THE SECRETARY
OF INTERIOR Mar 6 1903

TRIBAL ENROLLMENT OF PARENTS

	Name of Father	Year	County	Name of Mother	Year	County
1	Josie Carnes	Dead	Atoka	Vicey Carnes	Dead	Atoka
2	Nat LeFlore	"	"	Silve-honia		"
3						
4						
5						
6						
7						
8						
9						
10						
11						
12						
13						
14						
15						
16						
17						

No1 on 1896 roll as Limon Carn
No2 " 1896 " " Sillis "

No.1 and No.2 have separated

Date of Application for Enrollment.

Date of Application for Enrollment
Sept 1/99

Choctaw By Blood Enrollment Cards 1898-1914

RESIDENCE: Atoka COUNTY. **Choctaw Nation** **Choctaw Roll** *(Not Including Freedmen)* CARD NO.
POST OFFICE: Lehigh, I.T. FIELD NO. 4378

Dawes' Roll No.		NAME		Relationship to Person First Named	AGE	SEX	BLOOD	TRIBAL ENROLLMENT Year	County	No.
I.W. 838	1	Self, Joseph M	51	First Named	48	M	I.W.			
12216	2	" Lillian O	22	Wife	19	F	1/8	1896	Atoka	11622
12217	3	" Martha G	6	Dau	3	"	1/16	1896	"	11623
12218	4	" Ruth	4	"	8mo	"	1/16			
12219	5	" Joseph Manning	2	Son	6w	M	1/16			
12220	6	" Earl	1	Son	2mo	M	1/16			
	7									
	8									
	9									
	10	ENROLLMENT								
	11	OF NOS. 1 HEREON								
	12	APPROVED BY THE SECRETARY OF INTERIOR May 21 1904								
	13									
	14									
	15	ENROLLMENT								
	16	OF NOS. 2 3 4 5 and 6 HEREON APPROVED BY THE SECRETARY								
	17	OF INTERIOR Mar 6 1903								

TRIBAL ENROLLMENT OF PARENTS

	Name of Father	Year	County	Name of Mother	Year	County
1	Thomas Self	Dead	Non Citz	Martha Self	Dead	Non Citz
2	J. S. Spruill	"	" "	Martha Spruill	"	Atoka
3	No1			No2		
4	No1			No2		
5	No1			No2		
6	No.1			No.2		

No1 Dec 8 '03 Decision Prepared
~~No1 admitted by Dawes Com Case~~
No 796, as J. M. Self. No appeal.

~~No2 on 1896 roll as Lily O. Self~~

No 4- Affiliate of birth to be
supplied:- Filed Oct 26/99
~~No 5 Enrolled January 24, 1901~~
~~No.6 Born Feby 2, 1902: enrolled April 2 1902~~
For child of Nos 1&2 see NB (Apr 26-06) Card #657
" " " " " " " " (Mar 3-05) " #1113

#1 to 4
Date of Application for Enrollment.
Sept 1/99

RESIDENCE: Jacks Fork COUNTY. **Choctaw Nation** Choctaw Roll (Not Including Freedmen) CARD NO.
POST OFFICE: Stringtown, I.T. FIELD NO. 4379

Dawes' Roll No.	NAME		Relationship to Person First Named	AGE	SEX	BLOOD	TRIBAL ENROLLMENT Year	County	No.
12221	1 Shults, John	26	First Named	23	M	3/16	1896	Atoka	11668
I.W. 1423	2 " Fannie	28	Wife	23	F	I.W.			
12222	3 " James	7	Son	4	M	3/32	1896	Atoka	11669
12223	4 " Ollie	5	Dau	2	F	3/32			
DEAD	5 ~~" Elvah Herman~~		~~Son~~	~~1mo~~	~~M~~	~~3/32~~			
12224	6 " Verner	1	"	3mo	M	3/32			

ENROLLMENT OF NOS. ~~~ 2 ~~~~ HEREON APPROVED BY THE SECRETARY OF INTERIOR Jun 12 1905

No.5 hereon dismissed under order of the Commission to the Five Civilized Tribes of March 31, 1905.

ENROLLMENT OF NOS. 1,3 4 & 6 HEREON APPROVED BY THE SECRETARY OF INTERIOR Mar 6 1903

TRIBAL ENROLLMENT OF PARENTS

	Name of Father	Year	County	Name of Mother	Year	County
1	John Shults	Dead	Non Citz	Haley Shults	Dead	Atoka
2	Polk Gentrey		" "	Mary Gentry[sic]		Non Citz
3	No1			No2		
4	No1			No2		
5	~~No.1~~			~~No.2~~		
6	No.1			No.2		

No 2 restored to roll by Departmental authority of January 19, 1909 (File 5-51)

~~Enrollment of No2 cancelled by order of Department March 4, 1907~~

No3 on 1896 roll as Johnnie Shults

No4- Affidavit of birth to be supplied:- Filed Oct 26/99

Dec 6/99 No2 See Dawes Commission record 1896X Case No 1067. Denied and no appeal

No.5 Enrolled July 14, 1900. No.5 died Jan 3d, 1901: Proof of death filed November 18-1902

No.6 Born Dec 1,1901: enrolled Feby 24, 1902

Affidavit as to birth of №4 received and filed Jany 26, 1903

P.O. McGee I.T. 11/12/02

P.O. Stratford I.T.

#1 to 4

Date of Application for Enrollment.

Sept 1/99

RESIDENCE: Chickasaw Nation COUNTY. **Choctaw Nation** **Choctaw Roll** *(Not Including Freedmen)* CARD NO.
POST OFFICE: McGee, I.T. FIELD NO. 4380

Dawes' Roll No.		NAME	Relationship to Person First Named	AGE	SEX	BLOOD	TRIBAL ENROLLMENT Year	County	No.
12225	1	Ellis, George 68 ✓	First Named	65	M	1/4	1893	Atoka	233
12226	2	" Isabelle 71 ✓	Wife	68	F	1/2	1893	"	234
12227	3	" Elizabeth 28 ✓	Dau	25	"	3/8	1893	"	235
12228	4	Carnes, Isaac 13 ✓	Ward	10	M	3/8	1893	Blue	238
	5								
	6								
	7								
	8								
	9								
	10								
	11								
	12								
	13								
	14								
	15	ENROLLMENT							
	16	OF NOS. 1 2 3 & 4 HEREON APPROVED BY THE SECRETARY							
	17	OF INTERIOR MAR 6 1903							

TRIBAL ENROLLMENT OF PARENTS

	Name of Father	Year	County	Name of Mother	Year	County
1	John Ellis	Dead	Non Citizen	Mary Ellis	Dead	Kiamitia
2	Sam Anderson	"	Red River		"	Red River
3	No.1			No.2		
4		Dead	Blue	Maggie Tumbler		Atoka
5						
6						
7						
8		All on	1893 Pay Roll, Atoka County, Page 23			
9		No2 "	1893 " " as Isabel Ellis			
10		~~No3 " 1893 " " " Betsey "~~				
10		No4 "	1893 " " Page 34, No 358, Blue			
11		County, as Isaac Carnes				
12						
13						
14						
15						
16						
17						Sept 1, 1899

Choctaw By Blood Enrollment Cards 1898-1914

RESIDENCE: Atoka COUNTY. **Choctaw Nation** **Choctaw Roll** (*Not Including Freedmen*) CARD NO.
POST OFFICE: Atoka, I.T. FIELD NO. 4381

Dawes' Roll No.	NAME	Relationship to Person First Named	AGE	SEX	BLOOD	TRIBAL ENROLLMENT Year	County	No.
12229	1 McKinney, John 27	First Named	24	M	Full	1896	Atoka	9438
	2							
	3							
	4							
	5							
	6							
	7							
	8							
	9							
	10							
	11							
	12							
	13							
	14							
	15 ENROLLMENT							
	16 OF NOS. 1 HEREON APPROVED BY THE SECRETARY							
	17 OF INTERIOR MAR 6 1903							

TRIBAL ENROLLMENT OF PARENTS

Name of Father	Year	County	Name of Mother	Year	County
1 Sim Liashubbee		Choctaw Roll	E-a-hokey	Dead	Atoka
2					
3					
4					
5					
6					
7					
8					
9					
10					
11					
12					
13					
14					
15					
16					
17					Sept 1, 1899

P.O. Pauls Valley IT 8/25-04

RESIDENCE: Atoka COUNTY. **Choctaw Nation** **Choctaw Roll** *(Not Including Freedmen)* CARD NO.
POST OFFICE: Atoka, I.T. FIELD NO. 4382

Dawes' Roll No.	NAME	Relationship to Person First Named	AGE	SEX	BLOOD	TRIBAL ENROLLMENT Year	County	No.
I.W. 1014	1 James, Florence 31	First Named	29	F	I.W.			
	2							
	3							
	4							
	5							
	6							
	7							
	8							
	9							
	10							
	11							
	12							
	13							
	14							
	15							
	16							
	17							

ENROLLMENT OF NOS. ~~~ 1 ~~~~ HEREON APPROVED BY THE SECRETARY OF INTERIOR Oct 12 1904

TRIBAL ENROLLMENT OF PARENTS

	Name of Father	Year	County	Name of Mother	Year	County
1	Jos. Wofford		Non Citz	Sarah Wofford	Dead	Non Citz
2						
3						
4						
5						
6						

Admitted by Dawes Com. Case No 458.
No.1 now wife of Claiborn W. James, on Choc Card #3585 11/19 '02
Evidence of marriage filed Sept. 17, 1903

Date of Application for Enrollment. Sept 1/99

Durant Nov. 19 1902

RESIDENCE: Atoka COUNTY. **Choctaw Nation** **Choctaw Roll** (*Not Including Freedmen*) CARD NO.
POST OFFICE: Atoka, I.T. FIELD NO. 4383

Dawes' Roll No.	NAME	Relationship to Person First Named	AGE	SEX	BLOOD	TRIBAL ENROLLMENT Year	County	No.
12230	1 Marston, Bulah 35	First Named	32	M	1/4	1896	Atoka	8845
15790	2 " Willie	Son	13	M	1/8	1896	"	8846
15791	3 " Johnnie	"	7	M	1/8	1896		8847
DP 1/29/07	4 " Mary	Wife	30	F	I.W			

No 4 Action approved by Secretary of Interior Feb. 28, 1907
Notice of Departmental action forwarded Attorneys for Choctaw and Chickasaw Nation Apr 17, 1907
Notice of Departmental action mailed applicant Apr 17, 1907

ENROLLMENT OF NOS. 2 and 3 HEREON APPROVED BY THE SECRETARY OF INTERIOR Mar 15 1905

ENROLLMENT OF NOS. 1 HEREON APPROVED BY THE SECRETARY OF INTERIOR Mar 6 1903

No.4 Refused Feb. 2-1907
Record forwarded Department Feb. 2-1907

TRIBAL ENROLLMENT OF PARENTS

	Name of Father	Year	County	Name of Mother	Year	County
1	Bulah Marston		Non Citz	Hannah Thomas		Atoka
2	No.1			Mary Marston		non citz col
3	No.1			" "		" " "

No.1 on 1896 roll as Bulo Mouston For children of No.1 see NB (Mar 3 '05) #459

Two children on Card No D404
Mother of Nos 2 and 3 is Mary Marston (nee M^c^Carty) a non citizen colored woman
No2 on 1893 Pay Roll, Atoka Co, page 74, No. 764
Surnames of Nos 2 and 3 on 1896 roll as Mouston
Nos 2 and 3 originally listed for enrollment on Choctaw card D-404 Sept 1/99:
transferred to this card Jan 23 1905. See decision of Jan. 7, 1905
No4 placed on this card September 28th 1905, in accordance with order
of the Commissioner to the Five Civilized Tribes of that date holding application
was made within time prescribed by Act of Congress approved July 1, 1902 (32 Stat. 641)

Date of Application for Enrollment.
Sept 1/99

Choctaw By Blood Enrollment Cards 1898-1914

RESIDENCE: Atoka COUNTY. **Choctaw Nation** **Choctaw Roll** *(Not Including Freedmen)* CARD NO.
POST OFFICE: Atoka, I.T. FIELD NO. 4384

Dawes' Roll No.	NAME	Relationship to Person First Named	AGE	SEX	BLOOD	TRIBAL ENROLLMENT Year	County	No.
14904	1 Scott, Ina 19	First Named	16	F	3/4	1896	Atoka	11651
	2							
	3 ENROLLMENT							
	4 OF NOS. 1 HEREON APPROVED BY THE SECRETARY							
	5 OF INTERIOR MAY 21 1903							
	6							
	7							
	8							
	9							
	10							
	11							
	12							
	13							
	14							
	15							
	16							
	17							

TRIBAL ENROLLMENT OF PARENTS

Name of Father	Year	County	Name of Mother	Year	County
1 Simon Scott	Dead	Atoka		Dead	Atoka
2					
3					
4					
5					
6 On 1896 roll as Inna Scott					
7					
8					
9					
10					
11					
12					
13					
14					Date of Application
15					for Enrollment. Sept 1/99
16					
17					

RESIDENCE: Red River COUNTY. **Choctaw Nation** Choctaw Roll CARD NO.

POST OFFICE: Garvin, I.T. FIELD NO. 4385

Dawes' Roll No.		NAME	Relationship to Person First Named	AGE	SEX	BLOOD	TRIBAL ENROLLMENT Year	County	No.
12231	1	Hopkins, Nova W 23	First Named	20	F	1/16	1896	Red River	5689
12232	2	" Edward 6	Son	2	M	1/32			
12233	3	" Wallace 4	"	1	"	1/32			
DEAD.	4	~~" John Kirk~~	~~Son~~	~~1mo~~	~~M~~	~~1/32~~			
I.W. 759	5	" Thomas W (49)	Husb	49	M	I.W.	1896	Red River	14635

ENROLLMENT OF NOS. ~~~~ 5 ~~~~ HEREON APPROVED BY THE SECRETARY OF INTERIOR MAY -7 1904

No4 died Feb 16, 1902:- proof of death filed Dec 2, 1902

ENROLLMENT OF NOS. 1 2 and 3 HEREON APPROVED BY THE SECRETARY OF INTERIOR MAR 6 1903

TRIBAL ENROLLMENT OF PARENTS

	Name of Father	Year	County	Name of Mother	Year	County
1	Edw. Ward	Dead	Atoka	Missouri Ward	Dead	Non Citz
2	Thos. W. Hopkins		Intermarried	No1		
3	" " "		"	No1		
4	~~" " "~~		~~"~~	~~No.1~~		
5	John H Hopkins	dead	non-citz	Eliz Hopkins	dead	non-citz

~~№5 transferred from Choctaw card #D407. See decision of Feby 29, 1904~~

No1 on 1896 roll as Nora Ward Hopkins

No. 4 HEREON DISMISSED UNDER ORDER OF THE COMMISSION TO THE FIVE CIVILIZED TRIBES OF MARCH 31, 1905.

~~No1 - As to marriage of parents, see~~ testimony of William York

For child of No1 see NB (March 3,1905) #1018

~~Nos 2-3 Affidavits of birth to be supplied:- Filed Oct 26/99~~

~~Thos. W. Hopkins on Card No D407~~

~~No.4 Enrolled July 16, 1900~~

Date of Application for Enrollment.

For Nos ~~1-2&3~~ Sept 1/99

RESIDENCE: Atoka COUNTY. **Choctaw Nation** **Choctaw Roll** *(Not Including Freedmen)* CARD NO.
POST OFFICE: Atoka, I.T. FIELD NO. 4386

Dawes' Roll No.		NAME		Relationship to Person First Named	AGE	SEX	BLOOD	TRIBAL ENROLLMENT Year	County	No.
I.W. 421	1	Bassett, William	38		34	M	IW	1896	Atoka	14342
12234	2	" Louisianna	32	Wife	29	F	1/16	1896	"	1757
12235	3	" Clara	16	Dau	13	"	1/32	1896	"	1758
12236	4	" Mamie	14	"	11	"	1/32	1896	"	1759
12237	5	" Leroy	7	Son	4	M	1/32	1896	"	1760

ENROLLMENT
OF NOS. 1 HEREON
APPROVED BY THE SECRETARY
OF INTERIOR SEP 12 1903

ENROLLMENT
OF NOS. 2 3 4 and 5 HEREON
APPROVED BY THE SECRETARY
OF INTERIOR MAR 6 1903

TRIBAL ENROLLMENT OF PARENTS

	Name of Father	Year	County	Name of Mother	Year	County
1	John Bassett		Non Citz	Annie Bassett	Dead	Non Citz
2	Oliver Hebert	Dead	" "	Isabinda Hebert	"	Atoka
3	No1			No2		
4	No1			No2		
5	No1			No2		

No1 admitted by Dawes Com., Case No 949

~~Nos 3-4-5 were also admitted in same Case, application was only made for No's 1 and 5.~~

All admitted under name of Basset

~~See if application was made for No2 and if she was rejected by Commission.~~

Date of Application for Enrollment.
Sept 1/99

Choctaw By Blood Enrollment Cards 1898-1914

RESIDENCE: Atoka COUNTY. **Choctaw Nation** **Choctaw Roll** (Not Including Freedmen) CARD NO.
POST OFFICE: Atoka, I.T. FIELD NO. 4387

Dawes' Roll No.	NAME	Relationship to Person First Named	AGE	SEX	BLOOD	TRIBAL ENROLLMENT Year	County	No.
12238	1 Hebert, Alice 31	First Named	28	F	1/16	1896	Atoka	5964
12239	2 " Czarina 29	Sister	26	"	1/16	1896	"	5963
	3							
	4							
	5							
	6							
	7							
	8							
	9							
	10							
	11							
	12							
	13							
	14							
	15							
	16							
	17							

ENROLLMENT OF NOS. 1 and 2 HEREON APPROVED BY THE SECRETARY OF INTERIOR MAR 6 1903

TRIBAL ENROLLMENT OF PARENTS

	Name of Father	Year	County	Name of Mother	Year	County
1	Oliver Hebert	Dead	Non Citz	Isabinda Hebert	Dead	Atoka
2	" "	"	" "	" "	"	"

No1 on 1896 roll as A Hebert

See note referring to No2, on Card No 4386.

Date of Application for Enrollment. Sept 1/99

RESIDENCE: Atoka COUNTY. **Choctaw Nation** **Choctaw Roll** *(Not Including Freedmen)* CARD NO.
POST OFFICE: Atoka, I T FIELD NO. 4388

Dawes' Roll No.	NAME		Relationship to Person First Named	AGE	SEX	BLOOD	TRIBAL ENROLLMENT Year	County	No.
I.W. 422	1 Bell, Thomas D	43		41	M	IW	1896	Atoka	14347
12240	2 " Sarah A	50	Wife	47	F	1/8	1896	"	1809
12241	3 " Hattie	19	Dau	16	"	1/16	1896	"	1810
12242	4 " Thomas D Jr	13	Son	10	M	1/16	1896	"	1812
12243	5 " Wilber T	9	"	6	"	1/16	1896	"	1813
12244	6 " Ward H	7	"	4	"	1/16	1896	"	1814

ENROLLMENT ~~OF NOS. 1 HEREON~~ APPROVED BY THE SECRETARY OF INTERIOR SEP 12 1903

ENROLLMENT OF NOS. 2 3 4 5 & 6 HEREON APPROVED BY THE SECRETARY OF INTERIOR MAR 6 1903

TRIBAL ENROLLMENT OF PARENTS

	Name of Father	Year	County	Name of Mother	Year	County
1	Gorden P. Bell	Dead	Non Citz	Martha A Bell	Dead	Non Citz
2	Joseph Ward	"	" "	Betsey E Ward	"	Atoka
3	No1			No2		
4	No1			No2		
5	No1			No2		
6	No1			No2		

No.1 admitted by Dawes Commission, Case No. 640, as J.D. Bell
No1 on 1896 roll as Thos. D. Bell
No2 " 1896 " " Sarah H "
~~No5 " 1896 " " Wilber W "~~
No4 " 1896 " " Thomas D "

Date of Application for Enrollment.
Sept 1/99

~~P.O. Kiowa, I.T.~~

RESIDENCE: Atoka COUNTY. **Choctaw Nation** Choctaw Roll (Not Including Freedmen) CARD NO.
POST OFFICE: Limestone, I.T. FIELD NO. 4389

Dawes' Roll No.	NAME		Relationship to Person First Named	AGE	SEX	BLOOD	TRIBAL ENROLLMENT Year	County	No.
12245	1 Kelly, William W	29	First Named	26	M	1/16	1896	Atoka	7647
I.W. 423	2 " Mollie	28	Wife	25	F	IW			
12246	3 " DeWitt C	4	Son	8mo	M	1/32			
DEAD	4 ~~" Walton Byrne~~		~~Son~~	~~4mo~~	~~M~~	~~1/32~~			
	5								
	6								
	7 No. 4 hereon dismissed under order of								
	8 the Commission to the Five Civilized								
	9 Tribes of March 31, 1905.								
	10								
	11								
	12 ENROLLMENT OF NOS. 2 HEREON								
	13 APPROVED BY THE SECRETARY								
	14 OF INTERIOR Sep 12 1903								
	15 ENROLLMENT OF NOS. 1 and 3 HEREON								
	16 APPROVED BY THE SECRETARY								
	17 OF INTERIOR Mar 6 1903								

TRIBAL ENROLLMENT OF PARENTS

Name of Father	Year	County	Name of Mother	Year	County
1 W. W. Kelly	Dead	Non Citz	Sarah A. Bell		Atoka
2 As Landon		" "	Maria Landon	Dead	Non Citz
3 No1			No2		
4 ~~No1~~			~~No2~~		
5					
6					
7					
8 ~~No3 Affidavit of birth to be~~					
9 supplied:- Filed Oct 26/99					
10 No1 on 1896 roll as W. W. Kelly					
No.4 Enrolled July 11, 1901					
11 ~~Nº4 Died July 19, 1902; proof of death filed Oct. 23, 1902~~					
12 For children of Nos 1&2 see NB (March 3, 1905) #819					
13					
14					#1 to 3
15				Date of Application for Enrollment.	Sept 1/99
16					
17 ~~P.O. seems to be Elmore I.T.~~					

P.O. Pauls Valley I.T. 4/8/05

RESIDENCE: Atoka COUNTY. **Choctaw Nation** **Choctaw Roll** *(Not Including Freedmen)* CARD NO.
POST OFFICE: Lehigh, I.T. FIELD NO. 4390

Dawes' Roll No.	NAME	Relationship to Person First Named	AGE	SEX	BLOOD	TRIBAL ENROLLMENT Year	County	No.
I.W. 676	1 Ball, Thomas J 39	First Named	36	M	IW	1896	Atoka	14345
12247	2 " Salena 39	Wife	36	F	1/4	1896	"	1779

ENROLLMENT OF NOS. ~~1~~ HEREON APPROVED BY THE SECRETARY OF INTERIOR MAR 26 1904

ENROLLMENT OF NOS. 2 HEREON APPROVED BY THE SECRETARY OF INTERIOR MAR 6 1903

TRIBAL ENROLLMENT OF PARENTS

	Name of Father	Year	County	Name of Mother	Year	County
1	W. H. Ball		Non Citz	Ann Ball	Dead	Non Citz
2	Willis	Dead	Blue	Salina Willis	"	Blue

No1 on 1896 roll as T. J. Ball

Date of Application for Enrollment. Sept 1/99

RESIDENCE: Atoka COUNTY. **Choctaw Nation** **Choctaw Roll** (Not Including Freedmen) CARD NO.
POST OFFICE: Coalgate, I.T. FIELD NO. 4391

Dawes' Roll No.	NAME	Relationship to Person First Named	AGE	SEX	BLOOD	TRIBAL ENROLLMENT Year	County	No.
12248	1 Smallwood, Lorenzo 17	First Named	14	M	1/4	1896	Atoka	11689
I.W. 1503	2 Seybold, Lola	Mother	32	F	I.W.			
	3							
	4							
	5							
	6							
	7							
	8							
	9							
	10							
	11							
	12							
	13							
	14							
	15							
	16							
	17							

ENROLLMENT OF NOS. 2 HEREON APPROVED BY THE SECRETARY OF INTERIOR Nov 27 1905

ENROLLMENT OF NOS. 1 HEREON APPROVED BY THE SECRETARY OF INTERIOR Mar 6 1903

TRIBAL ENROLLMENT OF PARENTS

Name of Father	Year	County	Name of Mother	Year	County
1 John Smallwood	Dead	Atoka	Lola Hardin		No[sic] Citz
2 Jas Harden[sic]		non citizen	Nicky Harden	dead	non citizen

On 1896 roll as Perry Smallwood

Evidence of marriage of parents to be supplied.-

No2 was formerly wife of John Smallwood, a Choctaw Indian who died in 1885; now wife of Henry Seybold a non citizen
No2 transferred from Choctaw Card D486 October 18, 1905
See decision of October 2, 1905

Date of Application for Enrollment. For No1 Sept 1/99

POST OFFICE: Atoka, I.T. **Choctaw Nation** Choctaw Roll (Not Including Freedmen) FIELD NO. 4392

Dawes' Roll No.	NAME		Relationship to Person First Named	AGE	SEX	BLOOD	TRIBAL ENROLLMENT Year	County	No.
	1 ~~Pate, Joel L C~~	61	Named	~~58~~	~~M~~	~~IW~~			
12249	2 " Soulie L	23	Dau	20	F	1/32	1896	Atoka	10537
12250	3 " Lavinia W	21	"	18	"	1/32	1896	"	10538
DEAD.	4 ~~" James C~~		~~Son~~	~~33~~	~~M~~	~~1/32~~	~~1896~~	"	~~10539~~

No. 4 HEREON DISMISSED UNDER ORDER OF THE COMMISSION TO THE FIVE CIVILIZED TRIBES OF MARCH 31, 1905.

ENROLLMENT OF NOS. 2 & 3 HEREON APPROVED BY THE SECRETARY OF INTERIOR MAR 6 1903

TRIBAL ENROLLMENT OF PARENTS

	Name of Father	Year	County	Name of Mother	Year	County
1	~~Jas D Pate~~	~~Dead~~	~~Non Citz~~	~~Ellen E Pate~~	~~Dead~~	~~Non Citz~~
2	No1			Ella A Pate	"	Choctaw
3	No1			" " "	"	"
4	~~No1~~			" " "	"	"

No1 denied in 96 Case #567

Nos 2 and 3 admitted by act of Choctaw Council of Oct 21 1885 #1 REFUSED JAN 31 190[illegible]

No1 now in C.C.C.C. Case #113

~~No1 admitted by U.S. Court, Central Dist, July 13/97, Case No 45. As to~~ residence, see his testimony

RECORD FORWARDED DEPARTMENT. JAN 31 1907

No3 on 1896 roll as Lorenia W Pate

~~No4 " 1896 " " J. C. "~~

No4 died Jany 5,1901 Proof of death filed Nov 22, 1902

ACTION APPROVED BY SECRETARY OF INTERIOR. MAR 1 1907

Judgment of U.S. Ct admitting No vacated and set aside by Decree of C.C.C.C. Dec' 17 '02

No1 Denied by C.C.C.C. March 28 '04 Case #113

~~For child of No3 see NB (Mar 3,1905) Card #313~~

See Petition Jacket C-79

NOTICE OF DEPARTMENTAL ACTION MAILED PARTIES HEREIN. APR 22 1907

Sept 1/99

RESIDENCE: Atoka COUNTY. **Choctaw Nation** **Choctaw Roll** *(Not Including Freedmen)* CARD NO.
POST OFFICE: Atoka, I.T. FIELD NO. 4393

Dawes' Roll No.	NAME	Relationship to Person First Named	AGE	SEX	BLOOD	TRIBAL ENROLLMENT Year	County	No.
12251	1 Merrill, Elinor A 33	First Named	30	F	1/32	1896	Atoka	10536
12252	2 " Soulie Miriam 1	Dau	2wks	F	1/64			

ENROLLMENT
OF NOS. 1 & 2 HEREON
APPROVED BY THE SECRETARY
OF INTERIOR MAR 6 1903

TRIBAL ENROLLMENT OF PARENTS

Name of Father	Year	County	Name of Mother	Year	County
1 Joel L. C. Pate		Intermarried	Ella A Pate	Dead	Choctaw
2 Ambrose M Merrill		noncitizen	No1		

On 1896 roll as Ella A Pate
No2 Enrolled Aug 23-1901

No1 admitted by act of Choctaw Council of Oct 21, 1885 as Ellen A Pate

Date of Application for Enrollment.
Sept 1/99

RESIDENCE: Atoka COUNTY. **Choctaw Nation** **Choctaw Roll** (Not Including Freedmen) CARD NO.
POST OFFICE: Atoka, I.T. FIELD NO. 4394

Dawes' Roll No.	NAME		Relationship to Person First Named	AGE	SEX	BLOOD	TRIBAL ENROLLMENT Year	County	No.
I.W. 424	1 Clower, Walter F	46	First Named	42	M	IW	1896	Jackson	14417
12253	2 " Sallie M	33	Wife	30	F	1/32	1896	Blue	2844
12254	3 " Joe E	9	Son	6	M	1/64	1896	"	2845
12255	4 " Walter G	7	"	4	"	1/64	1896	"	2846
12257	5 " Oliver M	5	Dau	2	F	1/64			
12256	6 " Anna H	2	Dau	4mo	F	1/64			

No5- Affidavit of birth to be supplied:- Filed Oct 26/99

ENROLLMENT OF NOS. 1 HEREON APPROVED BY THE SECRETARY OF INTERIOR SEP 12 1903

ENROLLMENT OF NOS. 2 3 4 5 & 6 HEREON APPROVED BY THE SECRETARY OF INTERIOR MAR 6 1903

TRIBAL ENROLLMENT OF PARENTS

	Name of Father	Year	County	Name of Mother	Year	County
1	G. A. Clower	Dead	Non Citz	Mary A Clower	Dead	Non Citz
2	Joel L C Pate		Intermarried	Ella A Pate	"	Choctaw
3	No1			No2		
4	No1			No2		
5	No1			No2		
6	No1			No2		

For child of Nos 1 and 2 see NB (Mar 3, 1905) card #312

No1 admitted by Dawes Com, Case No 770, as W. F. Clower

~~No3 on 1896 roll as Zalla Clower~~

~~No4 " 1896 " " W. George "~~

No2- Certified copy of Act of Council of Oct 21, 1885 admitting No2 to citizenship, filed with ~~Com in 1896 in Case of W. F. Clower vs Choctaw Nation~~

No1 on 1896 roll as Walter F Clowet

No.6 Enrolled February 13, 1901.

~~Post Office address now~~ Caddo, Indian Territory, February 13, 1901.

Date of Application for Enrollment. Sept 1/99

~~11/21/02 PO Caddo IT~~

Choctaw By Blood Enrollment Cards 1898-1914

RESIDENCE: Atoka COUNTY. **Choctaw Nation** **Choctaw Roll** (Not Including Freedmen) CARD NO.
POST OFFICE: Atoka, I.T. FIELD NO. 4395

Dawes' Roll No.	NAME	Relationship to Person First Named	AGE	SEX	BLOOD	TRIBAL ENROLLMENT Year	County	No.
14334	1 Standley, James W 30	First Named	27	M	1/16			
	2							
	3							
	4							
	5							
	6							
	7							
	8							
	9							
	10							
	11							
	12							
	13							
	14							
	15							
	16							
	17							

ENROLLMENT OF NOS. 1 HEREON APPROVED BY THE SECRETARY OF INTERIOR APR 11 1903

TRIBAL ENROLLMENT OF PARENTS

Name of Father	Year	County	Name of Mother	Year	County
1 W. P. Standley	Dead	Choctaw	Mary H Standley	Dead	Non Citz
2					
3					
4					
5					
6					
7					
8					
9					
10					
11					
12					
13					
14					Date of Application for Enrollment.
15					Sept 1/99
16					
17 P.O. Caddo, I.T.					

Admitted by Dawes Com. Case No 1068. No appeal.

RESIDENCE: Atoka COUNTY. **Choctaw Nation** **Choctaw Roll** *(Not Including Freedmen)* CARD NO.
POST OFFICE: Atoka, I.T. FIELD NO. 4396

Dawes' Roll No.	NAME	Relationship to Person First Named	AGE	SEX	BLOOD	TRIBAL ENROLLMENT Year	County	No.
12258	1 Homer, Peter 11	First Named	8	M	Full	1893	Atoka	50
	2							
	3							
	4							
	5							
	6							
	7							
	8							
	9							
	10							
	11							
	12							
	13							
	14							
	15							
	16							
	17							

ENROLLMENT OF NOS. 1 HEREON APPROVED BY THE SECRETARY OF INTERIOR MAR 6 1903

TRIBAL ENROLLMENT OF PARENTS

	Name of Father	Year	County	Name of Mother	Year	County
1		Dead	Atoka	Mary Billy		Jackson
2						
3						
4						
5						
6						
7						
8						
9						
10						
11						
12						
13						
14						
15						
16						
17						

On 1893 Pay Roll, Page 5, No 50, Atoka Co., as Peter Billy

On 1896 Choctaw roll, page 300: No. 11621, as Peter Sexton.

March 7, 1900.

Date of Application for Enrollment.

Sept 1/99

RESIDENCE: Atoka COUNTY. **Choctaw Nation** **Choctaw Roll** (Not Including Freedmen) CARD NO.
POST OFFICE: Glove, I.T. FIELD NO. 4397

Dawes' Roll No.	NAME	Relationship to Person First Named	AGE	SEX	BLOOD	TRIBAL ENROLLMENT Year	County	No.
12259	1 Jackson, Greenwood 31	First Named	28	M	1/8	1896	Blue	7233
I.W. 425	2 " Belle Z. 29	Wife	26	F	I.W.			
12260	3 " Leona 9	Dau	6	"	1/16	1896	Blue	7234
12261	4 " Cora 7	"	4	"	1/16	1896	"	7235
12262	5 " Alfred 4	Son	7mo	M	1/16			
12263	6 " Laura A. 2	Dau	4mo	F	1/16			

ENROLLMENT OF NOS. 2 HEREON APPROVED BY THE SECRETARY OF INTERIOR Sep 12 1903

ENROLLMENT OF NOS. 1 3 4 5 & 6 HEREON APPROVED BY THE SECRETARY OF INTERIOR Mar 6 1903

TRIBAL ENROLLMENT OF PARENTS

	Name of Father	Year	County	Name of Mother	Year	County
1	William Jackson	Dead	Non Citz	Laura Kelly		Blue
2	Simon Thompson		" "	Margret Thompson		Non Citz
3	No1			No2		
4	No1			No2		
5	No1			No2		
6	No1			No2		
7	No1			No2		
8	No.1			No.2		

No3 on 1896 roll as Linie Jackson

~~No.5 Affidavit of birth to be~~ supplied:- Filed Oct 26/99

No.6 Enrolled June 4th, 1901.

For children of Nos 1&1 see NB (March 3, 1905) #1356

For Nos. 1 to 5 Incl.

Date of Application for Enrollment. Sept 1/99

RESIDENCE: Atoka COUNTY. **Choctaw Nation** **Choctaw Roll** *(Not Including Freedmen)* CARD NO.
POST OFFICE: Atoka, I.T. FIELD NO. 4398

Dawes' Roll No.	NAME	Relationship to Person First Named	AGE	SEX	BLOOD	TRIBAL ENROLLMENT Year	County	No.
12264	1 Betts, David C 32	First Named	29	M	1/4	1896	Blue	1654
I.W. 426	2 " Emma 26	Wife	23	F	I.W.	1896	"	14337
12265	3 " Bethel L 6	Dau	3	"	1/8	1896	"	1656
12266	4 " Ada M B 4	"	7mo	"	1/8			
12267	5 " Charlie Walker 2	Son	2½mo	M	1/8			

ENROLLMENT OF NOS. 2 HEREON APPROVED BY THE SECRETARY OF INTERIOR Sep 12 1903

ENROLLMENT OF NOS. 1, 3 4 & 5 HEREON APPROVED BY THE SECRETARY OF INTERIOR Mar 6 1903

TRIBAL ENROLLMENT OF PARENTS

Name of Father	Year	County	Name of Mother	Year	County
1 R. D. Betts		Atoka	Emiline Betts		Atoka
2 John Baxter		Non Citz		Dead	Non Citz
3 No1			No2		
4 No1			No2		
5 No1			No2		

No4- Affidavit of birth to be supplied:- Filed Nov 2/99
No.5 Enrolled April 10, 1901
~~Evidence of marriage of Nos 1 and 2 Filed May 9, 1901~~
For children of Nos 1&2 see NB (March 3 1905) #556

Date of Application for Enrollment.
Sept 1/99

Choctaw By Blood Enrollment Cards 1898-1914

RESIDENCE: Atoka COUNTY. **Choctaw Nation** **Choctaw Roll** (Not Including Freedmen) CARD NO.
POST OFFICE: Atoka I.T. FIELD NO. 4399

Dawes' Roll No.	NAME		Relationship to Person First Named	AGE	SEX	BLOOD	TRIBAL ENROLLMENT Year	County	No.
12268	1 Carnes, Sam	29	First Named	26	M	Full	1896	Atoka	2928
14941	2 " Silvey	25	Wife	22	F	"	1896	"	6085
12269	3 Nelson, Eli	19	Ward	16	M	"	1893	Jackson	127
DEAD	4 ~~Carnes Sally~~		~~Dau~~	~~4mo~~	~~F~~	~~"~~			

No. 4 hereon dismissed under order of the Commission to the Five Civilized Tribes of March 31, 1905.

ENROLLMENT OF NOS. 1 & 3 HEREON APPROVED BY THE SECRETARY OF INTERIOR Mar 6 1903

ENROLLMENT OF NOS. ~~~ 2 ~~~ HEREON APPROVED BY THE SECRETARY OF INTERIOR Oct 15 1903

TRIBAL ENROLLMENT OF PARENTS

Name of Father	Year	County	Name of Mother	Year	County
1 Jackson Carnes	Dead	Atoka	Nicey Carnes	Dead	Atoka
2 Lewis Hokey	"	Tobucksy	Louisianna Hokey		"
3 Solomon Nelson	"	Jackson	Lucy Nelson	"	Jackson
4 ~~No1~~			~~No2~~		

No1 on 1896 roll as Sam Carn
No2 " 1896 " " Selina Hoker
No3 on 1893 Pay Roll, Page 14, No. 127, Jackson Co., as Eliza Nelson.

No4 died June 1902, proof of death filed Nov 26, 1902

Date of Application for Enrollment.
Sept 1/99

No4 enrolled Jany 17, 1900

Choctaw By Blood Enrollment Cards 1898-1914

RESIDENCE: Atoka COUNTY. **Choctaw Nation** **Choctaw Roll** *(Not Including Freedmen)* CARD NO.
POST OFFICE: Atoka, I.T. FIELD NO. **4400**

Dawes' Roll No.	NAME	Relationship to Person First Named	AGE	SEX	BLOOD	TRIBAL ENROLLMENT Year	County	No.
12270	1 Williams, Warneta F 22	First Named	19	F	1/4	1896	Blue	1586
12271	2 " Jesse F 5	Son	1½	M	1/8			
12272	3 " Effie H 2	Dau	4mo	F	1/8			
	4							
	5							
	6							
	7							
	8							
	9							
	10							
	11							
	12							
	13							
	14							
	15 ENROLLMENT							
	16 OF NOS. 1 2 & 3 HEREON APPROVED BY THE SECRETARY							
	17 OF INTERIOR Mar 6 1903							

TRIBAL ENROLLMENT OF PARENTS

Name of Father	Year	County	Name of Mother	Year	County
1 R. D. Betts		Ataka[sic]	Emeline Betts		Atoka
2 T.R. Williams		Non Citz	No1		
3 " "		" "	No.1		
4					
5					
6					
7 For child of No.1 see NB (Mar. 3 1905) Card #314					
8					
9 No1 on 1896 roll as Juanita Betts					
10 No2- Affidavit of birth to be					
11 supplied:- Filed Nov. 2/99					
12					
13					
14		No.3 Enrolled May 24, 1900			Date of Application for Enrollment.
15					Sept 1/99
16					
17					

Choctaw By Blood Enrollment Cards 1898-1914

RESIDENCE: Atoka COUNTY. **Choctaw Nation** **Choctaw Roll** (Not Including Freedmen) CARD NO.
POST OFFICE: Coalgate, I.T. FIELD NO. 4401

Dawes' Roll No.	NAME	Relationship to Person First Named	AGE	SEX	BLOOD	TRIBAL ENROLLMENT Year	County	No.
12273	1 Marshall, Henry 62	First Named	59	M	1/4	1896	Atoka	8815
15690	2 " Robert L. 23	Son	21	M	1/4	1896	Atoka	8817
I.W. 1424	3 " Nancy	Wife	63	F	I.W.			

ENROLLMENT OF NOS. ~~~ 3 ~~~ HEREON APPROVED BY THE SECRETARY OF INTERIOR Jun 12 1905

ENROLLMENT OF NOS. ~~ 2 ~~ HEREON APPROVED BY THE SECRETARY OF INTERIOR Dec 2 1904

ENROLLMENT OF NOS. 1 HEREON APPROVED BY THE SECRETARY OF INTERIOR Mar 6 1903

TRIBAL ENROLLMENT OF PARENTS

Name of Father	Year	County	Name of Mother	Year	County
1 John C. Marshall	Dead	Non Citz	Matilda Marshall	Dead	Choctaw
2 No.1	1896	Atoka	Nancy Marshall		noncitizen
3 Allen Screws		non citz	Barbara Screws		non-citz

No.1 Admitted by Act of Choctaw Council No 62, Approved Nov 4-1886

No.1 is the husband of Nancy Marshal on Choctaw Card #D.600, December 11, 1900.

No.2 transferred from Choctaw card #D-599 Oct 31, 1904: See decision of Oct 15, 1904

No.3 originally listed for enrollment on Choctaw card #D-600 Dec. 11, 1900: transferred to this card May 15, 1905. See decision of March 29, 1905

Date of Application for Enrollment. Sept 1/99

For No.1 ↗

Choctaw By Blood Enrollment Cards 1898-1914

RESIDENCE: Gaines COUNTY. **Choctaw Nation** **Choctaw Roll** (Not Including Freedmen) CARD NO.
POST OFFICE: Wilburton, I.T. FIELD NO. **4402**

Dawes' Roll No.	NAME	Relationship to Person First Named	AGE	SEX	BLOOD	TRIBAL ENROLLMENT Year	County	No.
12274	1 Wright, Sarah 19 ✓	First Named	16	F	Full	1896	Gaines	12978
	2							
	3							
	4							
	5							
	6							
	7							
	8							
	9							
	10							
	11							
	12							
	13							
	14							
	15							
	16							
	17							

ENROLLMENT OF NOS 1 HEREON APPROVED BY THE SECRETARY OF INTERIOR MAR 6 1903

TRIBAL ENROLLMENT OF PARENTS

Name of Father	Year	County	Name of Mother	Year	County
1 John Wright	Dead	Red River	Susan Wright	Dead	Red River
2					
3					
4					
5					
6					
7					
8					
9					
10					
11 On 1896 Roll as Sallie Wright					
12					
13					
14					
15					
16					
17					Sept 1, 1899

RESIDENCE: Atoka COUNTY. **Choctaw Nation** Choctaw Roll (Not Including Freedmen) CARD NO.
POST OFFICE: Coalgate, I.T. FIELD NO. 4403

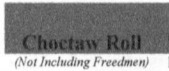

Dawes' Roll No.		NAME		Relationship to Person First Named	AGE	SEX	BLOOD	TRIBAL ENROLLMENT Year	County	No.
12275	1	Barker, Dora E	23	First Named	20	F	1/16	1896	Atoka	9437
12276	2	McGahey, Arthur D	21	Bro	18	M	1/16	1896	"	9434
12277	3	" Elijah W	18	"	15	"	1/16	1896	"	9435
12278	4	" Effie	8	Sister	5	F	1/16	1896	"	9436
12279	5	" Joel J	6	Bro	3	M	1/16	1896	"	9433
12280	6	Barker, James F. H.	2	Son	2mo	M	1/32			
12281	7	" Arthur L.H.A.	1	Son	1mo	M	1/32			

Nos 2,3,4 and 5 children of A.R. McGahey who was admitted by Act of Choctaw Council of Nov. 5 1880.

No.7 Born May 13th 1902: Enrolled June 19th 1902:

Martha Allen, Mother of Nos. 1-5 inclusive on Choctaw card D 837

Wife of No2 on Card No 6052

ENROLLMENT OF NOS. 1 2 3 4 5 6 & 7 HEREON APPROVED BY THE SECRETARY OF INTERIOR Mar 6 1903

TRIBAL ENROLLMENT OF PARENTS

	Name of Father	Year	County	Name of Mother	Year	County
1	A. R. McGahey	Dead	Jacks Fork	Martha Allen		Non Citz
2	" " "	"	" "	" "		" "
3	" " "	"	" "	" "		" "
4	" " "	"	" "	" "		" "
5	" " "	"	" "	" "		" "
6	Wm. N. Barker		Choctaw #D.501	No.1		
7	" " "		" " "	No1		

No.1 is now the wife of William N Barker on Choctaw card D #501

No1 was admitted by Act of Choctaw Council No 31, approved Nov. 5 1880 as Dora McGahey

Sept. 6, 1900.

For child of No2 see NB (Mar 3-05) #509

No2 on 1896 roll as Arthur L. McGahey

No3 " 1896 " " Eliza W "

No5 " 1896 " " Joseph J "

No.2 See note opposite name of No2 on 1896 roll which says "enrollment refused." Sept 28/99

For child of No.1 see NB (Apr 26-06) No.937

No6 Enrolled Sept 6th, 1900

#1 to 5
Date of Application for Enrollment.
Sept 1/99

No2 P.O. Cliff I.T. July 1-1904

RESIDENCE: Sugar Loaf COUNTY. **Choctaw Nation** **Choctaw Roll** *(Not Including Freedmen)* CARD NO.
POST OFFICE: LeFlore, I.T. FIELD NO. 4404

Dawes' Roll No.	NAME	Relationship to Person First Named	AGE	SEX	BLOOD	TRIBAL ENROLLMENT Year	County	No.
12282	1 Benton, John 15	First Named	12	M	Full	1893	Sugar Loaf	398

ENROLLMENT OF NOS. 1 HEREON APPROVED BY THE SECRETARY OF INTERIOR MAR 6 1903

TRIBAL ENROLLMENT OF PARENTS

	Name of Father	Year	County	Name of Mother	Year	County
1	Thomas Benton	Dead	Sugar Loaf	Meaby Benton		Sugar Loaf

On 1893 Pay Roll, Page 49, No 398, Sugar Loaf as Ealey Benton

No.1 "Duplicate enrollment of Elie Benton No 8924- "Not entitled to land or money." See Indian Office Letter February 28, 1908 (I.T. 4054-1908)

No1 is duplicate of Elie Benton #6 on 7-3050

Date of Application for Enrollment.

Sept 1/99

RESIDENCE: Atoka COUNTY. **Choctaw Nation** **Choctaw Roll** *(Not Including Freedmen)* CARD NO.

POST OFFICE: Atoka, I.T. FIELD NO. 4405

Dawes' Roll No.		NAME	Relationship to Person First Named	AGE	SEX	BLOOD	TRIBAL ENROLLMENT Year	County	No.
	1	~~Pate, George A~~	~~First Named~~	~~44~~	~~M~~	~~IW~~	~~1896~~	~~Atoka~~	~~14948~~
12283	2	" Josie L [37]	Wife	34	F	1/8	1896	"	10534
12284	3	" Arden [5]	Son	1½	M	1/16			
12285	4	" Milton [3]	Son	1mo	M	1/16			
	5								
	6	No1 denied in 96 Case #568							
	7	No.2 admitted by Act of Choctaw Council of Oct. 21, 1885.							
	8	No appeal to C.C.C.C.							
	9								
	10	No1 DISMISSED							
	11	SEP 22 1904							
	12								
	13								
	14	ENROLLMENT							
	15	OF NOS. 2 3 & 4 HEREON							
	16	APPROVED BY THE SECRETARY OF INTERIOR MAR 6 1903							
	17								

TRIBAL ENROLLMENT OF PARENTS

	Name of Father	Year	County	Name of Mother	Year	County
1	~~Jeff C. Pate~~	~~Dead~~	~~Non Citz~~	~~Eliza F. Pate~~	~~Dead~~	~~Non Citz~~
2	Joel L. C. Pate		Intermarried	Ella A Pate	"	Choctaw
3	No1			No2		
4	No1			No2		
5						
6						
7	~~No1- Admitted by U.S. Court, Central~~					
8	Dist, July 13/97 – Case No 43 as G.A.					
9	Pate- intermarried.					
	Judgement(s) of U.S. Court vacated and set aside by Decree of Choctaw Chickasaw Citizenship Court Dec 17 '02					
10	~~Milton Pate, born Dec 21/99, on~~					
11	Card No D-548					
12	No4 born December 21, 1899; transferred to this card May 24, 1902					
13						
14						
15				Date of Application for Enrollment.		Sept 1/99
16						1 to 3
17	P.O. Caddo I.T. 12/20/02					

Choctaw By Blood Enrollment Cards 1898-1914

RESIDENCE: Atoka COUNTY. **Choctaw Nation** **Choctaw Roll** *(Not Including Freedmen)* CARD NO.
POST OFFICE: Atoka, I.T. FIELD NO. 4406

Dawes' Roll No.		NAME	Relationship to Person First Named	AGE	SEX	BLOOD	TRIBAL ENROLLMENT Year	County	No.
12286	1	Folsom, William W [24]	First Named	21	M	1/4	1896	Atoka	4447
	2								
	3								
	4								
	5								
	6								
	7								
	8								
	9								
	10								
	11								
	12								
	13								
	14								
	15								
	16								
	17								

ENROLLMENT
OF NOS. 1 HEREON
APPROVED BY THE SECRETARY
OF INTERIOR MAR 6 1903

TRIBAL ENROLLMENT OF PARENTS

	Name of Father	Year	County	Name of Mother	Year	County
1	I. W. Folsom		Chick Natn	Lula B. Folsom		Intermarried
2						
3						
4						
5						
6						
7						
8						
9						
10						
11						
12						
13						
14						
15						
16						
17						

On 1896 roll as Willie Folsom

As to marriage of parents, see testimony of Allington Telle

Date of Application for Enrollment. Sept 1/99

RESIDENCE: Atoka COUNTY. Chocta[redacted] (Not Including Freedmen) CARD NO.
POST OFFICE: Atoka, I.T. FIELD NO. 4407

Dawes' Roll No.	NAME		Relationship to Person First Named	AGE	SEX	BLOOD	TRIBAL ENROLLMENT Year	TRIBAL ENROLLMENT County	
12287	1 Durant, Wesley	24	First Named	21	M	Full	1893	Blue	
12288	2 " Albert	5	Son	2	"	"			
I.W. 1344	3 " Nancy	22	Wife	22	F	I.W.			

ENROLLMENT OF NOS. 3 HEREON APPROVED BY THE SECRETARY OF INTERIOR MAR 14 1905

ENROLLMENT OF NOS. 1 & 2 HEREON APPROVED BY THE SECRETARY OF INTERIOR MAR 6 1903

TRIBAL ENROLLMENT OF PARENTS

Name of Father	Year	County	Name of Mother	Year	County
1 Watson Durant	Dead	Atoka	Lucy Durant	Dead	Atoka
2 No1			Mary Durant	"	"
3 Rollen Wallace		non citizen	Merggret[sic] Wallace		non citizen

On 1893 Pay Roll, Page 118, No 29, Blue Co.

Also on 1896 roll, Page 87, No 3620 as Wesley Duct Atoka Co.

Nos 1 and 3 were married May 1, 1901

No.3 originally listed for enrollment on Choctaw card D-973 Dec. 12, 1902 transferred to this card Feb. 1, 1905: See decision of Jan. 16, 1905

#1&2

Date of Application for Enrollment. Sept 1/99

No2 enrolled Dec 16/99

No 2 P.O. Wilburton I T. 12/9/04

RESIDENCE: Atoka COUNTY. **Choctaw Nation** **Choctaw Roll** *(Not Including Freedmen)* CARD NO.
POST OFFICE: Atoka, I.T. FIELD NO. 4408

Dawes' Roll No.	NAME	Relationship to Person First Named	AGE	SEX	BLOOD	TRIBAL ENROLLMENT Year	County	No.
12289	1 Colbert, Jasper [13]		10	M	Full	1893	Sans Bois	193

ENROLLMENT
OF NOS. 1 HEREON
APPROVED BY THE SECRETARY
OF INTERIOR MAR 6 1903

TRIBAL ENROLLMENT OF PARENTS

	Name of Father	Year	County	Name of Mother	Year	County
1	Jasper Lewis	Dead			Dead	

On 1893 Pay Roll, Page 19, No 193, Sans Bois Co

Duplicate enrollment of No 7926 and not entitled to land or money under No. 12289 (I.T. Ind. Office letter Aug 5, 1910 [Illegible]

Date of Application for Enrollment.
Sept 1/99

Choctaw By Blood Enrollment Cards 1898-1914

RESIDENCE: Chickasaw Nation ~~COUNTY.~~ **Choctaw Nation** **Choctaw Roll** *(Not Including Freedmen)* CARD NO.
POST OFFICE: Courtney, I.T. FIELD NO. 4409

Dawes' Roll No.		NAME	Relationship to Person First Named	AGE	SEX	BLOOD	TRIBAL ENROLLMENT Year	County	No.
✓ ✓	1	~~McCarty, Alphonzo~~ *	~~First Named~~	~~39~~	~~M~~	~~1/16~~			
✓ ✓	2	~~" Joseph~~ *	~~Son~~	~~3~~	~~M~~	~~1/32~~			
DP	3	~~" Kona~~	~~Dau~~	~~2mo~~	~~F~~	~~1/32~~			
	4								
	5								
	6	DENIED CITIZENSHIP BY THE CHOCTAW AND							
Nos 1 and 2	7	CHICKASAW CITIZENSHIP COURT							
	8								
	9								
3	10	DISMISSED	MAY 27 1904						
	11								
	12								
	13								
	14								
	15								
	16								
	17								

TRIBAL ENROLLMENT OF PARENTS

	Name of Father	Year	County	Name of Mother	Year	County
1	~~Press McCarty~~	~~Dead~~	~~Choctaw~~	~~Nancy McCarty~~	~~Dead~~	~~Non Citz~~
2	~~No1~~			~~Pennie McCarty~~		" "
3	~~No1~~			" "		" "
4						
5						
6						
7						
8						

Nos 1 and 2 denied on 96 Case #27
Admitted by U.S. Court, Central Dist, Jany 19/98, Case No 78. As ~~to residence, see testimony of No1~~
Judgment of U.S. Ct admitting No1&2 vacated and set aside by Decree of Choctaw Chickasaw Citizenship Court Dec 17'02
Evidence of marriage of parents of No3 to be supplied:-
Nos 1 and 2 now in C.C.C.C. Case #27

Date of Application for Enrollment.
Sept 1/99

RESIDENCE: Jackson COUNTY. **Choctaw Nation** Choctaw Roll (Not Including Freedmen) CARD NO.
POST OFFICE: Mayhew, I.T. FIELD NO. 4410

Dawes' Roll No.	NAME	Relationship to Person First Named	AGE	SEX	BLOOD	TRIBAL ENROLLMENT Year	County	No.
12290	1 Smallwood, Ruthie 9	First Named	6	F	1/4	1893	Kiamitia	751
I.W. 1584	2 Sisney, Emmer[sic]	Mother	35	F	I.W.			

No.2 was formerly wife of Robert Smallwood Choctaw card #1791 Roll 5708

ENROLLMENT OF NOS. ~~~~ 2 ~~~~ HEREON APPROVED BY THE SECRETARY OF INTERIOR Nov 26 1906

ENROLLMENT OF NOS. 1 HEREON APPROVED BY THE SECRETARY OF INTERIOR Mar 6 1903

TRIBAL ENROLLMENT OF PARENTS

Name of Father	Year	County	Name of Mother	Year	County
1 Robt. Smallwood		Kiamitia	Emma Smallwood		Non Citz
2 Fletcher Murphy		non citizen	Jane Meredith		non citizen

No2 placed hereon under order of Commissioner to Five Civilized Tribes of February 26, 1906 holding that application was made for her enrollment within the time provided by the Act of Congress approved July 1, 1902

On 1893 Pay Roll, Page 89, No 751, Kiamitia County

See testimony of Isabelle Kelly as to marriage of parents.

Also on 1896 roll as Rosie Smallwood Page 299, No 11566, Jackson Co.

Notify Apple & Franklin, Muskogee I.T. as to No2 2-26-06

For child of No2 see NB (Apr 26-06) #1264

Guardian of No 1 is Emma Sisney Boswell City I.T. 11/14 '02

2/26/06

Date of Application for Enrollment. Sept 1/99

P.O. Boswell I.T. 10/18/1905

3/5/06

Choctaw By Blood Enrollment Cards 1898-1914

RESIDENCE: Atoka COUNTY. **Choctaw Nation** **Choctaw Roll** *(Not Including Freedmen)* CARD NO.
POST OFFICE: Lehigh, I.T. FIELD NO. 4411

Dawes' Roll No.	NAME	Relationship to Person First Named	AGE	SEX	BLOOD	TRIBAL ENROLLMENT Year	County	No.
12291	1 Hawkins, Lucinda 22	First Named	19	F	1/2	1896	Atoka	9458
12292	2 " Loman A 4	Son	5mo	M	1/4			
12293	3 " Stella 2	Dau	4mo	F	1/4			

ENROLLMENT OF NOS. 1 2 & 3 HEREON APPROVED BY THE SECRETARY OF INTERIOR Mar 6 1903

TRIBAL ENROLLMENT OF PARENTS

Name of Father	Year	County	Name of Mother	Year	County
1 John M^c^Cartey	Dead	Colored man	Theresa M^c^Cartey	Dead	Atoka
2 Sam Hawkins		" "	№1		
3 " "		" "	№1		

No1 on 1896 roll as Silla M^c^Cartey

See enrollment of Martin Dick

No2- Affidavit of birth to be supplied:- Filed Oct 26/99

№3 Born Dec. 25, 1900: enrolled April 25, 1902

Child of No1 on NB Card (Apr 26-06) #279.

#1 to 2

Date of Application for Enrollment. Sept 1/99

P.O. Coalgate I.T. 5/14/06

RESIDENCE: Atoka COUNTY. **Choctaw Nation** **Choctaw Roll** *(Not Including Freedmen)* CARD NO.

POST OFFICE: Atoka, I.T. FIELD NO. **4412**

Dawes' Roll No.	NAME	Relationship to Person First Named	AGE	SEX	BLOOD	TRIBAL ENROLLMENT		
						Year	County	No.
I.W. 427	1 Vail, James W 65		62	M	I.W.			
12294	2 " Frances 45	Wife	42	F	1/4	1896	Atoka	12617
12295	3 " James T 26	Son	23	M	1/8	1896	"	12618
12296	4 " William E 24	"	21	"	1/8	1896	"	12619
12297	5 " Charles E 19	"	16	"	1/8	1896	"	12620
12298	6 " Mary M 16	Dau	13	F	1/8	1896	"	12621
12299	7 " Junior E 14	"	11	"	1/8	1896	"	12622
12300	8 " Lois M 11	"	8	"	1/8	1896	"	12623
12301	9 " Eunice 10	"	7	"	1/8	1896	"	12624
12302	10 " Ruth 7	"	4	"	1/8	1896	"	12625
12303	11 " Olive 5	"	2	"	1/8			
~~12304~~	12 ~~" Vergie 1~~	~~Gr. Dau~~	~~2mo~~	~~F~~	~~1/16~~			
	13 No6 on 1896 roll as Maud Vail							
	14 No2 was adopted by							
	15 Act of Choctaw Council Approved Oct 11 1871							
	16 No11 Affidavit of birth to							
	17 be supplied:- Filed Oct 26/99							

TRIBAL ENROLLMENT OF PARENTS

Name of Father	Year	County	Name of Mother	Year	County
1 Dan'l W. Vail	Dead	Non Citz	Betsy E. Vail	Dead	Non Citz
2 Coleman Folsom	"	Skullyville	Eliz. Folsom		white woman
3 No1			No2		
4 No1			No2		
5 No1			No2		
6 No1			No2		
7 No1			No2		
8 No1			No2		
9 No1			No2		
10 No1			No2		
11 No1			No2		
12 ~~Nº4~~			~~Rebecca Vail~~		~~non citizen~~
13 No1 admitted by Dawes Com. Case			No7 on 1896 roll as		
14 No 252 as J.W. Vail			Junia Vail.		
15 No2 on 1896 roll as Mrs. Frances Vail				Date of Application for Enrollment.	Sept 2/99
15 No3 " 1896 " " Jas T. "					
16 No4 " 1896 " " Willie C. "			No12 cancelled upon approval of Sec		
17 No5 " 1896 " " Chas E "			of the Interior. Letter of June 11, 1903. 7/18/03		

ENROLLMENT OF NOS. 1 HEREON APPROVED BY THE SECRETARY OF INTERIOR Sep 12 1903

ENROLLMENT OF NOS. 2,3,4,5,6,7,8,9,10,11,~~12~~ HEREON APPROVED BY THE SECRETARY OF INTERIOR ~~Mar 6 1903~~

~~No4 is now husband of Rebecca Vail noncitizen. Evidence of marriage filed Oct 29,1902~~

~~Nº12 born Aug 16,1902 enrolled Oct 29, 1902~~

RESIDENCE: Jackson COUNTY. **Choctaw Nation** **Choctaw Roll** *(Not Including Freedmen)* CARD NO.
POST OFFICE: Mayhew, I.T. FIELD NO. **4413**

Dawes' Roll No.	NAME		Relationship to Person First Named	AGE	SEX	BLOOD	TRIBAL ENROLLMENT Year	County	No.
~~12305~~	1	~~Harris, Jincey~~ 63 DIED PRIOR TO SEPTEMBER 25, 1902	~~First Named~~	~~60~~	~~F~~	~~3/4~~	~~1893~~	~~Jackson~~	~~321~~
12306	2	" Elisha 16	Son	13	M	3/8			323
12307	3	" Evelina 6	Dau	3	F	3/8			

ENROLLMENT OF NOS. 1, 2 & 3 HEREON APPROVED BY THE SECRETARY OF INTERIOR Mar 6 1903

TRIBAL ENROLLMENT OF PARENTS

	Name of Father	Year	County	Name of Mother	Year	County
1	~~Gilbert Edward~~	~~Dead~~	~~Cedar~~	~~Monte-hu-na~~	~~Dead~~	~~Cedar~~
2	Nelson Harris		Non Citz Col.	No1		
3	" "		" " "	No1		

No1 on 1893 Pay Roll, Page 37, No 321, Jackson Co
No2 " 1893 " " " 37, " 323 " "
as Elishi Harris
~~No3- Affidavit of birth to be supplied.-~~
Filed Oct 26/99
No.1 died Feb. - 1900: Enrollment cancelled by Department July 8, 1904

Date of Application for Enrollment.
Sept 2/99

Choctaw By Blood Enrollment Cards 1898-1914

RESIDENCE: COUNTY. **Choctaw Nation** **Choctaw Roll** *(Not Including Freedmen)* CARD NO.
POST OFFICE: Tuskahomma[sic], I.T. FIELD NO. **4414**

Dawes' Roll No.	NAME	Relationship to Person First Named	AGE	SEX	BLOOD	TRIBAL ENROLLMENT Year	County	No.
✓ ✓	1 Beck, Mattie *		30	F	1/8			
	2							
	3							
	4 Denied Citizenship by the Choctaw Chickasaw Citizenship Court Case #112 April 30 '04.							
	5							
	6							
	7							
	8							
	9							
	10							
	11							
	12							
	13							
	14							
	15							
	16							
	17							

TRIBAL ENROLLMENT OF PARENTS

	Name of Father	Year	County	Name of Mother	Year	County
1	B.P. Henderson		non cit	Nancy Henderson		Jacks Fork
2						
3						
4						
5						
6						
7	No1 Denied ion 96 Case #425					
8	No1 now in C.C.C.C. Case #112					
9	Admitted by U.S. Court at South M^c^Alester Jan 18, 1898					
10	case No.44 As to residence see her testimony					
11	Judgement[sic] of U.S. Ct admitting No1 vacated and set aside by Decree of Choctaw Chickasaw Citizenship Court Decr 17'02					
12	No.1 is the Mother of Nos 1 to 5 inclusive on Choctaw					
13	rejected card #R 387					
14						
15						
16						Date of Application for Enrollment.
17	P.O. Bailey, I.T. 1/19/05					9/2/99

RESIDENCE: Atoka COUNTY. **Choctaw Nation** **Choctaw Roll** *(Not Including Freedmen)* CARD NO.
POST OFFICE: Stringtown, I.T. FIELD NO. 4415

Dawes' Roll No.	NAME	Relationship to Person First Named	AGE	SEX	BLOOD	TRIBAL ENROLLMENT Year	County	No.
DEAD ✓	1 M[c]Bride, Mary DEAD	First Named	27	F	1/8			
✓DP	2 " Emma A	Dau	2	F	1/16			

No2 DISMISSED MAY 27 1904

Nº1 DENIED CITIZENSHIP BY THE CHOCTAW AND CHICKASAW CITIZENSHIP COURT [Illegible]

TRIBAL ENROLLMENT OF PARENTS

Name of Father	Year	County	Name of Mother	Year	County
1 B.P. Henderson		Non Cit.	Nancy Henderson		Jacks Fork
2 John M[c]Bride		" "	Nº1		

No1 denied in 96 Case #425

Judgment admitting No1 by U.S. Ct vacated and set aside by Decree of Choctaw Chickasaw Cit Court Dec 17 02

Nos 1&2 now in C.C.C.C. Case #112

Nº1 Original application filed with Dawes Commission Sept. 7, 1896

Admitted by U.S. Court at So M[c]Alester Jan 18 1898

Case No.44

As to residence see her testimony.

See Choctaw card #R.749 for children

Nº2 Born Dec 24 1896, was enrolled on Choctaw card #R749 Sept 2, 1899: Proper proof of birth subsequent to filing original application for Nº1, having been received, Nº2 was transferred from Choctaw card #R749 to this card July 23, 1902

Nº1 Died March 4 1900: proof of death filed July 23, 1902

Date of Application for Enrollment.

9/2/99

RESIDENCE: COUNTY. **Choctaw Nation** **Choctaw Roll** *(Not Including Freedmen)* CARD NO.

POST OFFICE: Tushkahomma[sic] I.T. FIELD NO. 4416

Dawes' Roll No.	NAME	Relationship to Person First Named	AGE	SEX	BLOOD	TRIBAL ENROLLMENT Year	County	No.
✓	1 ~~Fields, Nancy E~~	~~Named~~	~~21~~	~~F~~	~~1/8~~			
	2							
	3							
	4							
	5							
	6							
	7							
	8							
	9							
	10							
	11							
	12							
	13							
	14							
	15							
	16							
	17							

DENIED CITIZENSHIP BY THE CHOCTAW AND CHICKASAW CITIZENSHIP COURT

April 30. [illegible]
Case [illegible]

TRIBAL ENROLLMENT OF PARENTS

	Name of Father	Year	County	Name of Mother	Year	County
1	~~B.P. Henderson~~		~~Non Cit.~~	~~Nancy Henderson~~		~~Jacks Fork~~
2						
3						
4						
5						
6						
7						
8						
9						

No1 denied in 96 Case #425

Judgment of U.S. Ct admitting No1 vacated and set aside by Decree of Choctaw Chickasaw Citizenship Court Dec' 17'02

No1 now in C.C.C.C. Case #112

~~Admitted by U.S. Court at So M^c^Alester, Jan 18-1898~~
Case No.44, as Bettie Henderson
As to residence see testimony of Wm A. Fields.

Date of Application for Enrollment.
9/2/99

Choctaw By Blood Enrollment Cards 1898-1914

RESIDENCE: Jackson COUNTY. **Choctaw Nation** **Choctaw Roll** *(Not Including Freedmen)* CARD NO.
POST OFFICE: Mayhew, I.T. FIELD NO. 4417

Dawes' Roll No.	NAME	Relationship to Person First Named	AGE	SEX	BLOOD	TRIBAL ENROLLMENT Year	County	No.
12308	* 1 Billy, Alfred 26		23	M	Full	1896	Jackson	1512
	2							
	3							
	4							
	5							
	6							
	7							
	8							
	9							
	10							
	11							
	12							
	13							
	14							
	15							
	16							
	17							

ENROLLMENT OF NOS. 1 HEREON APPROVED BY THE SECRETARY OF INTERIOR MAR 6 1903

TRIBAL ENROLLMENT OF PARENTS

Name of Father	Year	County	Name of Mother	Year	County
1 Esau Billy	Dead	Atoka	Liza A Billy	Dead	Jacks Fork
2					
3					
4					
5					
6					
7					
8					
9					
10					
11					
12					
13					
14					
15					
16					
17					

* "Died prior to Sept 25, 1902 not entitled to land or money"
See Indian Office letter of Aug 18 [remainder illegible]

Sept 2/99
Date of Application for Enrollment.

Choctaw By Blood Enrollment Cards 1898-1914

RESIDENCE: Jackson COUNTY. **Choctaw Nation** **Choctaw Roll** *(Not Including Freedmen)* CARD NO.
POST OFFICE: Mayhew, I.T. FIELD NO. 4418

Dawes' Roll No.	NAME	Relationship to Person First Named	AGE	SEX	BLOOD	TRIBAL ENROLLMENT Year	County	No.
I.W. 428	1 Kennedy, Michael 59	First Named	57	M	IW	1896	Jackson	14412
	2							
	3							
	4							
	5							
	6							
	7							
	8							
	9							
	10							
	11							
	12							
	13							
	14							
	15							
	16							
	17							

ENROLLMENT
OF NOS. 1 HEREON
APPROVED BY THE SECRETARY
OF INTERIOR SEP 12 1903

TRIBAL ENROLLMENT OF PARENTS

Name of Father	Year	County	Name of Mother	Year	County
1 Murdick[sic] Kennedy	Dead	Non Citz	Mary Kennedy	Dead	Non Citz
2					
3					
4					
5					
6					
7 On 1896 roll as Michael [Illegible]					
8					
9					
10					
11					
12					
13					
14					
15		Date of application for enrollment			Sept 2/99
16					Date of Application for Enrollment.
17 12/23/02 PO Boswell IT					

Choctaw By Blood Enrollment Cards 1898-1914

RESIDENCE: Jacks Fork COUNTY. **Choctaw Nation** **Choctaw Roll** *(Not Including Freedmen)* CARD NO.
POST OFFICE: Tushkahomma[sic] I.T. FIELD NO. 4419

Dawes' Roll No.	NAME	Relationship to Person First Named	AGE	SEX	BLOOD	TRIBAL ENROLLMENT Year	County	No.
✓	1 ~~Henderson, Nancy~~ *	~~Named~~	~~60~~	~~F~~	~~1/4~~			
✓	2 ~~" Adam~~ *	~~Son~~	~~22~~	~~M~~	~~1/8~~			
✓	3 ~~" Sarah A~~ *	~~Dau~~	~~18~~	~~F~~	~~1/[illegible]~~			
	4							
	5							
	6							
	7							
	8							
	9							
	10							
	11							
	12							
	13							
	14							
	15							
	16							
	17							

DENIED CITIZENSHIP BY THE CHOCTAW AND CHICKASAW CITIZENSHIP COURT

April 30 [illegible] Case #[illegible]

TRIBAL ENROLLMENT OF PARENTS

	Name of Father	Year	County	Name of Mother	Year	County
1	~~John Vincent~~	~~Dead~~	~~Non Citz~~	~~Nancy Vincent~~	~~Dead~~	~~Choctaw~~
2	~~B.P. Henderson~~		~~" "~~	~~No1~~		
3	~~" "~~		~~" "~~	~~No1~~		
4						
5						
6						
7						
8						
9						
10						
11						
12						
13						
14						Date of Application for Enrollment.
15						Sept 2/99
16						
17						

Nos 1,2&3 denied in 96 Case #425
Admitted by U.S. Court, Central Dist, Jany 18/98, Case No 44. As to residence ~~see testimony of No1~~
No3 admitted as Sarah Henderson
Judgment of U.S. Ct admitting vacated and set aside by Decree of Choctaw Chickasaw Citizenship Court Dec' 17'02
Nos 1,2 and 3 now in C.C.C.C. Case #112

No2 Ashland IT 3/6/02
No2 P.O. Bailey 1/16/03
No2 P.O. Kiowa IT 12/24/05

Choctaw By Blood Enrollment Cards 1898-1914

RESIDENCE: Jacks Fork COUNTY. **Choctaw Nation** **Choctaw Roll** *(Not Including Freedmen)* CARD NO.
POST OFFICE: Tushkahomma[sic] I.T. FIELD NO. 4420

Dawes' Roll No.	NAME	Relationship to Person First Named	AGE	SEX	BLOOD	TRIBAL ENROLLMENT Year	County	No.
✓ ✓	1 Henderson, David *		32	M	1/8			
	2							
	3							
	4							
	5							
	6							
	7							
	8							
	9							
	10							
	11							
	12							
	13							
	14							
	15							
	16							
	17							

DENIED CITIZENSHIP BY THE CHOCTAW AND CHICKASAW CITIZENSHIP COURT Case #112 April 30 '04

TRIBAL ENROLLMENT OF PARENTS

	Name of Father	Year	County	Name of Mother	Year	County
1	Bailey P Henderson		Non Citz	Nancy Henderson		Choctaw
2						
3						
4						
5						

No1 denied in 96 Case #425

Admitted by U.S. Court, Central Dist, Jany 18/98 Case No 44. As to residence, see his testimony.

Judgment of U.S. Ct admitting No1 vacated and set aside by Decree of Choctaw Chickasaw Citizenship Court Dec 17'02

No1 now in C.C.C.C. Case #112

Date of Application for Enrollment.
Sept 2/99

RESIDENCE: Jacks Fork COUNTY. **Choctaw Nation** **Choctaw Roll** (*Not Including Freedmen*) CARD NO.
POST OFFICE: Tushkahomma[sic] I.T. FIELD NO. 4421

Dawes' Roll No.		NAME	Relationship to Person First Named	AGE	SEX	BLOOD	TRIBAL ENROLLMENT Year	County	No.
✓ ✓	1	Henderson, John F	First Named	26	M	1/8			
✓DP	2	" Louisa	Wife	17	F	IW			
✓DP	3	" Ruby Josephene	Dau. ~~Son~~	3mo	F	1/16			
	4								
	5								
	6								
Nos 2&3	7	MAY 27 1904 DISMISSED							
	8								
	9								
	10								
	11								
	12								
	13								
	14								
Nº1	15	DENIED CITIZENSHIP BY THE CHOCTAW AND							
	16	CHICKASAW CITIZENSHIP COURT							
	17							Case #112 April 30 1904	

TRIBAL ENROLLMENT OF PARENTS

	Name of Father	Year	County	Name of Mother	Year	County
1	B.P. Henderson		Non Citz	Nancy Henderson		Choctaw
2	I. F. Fields	Dead	" "	Permelia Fields	Dead	Non Citz
3	No1			No2		

No1 Denied in 96 Case #425
No1 Admitted by U.S. Court, Central Dist, Case No 44, Jany 18/98 as John Henderson.
As to residence and marriage see testimony of No1
Judgment of U.S. Ct admitting No1 vacated and set aside by Decree of Choctaw Chickasaw Citizenship Court Dec' 17'02
No1 now in C.C.C.C. Case ~~#112~~

7-27-01
PO Stringtown IT

Date of Application for Enrollment.
Sept 2/99

Choctaw By Blood Enrollment Cards 1898-1914

RESIDENCE: Jacks Fork COUNTY. **Choctaw Nation** **Choctaw Roll** *(Not Including Freedmen)* CARD NO.
POST OFFICE: Tushkahomma[sic], I.T. FIELD NO. 4422

Dawes' Roll No.	NAME	Relationship to Person First Named	AGE	SEX	BLOOD	TRIBAL ENROLLMENT Year	County	No.
DP Denied	~~Henderson, James H~~ *	~~First Named~~	~~36~~	~~M~~	~~1/8~~			
12309	" Edna E 31	Wife	28	F	1/2	1896	Jacks Fork	6106
12310	" Willie M 13	Dau	10	"	5/16	1896	" "	6107
12311	" Leonidas W 10	Son	7	M	5/16	1896	" "	6108
12312	" Viola B 6	Dau	3	F	5/16	1896	" "	6110
12313	" Mattie 3	Dau	4mo	F	5/16			
12314	" Robert David 1	Son	1mo	M	5/16			

~~Feb 6 1905 Decision rendered denying No1 as I.W.~~
Feb 6 1905 Record forwarded Department
March 14 1905. Decision of Commission ~~of February 6 1905 refusing No1 affirmed~~ ~~by Department~~
For child of No.1 see NB (March 3 1905) #753

ENROLLMENT OF NOS. 2,3,4,5,6 & 7 HEREON APPROVED BY THE SECRETARY OF INTERIOR Mar 6 1903

TRIBAL ENROLLMENT OF PARENTS

Name of Father	Year	County	Name of Mother	Year	County
~~B P Henderson~~		~~Non Citz~~	~~Nancy Henderson~~		~~Choctaw~~
Alexander	Dead	" "	Sarah Woods		Blue
No1			No2		
No1			No2		
No1			No2		
No1			No2		
No.1			No.2		

~~No1 denied in 96 Case #425~~
No1 now in C.C.C.C. Case #112
No1 admitted by U.S. Court, Central ~~Dist, Jany 18/98, Case No 44 as Henry~~ ~~Henderson~~ ~~As to residence, see his~~ testimony

~~No1 Denied Citizenship by the Choctaw and~~ Chickasaw Citizenship Court April 30-1904 Case #112
Judgement[sic] of U.S. Court admitting No1 vacated ~~and set aside by Decree of C.C.C.C. Decr 17 '02~~

No3 on 1896 roll as Wm Henderson
~~No4 " 1896 " " Leonidas "~~
~~No5 " 1896 " " Viola V "~~
No.6 Enrolled May 24, 1900
No.7 born June 12, 1902: Enrolled July 8, 1902

Date of Application for Enrollment.
Sept 2/99

Bailey I.T.

Choctaw By Blood Enrollment Cards 1898-1914

RESIDENCE: Chickasaw Nation ~~COUNTY.~~ **Choctaw Nation** Choctaw Roll (Not Including Freedmen) CARD NO.
POST OFFICE: Iona, I.T. FIELD NO. 4423

Dawes' Roll No.	NAME		Relationship to Person First Named	AGE	SEX	BLOOD	TRIBAL ENROLLMENT Year	County	No.
15155	1 Moran, Charles W	30	First Named	27	M	1/16	1893	Kiamitia	page 119
I.W. 1015	2 " Fannie	25	Wife	22	F	IW			
15156	3 " Bertie	7	Dau	4	"	1/32			
15157	4 " Cora	5	"	2	"	1/32			
15158	5 " Bessie Lee	1	"	1mo	"	1/32			

ENROLLMENT OF NOS. 1,3,4 and 5 HEREON APPROVED BY THE SECRETARY OF INTERIOR MAR 26 1904

ENROLLMENT OF NOS. ~~~~ 2 ~~~~ HEREON APPROVED BY THE SECRETARY OF INTERIOR OCT 21 1904

TRIBAL ENROLLMENT OF PARENTS

	Name of Father	Year	County	Name of Mother	Year	County
1	Marmaduke Moran		Choctaw	Catherine Moran	Dead	Non Citz
2	Chas Magby		Non Citz	Martha Magby		" "
3	No1			No2		
4	No1			No2		
5	No1			No2		

No1 Admitted by Act of Choctaw Council approved Nov 3/79 as Charles Moran
No.1 on 1893 Choctaw payment roll: Kiamitia County, page 119 as Chas. Moran
~~Nos 3-4- Affidavits of birth to be supplied:- Filed Oct 26/99 as to No3, as to No4 filed Nov 2/99~~
No2 admitted by Dawes Com, ~~Case No 394~~
~~No 5 born June 4, 1901: Enrolled July 7, 1902~~
For child of Nos 1&2 see NB (March 3, 1905) #1383 #1 to 4

DATE OF APPLICATION FOR ENROLLMENT. Sept 2/99

P.O. Roff, I.T.

RESIDENCE: Atoka COUNTY. **Choctaw Nation** **Choctaw Roll** *(Not Including Freedmen)* CARD NO.
POST OFFICE: Atoka, I.T. FIELD NO. 4424

Dawes' Roll No.	NAME		Relationship to Person First Named	AGE	SEX	BLOOD	TRIBAL ENROLLMENT		
							Year	County	No.
12315	1 Betts, William W	35		32	M	1/2	1896	Atoka	1761
I.W. 429	2 " Bettie	30	Wife	27	F	I.W.			14343
12316	3 " Claude	11	Son	8	M	1/4			1762
~~12317~~	4 ~~" Idell~~ DIED PRIOR TO SEPTEMBER 25, 1902	9	~~Dau~~	~~6~~	~~F~~	~~1/4~~			~~1764~~
12318	5 " Clyde	7	Son	4	M	1/4			1763
12319	6 " Cordie Lee	2	Dau	1mo	F	1/4			
	7								
	8								
	9								
	10								
	11								
	12								
	13								
	14								
	15								
	16								
	17								

ENROLLMENT OF NOS. 2 HEREON APPROVED BY THE SECRETARY OF INTERIOR Sept 12 1903

ENROLLMENT OF NOS. 1 3 4 5 & 6 HEREON APPROVED BY THE SECRETARY OF INTERIOR Mar 6 1903

TRIBAL ENROLLMENT OF PARENTS

Name of Father	Year	County	Name of Mother	Year	County
1 R D Betts		Atoka	Emeline Betts		Atoka
2 George Street		Non Citz			Non Citz
3 No1			No2		
4 ~~No1~~			~~No2~~		
5 No1			No2		
6 No.1			No.2		
7					
8					

For child of Nos 1&2 see NB (Mar 3,1905) card #315
No2 Evidence of marriage to be supplied:- Filed Nov 2/99
No1 on 1896 roll as Wallace Betts
No3 " 1896 " " Claude Bells
No4 " 1896 " " Idell
No5 " 1896 " " Clide
No2 " 1896 " " Billy
No.6 Enrolled December 19, 1900
№4 Died Oct 22, 1899 proof of death filed Jany 26, 1903
~~No 4 died Oct 22 1899: Enrollment cancelled by Department July 8, 1904~~

#1 to 5
Date of Application for Enrollment. Sept 2/99

For child of Nos 1&2 see NB (Apr 26-06) Card #1230

Choctaw By Blood Enrollment Cards 1898-1914

RESIDENCE: Atoka COUNTY. **Choctaw Nation** **Choctaw Roll** *(Not Including Freedmen)* CARD NO.
POST OFFICE: Atoka, I.T. FIELD NO. 4425

Dawes' Roll No.	NAME	Relationship to Person First Named	AGE	SEX	BLOOD	TRIBAL ENROLLMENT Year	County	No.
12320	1 Ward, Edward A 27	First Named	24	M	1/16	1896	Atoka	13942
I.W. 639	2 " Mary (21)	Wife	21	F	IW			
	3							
	4							
	5							
	6							
	7							
	8							
	9							
	10							
	11							
	12							
	13							
	14							
	15							
	16							
	17							

ENROLLMENT OF NOS. 2 HEREON APPROVED BY THE SECRETARY OF INTERIOR May 21 1904

ENROLLMENT OF NOS. 1 HEREON APPROVED BY THE SECRETARY OF INTERIOR Mar 6 1903

TRIBAL ENROLLMENT OF PARENTS

Name of Father	Year	County	Name of Mother	Year	County
1 Ed Ward	Dead	Atoka	Hannah Ward	Dead	Non Citz
2 Louis Couch		non citizen	Sallie Couch		non citizen

As to marriage of parents see enrollment of sister, Nova Hopkins

For child of Nos 1 and 2 see NB (Apr 26-06) No. 545

~~Nº1 is husband of Mary Ward on Choctaw Card D823: Nov. 11, 1902~~

No2 transferred from Choctaw card D823 April 15, 1904

See decision of March 15, 1904

Date of Application for Enrollment. Sept 2/99

~~P.O. Jesse I.T.~~

P.O. Folsom I.T. 12/1/03

RESIDENCE: Atoka COUNTY. **Choctaw Nation** **Choctaw Roll** *(Not Including Freedmen)* CARD NO.
POST OFFICE: Lehigh, I.T. FIELD NO. 4426

Dawes' Roll No.	NAME	Relationship to Person First Named	AGE	SEX	BLOOD	TRIBAL ENROLLMENT Year	County	No.
✓ *	1 Lancaster, Hiram		43	M	5/32			
✓ *	2 " Margaret	Wife	32	F	IW			
✓ *	3 " Robert B	Son	19	M	5/64			
✓ *	4 " Knox R	"	14	"	5/64			
✓ *	5 " Harry	"	11	"	5/64			
✓ *	6 " Russ	"	6	"	5/64			
	7							
	8							
	9							
	10							
	11							
	12							
	13							
	14							
	15							
	16							
	17							

TRIBAL ENROLLMENT OF PARENTS

Name of Father	Year	County	Name of Mother	Year	County
1 Hiram Lancaster	Dead	Choctaw	Sarah Lancaster		Choctaw
2 Elum Hobbs	"	Non Citz	Mary Hobbs		Non Citz
3 No1			No2		
4 No1			No2		
5 No1			No2		
6 No1			No2		

7 Denied Citizenship by the Choctaw and Chickasaw Citizenship Court Mar 28 '04

8 Nos 1 to 6 incl denied Case #1218

9 Admitted by U.S. Court, Central Dist.

10 Aug 24/97, Case No 29. As to residence see testimony of No1.

11 No3 admitted as Robert Baw Lancaster

12 No4 " " Knox Reed "

Cora Lancaster, wife of No.3 on Choctaw card #D.621

13 Judgement[sic] of U.S. Court admitting Nos 1 to 6 incl vacated and set aside by Decree of Choctaw Chickasaw Citizenship Court Dec 17'02

14 Nos 1 to 6 incl now in C.C.C.C. Case #82

15 Nos 1 to 6 incl Denied C.C.C.C. March 28 '04

Date of Application for Enrollment.
Sept 2/99

RESIDENCE: Atoka COUNTY. **Choctaw Nation** **Choctaw Roll** *(Not Including Freedmen)* CARD NO.
POST OFFICE: Lehigh, I.T. FIELD NO. 4427

Dawes' Roll No.	NAME	Relationship to Person First Named	AGE	SEX	BLOOD	TRIBAL ENROLLMENT Year	County	No.
✓ *	1 ~~Lancaster, Mary W~~	~~First Named~~	~~17~~	~~F~~	~~5/64~~			
✓	2 ~~Stoops, Esther~~	~~Dau~~	~~2~~	~~"~~	~~5/128~~			
	3							
	4							
No2	5 DISMISSED	MAY 27 1904						
	6							
	7							
	8							
	9							
	10							
	11							
	12							
	13							
	14							
	15							
	16							
	17							

No1 DENIED CITIZENSHIP BY THE CHOCTAW AND CHICKASAW CITIZENSHIP COURT Mar 28 '04

TRIBAL ENROLLMENT OF PARENTS

Name of Father	Year	County	Name of Mother	Year	County
1 ~~Hiram Lancaster~~		~~Choctaw~~	~~Margaret Lancaster~~		~~Intermarried~~
2 ~~Jesse Stoops~~		~~Non Citz~~	~~No1~~		

No1 denied in 96 Case #1218

Admitted by U.S. Court, Central Dist, ~~Aug 24/97, Case No 28 as Mary Willie Lancaster. As to residence and birth~~ of child, see her testimony

Judgment of U.S. Ct admitting No1 vacated and set aside by Decree of Choctaw Chickasaw Citizenship Court Dec' 17'02

No2- Affidavit of birth to be ~~supplied: Filed Oct 26/99~~

No1 now in C.C.C.C. Case #82

No1 Denied by C.C.C.C. March 28 '04

Date of Application for Enrollment.
Sept 2/99

RESIDENCE: Atoka COUNTY. **Choctaw Nation** **Choctaw Roll** *(Not Including Freedmen)* CARD NO.
POST OFFICE: Lehigh, I.T. FIELD NO. 4428

Dawes' Roll No.		NAME	Relationship to Person First Named	AGE	SEX	BLOOD	TRIBAL ENROLLMENT Year	County	No.
	1								
12321	2	Davis, Lorena 34		31	F	1/2	1896	Atoka	3607
12322	3	" Alice A 14	Dau	11	"	1/4	1896	"	3608
12323	4	" Carrie J 12	"	9	"	1/4	1896	"	3609
12324	5	" Royal E 10	Son	7	M	1/4	1896	"	3610
12325	6	" Winnie H 8	Dau	5	F	1/4	1896	"	3611
12326	7	" Jefferson Harris 4	Son	4mo	M	1/4			

ENROLLMENT OF NOS. 2 3 4 5 6 & 7 HEREON APPROVED BY THE SECRETARY OF INTERIOR MAR 6 1903

TRIBAL ENROLLMENT OF PARENTS

	Name of Father	Year	County	Name of Mother	Year	County
1						
2	John Choate	Dead	Tobucksy	Tennessee Choate	Dead	Tobucksy
3	Alonzo M Davis		white man	No2		
4	" " "		" "	No2		
5	" " "		" "	No2		
6	" " "		" "	No2		
7	" " "		" "	No.2		

No3 on 1896 roll as Alice E. Davis
No5 " 1896 " " Royal "
No.2 is the wife of Alonzo M Davis on Choctaw card #4446: June 15, 1901
~~No.7 Enrolled June 15th, 1901~~
For child of No 1 see NB (March 3, 1905) #746

#1 to 6
Date of Application for Enrollment.
Sept 2/99

~~P.O. Johnson, I.T. 10/24/02~~
P.O. Byars I.T. 4/5/05

Choctaw By Blood Enrollment Cards 1898-1914

RESIDENCE: Chickasaw Nation ~~COUNTY.~~ **Choctaw Nation** **Choctaw Roll** *(Not Including Freedmen)* CARD NO.
POST OFFICE: Ardmore, I.T. FIELD NO. 4429

Dawes' Roll No.	NAME	Relationship to Person First Named	AGE	SEX	BLOOD	TRIBAL ENROLLMENT Year	County	No.
✓ ✓	1 ~~Dillard, Dora~~	~~Named~~	~~20~~	~~F~~	~~I.W.~~			
✓	2 ~~" Bertha May~~	~~Dau~~	~~10da~~	~~F~~				
	3							
	4							
	5							
	6							
	7							
	8 No1 Dismissed May 7, 1904							
	9							
	10 No2- Dismissed May 27, 1904							
	11							
	12							
	13							
	14							
	15							
	16							
	17							

TRIBAL ENROLLMENT OF PARENTS

Name of Father	Year	County	Name of Mother	Year	County
1 ~~John Baker~~		~~Non Citz~~	~~Jane Baker~~		~~Non Citz~~
2 ~~Robert L Dillard~~			~~No.1~~		
3					
4					
5					
6					
7					
8					

See Card of husband Robert L. Dillard
admitted by U.S. Court, Sept 9/97
Case No 63
~~No1 is the wife of Robert L Dillard on Choc. Card #4966~~
No 2 born Dec 17, 1901· Enrolled Dec 27, 1901
Husband of No1 Robert L Dillard denied by C.C.C.C. Case #43

Date of Application for Enrollment.
Sept 2/99

RESIDENCE: Chickasaw Nation ~~COUNTY.~~ **Choctaw Nation** **Choctaw Roll** *(Not Including Freedmen)* CARD NO.
POST OFFICE: M^c^Gee I.T. FIELD NO. **4430**

Dawes' Roll No.		NAME		Relationship to Person First Named	AGE	SEX	BLOOD	TRIBAL ENROLLMENT Year	County	No.
I.W. 430	1	Orr, William E	42		38	M	I.W.	1896	Atoka	14920
12327	2	" Catherine	42	Wife	39	F	3/4	1896	Atoka	10016
12328	3	" Ella	15	Dau	12	"	3/8	1896	"	10018
12329	4	" Etta	12	"	9	"	3/8	1896	"	10019
12330	5	" George	10	Son	7	M	3/8	1896	"	10017
void	6	~~Carnes, Isaac~~		~~Nephew~~	~~10~~	~~"~~	~~7/8~~	~~1893~~	~~Blue~~	~~358~~
	7									
	8									
	9									
	10									
	11	ENROLLMENT								
	12	OF NOS. 1 HEREON APPROVED BY THE SECRETARY								
	13	OF INTERIOR Sep 12 1903								
	14									
	15	ENROLLMENT								
	16	OF NOS. 2 3 4 and 5 HEREON APPROVED BY THE SECRETARY								
	17	OF INTERIOR Mar 6 1903								

TRIBAL ENROLLMENT OF PARENTS

	Name of Father	Year	County	Name of Mother	Year	County
1	William Orr	Dead	Non Citz	Catherine Orr	Dead	Non Citz
2	Jack Ellis	"	Blue	Isabelle Ellis		Atoka
3	No1			No2		
4	No1			No2		
5	No1			No2		
6		~~Dead~~	~~Blue~~	~~Maggie Tumbler~~		~~Atoka~~
7						
8						
9	No1 admitted by Dawes Com., Case No 249					
10	as W. E. Orr – On 1896 roll as William Orr					
11	No.6 is on Choctaw Card #4380 with his grandfather, George Ellis					
11	~~For child of No.4 see NB (Apr 26, 1906) Card No. 140~~					
12	~~" " "Nos1&2 " " (March4,1905) " " 778~~					
13						
14						Date of Application for Enrollment.
15						Sept 2/99
16						
17	P.O. Brady I.T. 1/17/03					

RESIDENCE: Atoka | COUNTY. **Choctaw Nation** | **Choctaw Roll** *(Not Including Freedmen)* | CARD NO.
POST OFFICE: Atoka, I.T. | FIELD NO. 4431

Dawes' Roll No.	NAME	Relationship to Person First Named	AGE	SEX	BLOOD	TRIBAL ENROLLMENT Year	County	No.
✓	1 York, William C ✓	First Named	47	M	I.W.			
	2 " Sarah ✓	Wife	40	F		1896	Atoka	14235
✓	3 " Maud E ✓	Dau	20	"		1896	"	13236
✓	4 " Leslie O ✓	Son	18	M		1896	"	14237
✓	5 " Mabel L ✓	Dau	17	F		1896	"	14238
✓	6 " Erda C ✓	"	15	"		1896	"	14239
✓	7 " Willie P ✓	"	13	"		1896	"	14240
✓	8 " Benjamin ✓	Son	8	M		1896	"	14241
	9 Dismissed Sep. 20, 1904							
	10 No2 on 1896 roll as Sarah A. York							
	11 No3 " 1896 " " Maud "							
	12 No4 " 1896 " " Leslie "							
	No5 " 1896 " " Mabel "							
	13 No6 " 1896 " " Erda "							
	14 No7 " 1896 " " Willie P "							
	No8 " 1896 " " Ben J "							
	15 See Petition #W-17							
	16							
	17							

TRIBAL ENROLLMENT OF PARENTS

	Name of Father	Year	County	Name of Mother	Year	County
1	A. H. York		Non Citz	Mary A York		Non Citz
2	Sam Ward	Dead	" "	Eliza Ward	Dead	Cherokee
3	No1			No2		
4	No1			No2		
5	No1			No2		
6	No1			No2		
7	No1			No2		
8	No1			No2		
9						
10						

Nos 1 to 8 incl. denied in 96 Case #241

Admitted by U.S. Court, Central Dist July 13/97, Case No 46. As to residence see testimony of No.1

No1 admitted as W.C. York
No6 " " Erda "
No8 " " Ben "

Judgements of U.S. Court admitting Nos 1 to 8 incl vacated and set aside by Decree of Choctaw Chickasaw Citizenship Court Dec 17 '02

No appeal to C.C.C.C.

Refused Jan. 16, 1907

Record forwarded: Department Jan. 16, 1907.

Date of Application for Enrollment.
Sept 2/99

For children of No4 see NB 942 (Apr. 26 '06)
" child " No5 " " 941 " "

Choctaw By Blood Enrollment Cards 1898-1914

RESIDENCE: Atoka COUNTY. **Choctaw Nation** **Choctaw Roll** (Not Including Freedmen) CARD NO.
POST OFFICE: Atoka, I.T. FIELD NO. 4432

Dawes' Roll No.	NAME	Relationship to Person First Named	AGE	SEX	BLOOD	TRIBAL ENROLLMENT Year	County	No.
12331	1 Kendle, Etta 23		20	F	1/32	1896	Atoka	3605
I.W. 840	2 " Charles J (35)	Hus.	35	M	I.W.			
	3							
	4							
	5							
	6							
	7							
	8							
	9							
	10							
	11							
	12							
	13							
	14							
	15							
	16							
	17							

ENROLLMENT
OF NOS. 2 HEREON
APPROVED BY THE SECRETARY
OF INTERIOR May 21 1904

ENROLLMENT
OF NOS. 1 HEREON
APPROVED BY THE SECRETARY
OF INTERIOR Mar 6 1903

TRIBAL ENROLLMENT OF PARENTS

Name of Father	Year	County	Name of Mother	Year	County
1 John Dillon	Dead	Non Citz	Susie Dillon		Atoka
2 Alex Kendle	Dead	non citizen	Sarah Kendle		non citizen
3					
4					
5					
6					
7					
8					
9					
10					
11					
12					
13					
14					
15					
16					
17					

~~On 1896 roll as Ettie Dillon~~

Husband on Card No D414

No2 transferred from Choctaw card D414, April 15, 1904
See decision of March 15, 1904

Date of Application for Enrollment.
Sept 2/99

Choctaw By Blood Enrollment Cards 1898-1914

RESIDENCE: Atoka COUNTY. **Choctaw Nation** **Choctaw Roll** *(Not Including Freedmen)* CARD NO.
POST OFFICE: Coalgate, I.T. FIELD NO. 4433

Dawes' Roll No.	NAME	Relationship to Person First Named	AGE	SEX	BLOOD	TRIBAL ENROLLMENT Year	County	No.
12332	1 Taaffe, Francis 25	First Named	22	M	1/16	1896	Tobucksy	12015
	2							
	3							
	4							
	5							
	6							
	7							
	8							
	9							
	10							
	11							
	12							
	13							
	14							
	15							
	16							
	17							

ENROLLMENT
OF NOS. 1 HEREON
APPROVED BY THE SECRETARY
OF INTERIOR MAR 6 1903

TRIBAL ENROLLMENT OF PARENTS

	Name of Father	Year	County	Name of Mother	Year	County
1	George Taaffe	Dead	Non Citz	Fredonia Taaffe	Dead	Red River
2						
3						
4						
5						
6	On 1896 roll as Frances Taffee					
7	For child of No.1 see NB (Apr 26, 1906) Card No. 46					
8						
9						
10						
11						
12						
13						Date of Application for Enrollment.
14						
15						Sept 2/99
16						
17	P.O. Hugo, I.T. 12/5/02					

RESIDENCE: Atoka COUNTY. **Choctaw Nation** Choctaw Roll (Not Including Freedmen) CARD NO.
POST OFFICE: Coalgate, I.T. FIELD NO. 4434

Dawes' Roll No.		NAME	Relationship to Person First Named	AGE	SEX	BLOOD	TRIBAL ENROLLMENT Year	County	No.
I.W. 431	1	Rainey, David F 43	First Named	40	M	IW			
12333	2	" Gertrude 25	Wife	22	F	1/16	1896	Red River	12322
12334	3	" William Franklin 3	Son	2mo	M	1/32			
12335	4	" Joseph Aloyious 1	Sons	2½mo	M	1/32			
	5								
	6								
	7								
	8								
	9								
	10								
	11								
	12	ENROLLMENT OF NOS. 1 HEREON							
	13	APPROVED BY THE SECRETARY							
	14	OF INTERIOR SEP 12 1903							
	15	ENROLLMENT OF NOS. 2 3 & 4 HEREON							
	16	APPROVED BY THE SECRETARY							
	17	OF INTERIOR MAR 6 1903							

TRIBAL ENROLLMENT OF PARENTS

	Name of Father	Year	County	Name of Mother	Year	County
1	W. R. Rainey		Non Citz	Jennetta Carter		Non Citz
2	George Taaffe	Dead	" "	Fredonia Taaffe	Dead	Red River
3	No.1			No2		
4	№2			№2		
5						
6						
7	~~No2 on 1896 roll as Gertrude Taaffe~~					
8	№4 Born Feby 25, 1902: enrolled May 14, 1902					
9						
10						
11						
12						
13						
14						Date of Application for Enrollment.
15						Sept 2/99
16						
17	P.O. Stringtown, I.T. 5/14/02			No.3 Enrolled May 24, 1900		

RESIDENCE: Atoka COUNTY. **Choctaw Nation** **Choctaw Roll** *(Not Including Freedmen)* CARD NO.
POST OFFICE: Atoka, I.T. FIELD NO. 4435

Dawes' Roll No.	NAME	Relationship to Person First Named	AGE	SEX	BLOOD	TRIBAL ENROLLMENT Year	County	No.
12336	1 Leader, Mary A 33	First Named	30	F	Full	1896	Atoka	13995
	2							
	3							
	4							
	5							
	6							
	7							
	8							
	9							
	10							
	11							
	12							
	13							
	14							
	15							
	16							
	17							

ENROLLMENT OF NOS. 1 HEREON APPROVED BY THE SECRETARY OF INTERIOR MAR 6 1903

TRIBAL ENROLLMENT OF PARENTS

Name of Father	Year	County	Name of Mother	Year	County
1 Willis Warhee	Dead	Blue	E-la-la-ho-ya	Dead	Blue
2					
3					
4					
5					
6					
7 ~~On 1896 roll as Mary A. Warhee~~					
8					
9					
10					
11					
12					
13					
14					Date of Application for Enrollment.
15					Sept 2/99
16					
17					

RESIDENCE: Atoka COUNTY. **Choctaw Nation** **Choctaw Roll** (Not Including Freedmen) CARD NO.
POST OFFICE: Atoka, I.T. FIELD NO. 4436

Dawes' Roll No.	NAME		Relationship to Person First Named	AGE	SEX	BLOOD	TRIBAL ENROLLMENT Year	County	No.
12337	1 Telle, Alinton	42		39	M	Full	1896	Atoka	12441
I.W. 432	2 " Emma	37	Wife	34	F	IW	1896	"	15114
12338	3 " Alinton R	9	Son	6	M	1/2	1896	"	12442
DEAD	4 ~~" Nanima L~~		~~Dau~~	~~1~~	~~F~~	~~1/2~~			

No. 4 HEREON DISMISSED UNDER ORDER OF THE COMMISSION TO THE FIVE CIVILIZED TRIBES OF MARCH 31, 1905.

ENROLLMENT OF NOS. 2 HEREON APPROVED BY THE SECRETARY OF INTERIOR SEP 12 1903

ENROLLMENT OF NOS. 1 & 3 HEREON APPROVED BY THE SECRETARY OF INTERIOR MAR 6 1903

TRIBAL ENROLLMENT OF PARENTS

	Name of Father	Year	County	Name of Mother	Year	County
1	Ina-no-lubbe	Dead	Bok Tuklo	Pisa-ho-te-ma	Dead	Bok Tuklo
2	W. W. Russell	"	Non Citz	Louisa Russell		Non Citz
3	No1			No2		
4	~~No1~~			~~No2~~		

No2 admitted by Dawes Com., Case No 293, as Mrs. Emma Telle
No3 on 1896 roll as A. R. Telle
~~No.4 died Oct. 11th, 1900. See testimony of Alinton Telle.~~

Date of Application for Enrollment.
Sept 2/99

RESIDENCE: Chickasaw Nation ~~COUNTY.~~ **Choctaw Nation** **Choctaw Roll** *(Not Including Freedmen)* CARD NO.
POST OFFICE: Jesse, I.T. FIELD NO. 4437

Dawes' Roll No.	NAME		Relationship to Person First Named	AGE	SEX	BLOOD	TRIBAL ENROLLMENT Year	County	No.
I.W. 433	1 Roach, Robert W	43	First Named	40	M	IW	1896	Atoka	14995
12339	2 " Joanna	29	Wife	26	F	3/4	1896	"	10985
12340	3 " Jewel I	9	Dau	6	"	3/8	1896	"	10986
12341	4 " Ruby W	8	"	5	"	3/8	1896	"	10987
12342	5 " Vinnie O	6	"	3	"	3/8	1896	"	10988
12343	6 " Garnet	5	Son	2	M	3/8			
12344	7 " Onyx	3	Son	2mo	M	3/8			
12345	8 " Diamond	1	Son	3wks	M	3/8			

ENROLLMENT OF NOS 1 HEREON APPROVED BY THE SECRETARY OF INTERIOR Sep. 12, 1903

ENROLLMENT OF NOS. 2 3 4 5 6 7 & 8 HEREON APPROVED BY THE SECRETARY OF INTERIOR Mar 6 1903

TRIBAL ENROLLMENT OF PARENTS

Name of Father	Year	County	Name of Mother	Year	County
1 W.H. Roach	Dead	Non Citz	Eliz. Roach	Dead	Non Citz
2 John Choate	"	Tobucksy	Tennessee Choate	"	Tobucksy
3 No1			No2		
4 No1			No2		
5 No1			No2		
6 No1			No2		
7 No1			No2		
8 №1			№2		

No1 admitted by Dawes Com, Case No 1188 as R. W. Roach

~~No2 on 1896 roll as Mrs. Joanna Roach~~

~~No6 Affidavit of birth to be~~ supplied: Filed Oct 26/99

No1 on 1896 roll as R. W. Roach

~~№8 Born July 6,19002: enrolled July 28, 1902~~

~~No.7 Enrolled May 24, 1900~~

For child of Nos 1&2 see NB (March 3, 1905) #747

~~P.O. Wapanucka I.T. 11/20/02~~

~~#1 to 6~~

Date of Application for Enrollment.

Sept 2/99

Choctaw By Blood Enrollment Cards 1898-1914

RESIDENCE: Atoka COUNTY. **Choctaw Nation** **Choctaw Roll** *(Not Including Freedmen)* CARD NO.
POST OFFICE: Lehigh, I.T. FIELD NO. 4438

Dawes' Roll No.	NAME		Relationship to Person First Named	AGE	SEX	BLOOD	TRIBAL ENROLLMENT Year	County	No.
I.W. 572	1 Link, Robert E	44	First Named	40	M	I.W.	1896	Atoka	14782
12346	2 " Ida	33	Wife	30	F	1/8	1896	"	8277
12347	3 " Minnie G	14	Dau	11	"	1/16	1896	"	8279
12348	4 " Edna M	12	"	9	"	1/16	1896	"	8280
12349	5 " Arthur C	10	Son	7	M	1/16	1896	"	8278
12350	6 " Ada B	8	Dau	5	F	1/16	1896	"	8281
12351	7 " Myrtle A	5	"	2	"	1/16			
12352	8 " Bertha J	3	"	2mo	"	1/16			

ENROLLMENT OF NOS. ~~~ 1 ~~~~ HEREON APPROVED BY THE SECRETARY OF INTERIOR Feb 8, 1904

ENROLLMENT OF NOS. 2 3 4 5 6 7 & 8 HEREON APPROVED BY THE SECRETARY OF INTERIOR Mar 6 1903

TRIBAL ENROLLMENT OF PARENTS

	Name of Father	Year	County	Name of Mother	Year	County
1	George Link	Dead	Non Citz	Nancy Link		Non Citz
2	William Chunn	"	" "	Nancy Hill		Tobucksy
3	No1			No2		
4	No1			No2		
5	No1			No2		
6	No1			No2		
7	No1			No2		
8	No1			No2		

No1 on 1896 roll as I.C. Link – as to marriage, see his testimony

~~No3 on 1896 roll as Minnie Link~~
~~No4 " 1896 " " May "~~
No5 " 1896 " " Arthur "
No6 " 1896 " " Ada "
~~Nos 7-8- Affidavits of birth to be supplied:- Filed Oct 26/99~~

Affidavits of N.A. Hill and John B. Boumert as to residence and marriage of Nos 1 and ~~2, filed July 3, 1903~~

Date of Application for Enrollment.
Sept 2/99

RESIDENCE: Atoka COUNTY. **Choctaw Nation** Choctaw Roll (Not Including Freedmen) CARD NO.
POST OFFICE: Limestone, I.T. FIELD NO. 4439

Dawes' Roll No.		NAME	Relationship to Person First Named	AGE	SEX	BLOOD	TRIBAL ENROLLMENT Year	County	No.
12353	1	Dilbeck, Alverado 32	First Named	29	F	1/4	1896	Atoka	3621
DEAD	2	~~" Artemissa L 11~~ DEAD	~~Dau~~	~~7~~	~~"~~	~~1/8~~	~~1896~~	~~"~~	~~3623~~
15476	3	" Benjamin H 8	Son	5	M	1/8	1896	"	3624
12354	4	" Bessie G 6	Dau	3	F	1/8	1896	"	3625
~~12355~~	5	~~" Andrew Jackson 2~~	~~Son~~	~~3m~~	~~M~~	~~1/8~~			
	6								
	7	ENROLLMENT							
	8	OF NOS. ~~~ 3 ~~~ HEREON							
	9	APPROVED BY THE SECRETARY OF INTERIOR May 9 1904							
	10								
	11	No2 hereon dismissed under order of							
	12	the Commission to the Five Civilized							
	13	Tribes of March 31, 1905.							
	14	For children of No1 see NB (Mar 3,1905) #770							
	15	ENROLLMENT							
	16	OF NOS. 1 4 & 5 HEREON APPROVED BY THE SECRETARY							
	17	OF INTERIOR Mar 6 1903							

TRIBAL ENROLLMENT OF PARENTS

	Name of Father	Year	County	Name of Mother	Year	County
1	Jackson Taylor	Dead	Atoka	Beckie Taylor	Dead	Non Citz
2	~~J. L. Dilbeck~~		~~Non Citz~~	~~No1~~		
3	" " "		" "	No1		
4	" " "		" "	No1		
5	~~" " "~~		~~" "~~	~~No1~~		
6						
7						

No.5 died in 1900 or 1901: Enrollment cancelled by Department May 2, 1906
No1 on 1896 roll as Alexander Dillbeck
~~No2 " 1896 " " Artimissa A~~
~~No3 " 1896 " " Ben H.~~
No4 " 1896 " " Bessie
No2- As to marriage of parents, see testimony of Oliver W. Taylor
~~No5 Enrolled January 14, 1901~~
~~No2 Died Nov. 27, 1899: Proof of death filed Dec 23, 1902~~
~~No3 " Aug. 17, 1901: " " " " " 23, 1902~~
~~Above notation is error: see testimony taken Dec. 18, 1903~~
~~No.3 is alive.~~ +

#1 to 4
Date of Application for Enrollment.
Sept 2/99

RESIDENCE: Atoka COUNTY. **Choctaw Nation** **Choctaw Roll** (*Not Including Freedmen*) CARD NO.

POST OFFICE: Atoka, I.T. FIELD NO. 4440

Dawes' Roll No.	NAME		Relationship to Person First Named	AGE	SEX	BLOOD	TRIBAL ENROLLMENT Year	County	No.
I.W. 434	1 Moore, Robert M	40		36	M	I.W.	1896	Atoka	14838
12356	2 " Olive M	27	Wife	23	F	1/4	1896	Atoka	8818
12357	3 " James H	6	Son	3	M	1/8	1896	"	8819
12358	4 " Lucile	4	Dau	9mo	F	1/8			
12359	5 " Selma	2	Dau	1 1/3	F	1/8			

ENROLLMENT OF NOS. 1 HEREON APPROVED BY THE SECRETARY OF INTERIOR Sep 12 1903

ENROLLMENT OF NOS. 2 3 4 & 5 HEREON APPROVED BY THE SECRETARY OF INTERIOR Mar 6 1903

TRIBAL ENROLLMENT OF PARENTS

	Name of Father	Year	County	Name of Mother	Year	County
1	James A Moore		Non Citz	Martha A Moore		Non Citz
2	Oliver Hebert	Dead	" "	Isabinda Hebert	Dead	Atoka
3	No1			No2		
4	No1			No2		
5	No.1			No.2		

No1 Admitted by Dawes Com, Case No 369 as R. M. Moore

~~No3 on 1896 roll as Jas. H. Moore~~

~~No4 Affidavit of birth to be~~ supplied:- Filed Oct 26/99

No2 See Card No 4386 and note thereon referring to No2

~~No1 on 1896 roll as Ira M Moore~~

No.5 Born March 24th 1901: Enrolled July 17th 1902

For child of Nos 1&2 see NB (March 3, 1905) #1119

#1 to 4 inc

Date of Application for Enrollment. Sept 2/99

Choctaw By Blood Enrollment Cards 1898-1914

RESIDENCE: Jacks Fork COUNTY. **Choctaw Nation** **Choctaw Roll** *(Not Including Freedmen)* CARD NO.
POST OFFICE: Antlers, I.T. FIELD NO. **4441**

Dawes' Roll No.	NAME	Relationship to Person First Named	AGE	SEX	BLOOD	TRIBAL ENROLLMENT Year	County	No.
DEAD ✓	Tronterhouse, Eliza A [30]		27	F	Full	1896	Jacks Fork	7354

No.1 hereon dismissed under order of the Commission to the Five Civilized Tribes of March 31, 1905.

CANCELLED

Applicant died prior to ratification of Choctaw-Chickasaw agreement Sept 25, 1902

TRIBAL ENROLLMENT OF PARENTS

Name of Father	Year	County	Name of Mother	Year	County
Stephen Noah	Dead	Jacks Fork	Elizabeth Noah	Dead	Jacks Fork

Husband on Card No D415

On 1896 roll as Elizann Jefferson

No1 died March 9, 1900: proof of death filed Dec 10, 1902

Date of Application for Enrollment.

Sept 2/99

RESIDENCE: Blue COUNTY. **Choctaw Nation** **Choctaw Roll** *(Not Including Freedmen)* CARD NO.
POST OFFICE: Boggy Depot, I.T. FIELD NO. 4442

Dawes' Roll No.	NAME	Relationship to Person First Named	AGE	SEX	BLOOD	TRIBAL ENROLLMENT Year	County	No.
12360	1 Harkins, William M 40	First Named	37	M	1/4	1896	Blue	5919

ENROLLMENT OF NOS. 1 HEREON APPROVED BY THE SECRETARY OF INTERIOR MAR 6 1903

TRIBAL ENROLLMENT OF PARENTS

Name of Father	Year	County	Name of Mother	Year	County
1 Geo Harkins	Dead	Blue	Sophie Harkins	Dead	Blue

On 1896 roll as Wm M. Harkins
Nº1 wife and children on Chickasaw card #774

Date of Application for Enrollment.
Sept 2/99

Choctaw By Blood Enrollment Cards 1898-1914

RESIDENCE: Atoka COUNTY. **Choctaw Nation** **Choctaw Roll** *(Not Including Freedmen)* CARD NO.
POST OFFICE: Atoka, I.T. FIELD NO. 4443

Dawes' Roll No.	NAME	Relationship to Person First Named	AGE	SEX	BLOOD	TRIBAL ENROLLMENT Year	County	No.
12361	1 Brinkley, Robert B 22	First Named	19	M	1/8	1896	Chick Dist	2039
15942	2 " Benjamin	Son	1	M	1/16			
I.W. 1608	3 " Carrie	Wife	32	F	I.W.			
	4							
	5 * 2. Ev of marriage of parents and testimony see Memo, app. for enrollment of Carrie Brinkley 8/19/03							

ENROLLMENT OF NOS. ~~~ 3 ~~~~ HEREON APPROVED BY THE SECRETARY OF INTERIOR Feb 12 1907

ENROLLMENT OF NOS. ~~~ 2 ~~~~~ HEREON APPROVED BY THE SECRETARY OF INTERIOR Nov 24 1905

ENROLLMENT OF NOS. 1 HEREON APPROVED BY THE SECRETARY OF INTERIOR Mar 6 1903

TRIBAL ENROLLMENT OF PARENTS

Name of Father	Year	County	Name of Mother	Year	County
1 Alfred Brinkley	Dead	Non Citz	Esther Brinkley	Dead	Atoka
2 No.1			Carrie Brinkley		
3 Henry Steed	Dead	Non Citz	Maria Steed	Dead	Non Citz

No3 placed hereon under Departmental instructions of November 20-1906 ordering her enrollment as an intermarried citizen of the Choctaw Nation

~~On 1896 roll as R. B. Brintley[sic] – claims to have been admitted by Secy of Interior~~ Oct. 12/89. Was admitted by U.S. Indian Agent Oct. 12, 1889 in case of Nancy Stewart

~~See papers on file in Office of Com. in Case of Jno. B. Stewart, et al~~

For child of No.1 see NB (Apr 26-06) No. 803

See also Card No D 420

~~No2 was born June 21, 1902: application received and No2 placed on this card March 4, 1905, under Act~~ of Congress approved March 3, 1905

Date of Application for Enrollment. Sept 2/99

Choctaw By Blood Enrollment Cards 1898-1914

See Petitions C-12-17-20-21-22-23 & 24

RESIDENCE: Atoka COUNTY. **Choctaw Nation** **Choctaw Roll** *(Not Including Freedmen)* CARD NO.

POST OFFICE: Lehigh, I.T. FIELD NO. 4444

Dawes' Roll No.	NAME	Relationship to Person First Named	AGE	SEX	BLOOD	TRIBAL ENROLLMENT Year	County	No.
	1 Davis, Rhoda L	Named	48	F			D	
	2 " Clarence	Son	19	M			D	
	3 " Neta	Dau	17	F			D	
	4 " Arthur	Son	12	M			D	
	5 " Mamie	Dau	10	F			D	
	6 " Virgil	Son	8	M			D	
	7 " James	"	6	"			D	
	8 Denied Citizenship by the Choctaw and Chickasaw Citizenship Court Nov 29 '04 11/29/04 100 M							
	9							
	10 See white petition No 29							
	11							
	12							
	13							
	14							
	15							
See Petition No C 22-23-24	16							
	17 For record see ALL 7=4448-See Petition #C-12							

TRIBAL ENROLLMENT OF PARENTS

Name of Father	Year	County	Name of Mother	Year	County
1 Stephen Pate	Dead	Non Citz	Louisa Pate	Dead	Non Citz
2 J.D. Davis	"	" "	No1		
3 " " "	"	" "	No1		
4 " " "	"	" "	No1		
5 " " "	"	" "	No1		
6 " " "	"	" "	No1		
7 " " "	"	" "	No1		
8	Nos 1 to 7 incl denied in 96 Case #317				
9	Admitted by U.S. Court Central Dist				
10	Aug 24/97 Case No 60 As to residence see testimony of No1				
11	No1 was admitted as R. L. Davis				
12	No3 " " " Neter "				
13 Judgement[sic] of U.S. Ct admitting Nos 1 to 7 incl vacated and set aside by Decree of C.C.C.C. Decr 17 '02					
14 Nos 1 to 7 incl now in C.C.C.C. Case #100					Date of Application for Enrollment.
15					Sept 2/99
16					
17					

No3 P.O. Olney, IT. 12/16/05

Choctaw By Blood Enrollment Cards 1898-1914

See Petitions C-12-17-20-21-22-23 & 24

RESIDENCE: Atoka COUNTY. **Choctaw Nation** **Choctaw Roll** *(Not Including Freedmen)* CARD NO.
POST OFFICE: Nixon, I.T. FIELD NO. 4445

Dawes' Roll No.	NAME	Relationship to Person First Named	AGE	SEX	BLOOD	TRIBAL ENROLLMENT Year	County	No.
	1 ~~Davis, Robert M~~	~~Named~~	~~27~~	~~M~~				
	2							
	3 Denied Citizenship by the Choctaw and Chickasaw Citizenship Court Nov. 29 '04							
	4						100 M	
	5							
	6							
	7							
	8							
	9							
	10							
	11							
	12							
	13							
	14							
	15							
	16							
	17 See Petition #C-12- For record see 7-4448							

TRIBAL ENROLLMENT OF PARENTS

Name of Father	Year	County	Name of Mother	Year	County
1 ~~J. D. Davis~~	~~Dead~~	~~Non Citz~~	~~Martha Davis~~	~~Dead~~	~~white woman~~
2					
3					
4					
5					
6		No1 denied in 96 Case #317			
7		Admitted by U.S. Court Central			
8		Dist Aug 24/97, Case No 60. As to			
9		~~residence, see his testimony~~			
9		Wife on rejected card Choctaw R. 482			
10 Judgment of U.S. Ct admitting No1 vacated and set aside by					June 4, 1900
11 Decree of Choctaw Chickasaw Citizenship Court Decr 17 '02					
11 ~~No1 now in C.C.C.C. Case #100~~					
12					
13					
14					Date of Application for Enrollment.
15					Sept 2/99
16					
17					

Choctaw By Blood Enrollment Cards 1898-1914

See Petitions C-12-17-20-21-22-23 & 24

RESIDENCE: Atoka COUNTY. **Choctaw Nation** **Choctaw Roll** *(Not Including Freedmen)* CARD NO.
POST OFFICE: Lehigh, I.T. FIELD NO. 4446

Dawes' Roll No.	NAME	Relationship to Person First Named	AGE	SEX	BLOOD	TRIBAL ENROLLMENT Year	County	No.
	1 Davis, Alonzo M		34	M				
	2							
	3							
	4							
	5							
	6							
	7							
	8							
	9							
	10							
	11							
	12							
	13							
	14							
	15							
	16							
	17							

DENIED CITIZENSHIP BY THE CHOCTAW AND CHICKASAW CITIZENSHIP COURT Nov 29 '04 10AM

TRIBAL ENROLLMENT OF PARENTS

Name of Father	Year	County	Name of Mother	Year	County
1 J. D. Davis	Dead	Non Citz	Martha Davis	Dead	white woman

No1 not in original appl Case #317 Admitted as an I.W. in 96 Case #325
Admitted by U.S. Court, Central Dist
Aug 24/97, Case No 60, as Alonzo L
Davis
As to residence, see his testimony
No.1 is the husband of Lorena Davis and the father of
on Choctaw card #4428, June 15, 1901
Judgment of U.S. Ct admitting No1 vacated and set aside by Decree of Choctaw Chickasaw Citizenship Court Dec 17 '02
No1 now in C.C.C.C. Case #100

See Petition #C-12- For record see 7-4448

Date of Application for Enrollment.
Sept 2/99

P.O. Johnson, I.T.

Choctaw By Blood Enrollment Cards 1898-1914

See Petitions C-12-17-20-21-22-23 & 24

RESIDENCE: Atoka COUNTY. **Choctaw Nation** **Choctaw Roll** *(Not Including Freedmen)* CARD NO.

POST OFFICE: Lehigh, I.T. FIELD NO. **4447**

Dawes' Roll No.	NAME	Relationship to Person First Named	AGE	SEX	BLOOD	TRIBAL ENROLLMENT Year	County	No.
	Standifer, Clara		29	F			D	
D.P.	Travel, Georgena Ethel	Dau	3mo	F			Dis	

No1 Denied Citizenship by the Choctaw and Chickasaw Citizenship Court Nov. 29 '04 100M

#2 Dismissed
Jan 21, 1905

See white petition #29

No1 Denied by C.C.C.C. as "Clara Louise Travel or Trowel or Clara Standifer"

No2 Denied by C.C.C.C. as "Georgina Ethel Travel or Trowel"

See Petition No C 20

~~See Pet......[sic] #C-12. For record see 7-4448.~~

TRIBAL ENROLLMENT OF PARENTS

Name of Father	Year	County	Name of Mother	Year	County
J.D. Davis	Dead	Non Citz	Martha Davis	Dead	white woman

No1 denied in 96 Case #317
Admitted by U.S. Court, Central Dist,
Aug 24/97 Case ~~No 60~~ 174. As to residence
~~see her testimony~~

Judgement[sic] of the U.S. Ct admitting No1 vacated and set aside by Decree of Choctaw Chickasaw Citizenship Court Decr 17'02

Child of No.1 on Choctaw Card #R.558

No.1 is now wife of Richard Travel a non citizen. Evidence of ~~marriage filed July 27, 1901~~

No.2 Enrolled July 27, 1901

Nos 1 and 2 now in C.C.C.C. Case #100.

Date of Application for Enrollment.
Sept 2/99

Choctaw By Blood Enrollment Cards 1898-1914

See Petitions C-12-17-20-21-22-23 & 24

RESIDENCE: Atoka COUNTY. **Choctaw Nation** **Choctaw Roll** *(Not Including Freedmen)* CARD NO. FIELD NO. 4448

POST OFFICE: Lehigh, I.T.

Dawes' Roll No.	NAME	Relationship to Person First Named	AGE	SEX	BLOOD	TRIBAL ENROLLMENT Year	County	No.
D.P.	~~Krebbs, Anna~~	~~Named~~	~~31~~	~~F~~	~~I.W.~~	~~1896~~	~~Atoka~~	~~14421~~

Denied Citizenship by the Choctaw and Chickasaw Citizenship Court Nov. 29'04 100M

Action approved by Secretary of Interior Feb 19,1907.

Action approved by Secretary of Interior Mar 1 1907. ⟵ Relative to petition. Notice of Departmental action forwarded attorneys for Choctaw and Chickasaw Nations May 7, 1907. Notice of Departmental action forwarded attorney for applicant May 7,1907

Notice of Departmental action forwarded Attorneys for Choctaw and Chickasaw Nations May 7-1907 Notice of Departmental action forwarded Attorney for applicant May 7-1907 Notice of Departmental action mailed applicant

Refused May 7-1907

Copy of decision forwarded attorney for Choctaw and Chickasaw Nations Nov 9,1906- Jan 17, 1906: Record returned to Department with report and recommendation Nov.9-1906.

Decision rendered May 6, 1905 Notice of decision forwarded Attorney for applicant May 6 1905 Copy of decision forwarded Attorneys for Choctaw and Chickasaw Nations May 6-1905 Copy of decision forwarded applicant May 6,1905

Copy of decision forwarded attorney for applicant Nov 9, 1906 Copy of decision forwarded applicant Nov 9, 1906 Record forwarded Department Nov. 9, 1906

TRIBAL ENROLLMENT OF PARENTS

Name of Father	Year	County	Name of Mother	Year	County
~~J.D. Davis~~	~~Dead~~	~~Non Citz~~	~~Martha Davis~~	~~Dead~~	~~white woman~~

No1 denied in 96 Case #317 as a citizen by blood
Admitted by U.S. Court, Central Dist
Case No 60- Aug 24/97. As to residence see her testimony.
Notice of Departmental action mailed applicant May 7-1907
On 1896 roll as Anna Crebbs

Proper P.O. address of No.1 is Roff, I.T. Nov. 23, 1901

Judgment of U.S. Ct admitting No1 vacated and set aside by Decree of Choctaw Chickasaw Citizenship Court Dec 17 '02

No1 does not appear in C.C.C.C. Case #100 ought to be

Denied by C.C.C.C. as "Anna James Mason or Annie Krebs (nee Davis)"

June 23 1905. Record returned by Department for further investigation July 18, 1905. Applicant her attorney and attorneys for Nation notified of further hearing on August 7, 1905.

Record forwarded Department May-6 1905

Date of Application for Enrollment. Sept 2/99

Choctaw By Blood Enrollment Cards 1898-1914

RESIDENCE: Sans Bois COUNTY. **Choctaw Nation** Choctaw Roll (Not Including Freedmen) CARD NO.
POST OFFICE: Stigler, I.T. FIELD NO. 4449

Dawes' Roll No.		NAME		Relationship to Person First Named	AGE	SEX	BLOOD	TRIBAL ENROLLMENT Year	County	No.
12362	1	Perry, Frank	43	First Named	40	M	Full	1896	Sans Bois	10053
12363	2	" Sally	22	Wife	19	F	"	1896	" "	2096
12364	3	" Davis	17	Son	14	M	"	1896	" "	10054
12365	4	" Gilbert	10	"	7	"	"	1896	" "	10055
DEAD	5	~~" Lizzie~~	3	~~Dau~~	~~1mo~~	~~F~~	~~"~~			
DEAD	6	~~" Sampson~~	1	~~Son~~	~~2mo~~	~~M~~	~~"~~			
	7									
	8									
	9									
	10	No.5 and 6 hereon dismissed under								
	11	order of the Commission to the Five								
	12	Civilized Tribes of March 31, 1905.								
	13									
	14									
	15	ENROLLMENT								
	16	OF NOS. 1,2,3 & 4 HEREON APPROVED BY THE SECRETARY								
	17	OF INTERIOR Mar 6 1903								

TRIBAL ENROLLMENT OF PARENTS

	Name of Father	Year	County	Name of Mother	Year	County
1	Boland Perry	Dead	Sans Bois	Nancy Perry	Dead	Sans Bois
2	Sam Cooper		" "	Sophie Cooper	"	" "
3	No1			Ellen Perry	"	" "
4	No1			" "	"	" "
5	~~No1~~			~~No2~~		
6	~~No1~~			~~No2~~		
7						
8						
9						
10						
11						
12	No2 on 1896 roll as Sally Cooper					
13	No5- Affidavit of birth to be					
14	~~supplied:- Filed Oct 26/99~~					Date of Application for Enrollment.
15	~~No.6 born Oct 7, 1901: Enrolled Nov. 30, 1901~~					Sept 4/99
15	No.6 Died March 5th 1902: Proof of Death filed Decr 23rd 1902					
16	No5 Died June 29th 1900: Proof of Death filed Decr 23rd 1902					
16	~~For child of Nos 1&2 see N.B. (Apr 25, 1906) Card No 40~~					
17	~~" " " " " " " (Mar 3, 1905) " " 633~~					

RESIDENCE: Sans Bois COUNTY. **Choctaw Nation** Choctaw Roll (Not Including Freedmen) CARD NO. 4450
POST OFFICE: Whitefield, I.T. FIELD NO. 44_

Dawes' Roll No.	NAME		Relationship to Person First Named	AGE	SEX	BLOOD	TRIBAL ENROLLMENT Year	County	No.
12366	1 Perry, Isham	48		45	M	Full	1896	Sans Bois	10046
12367	2 " Mary	63	Wife	60	F	"	1896	" "	10047
12368	3 " Louis	23	Son	20	M	"	1896	" "	10048
	4								
	5								
	6								
	7								
	8								
	9								
	10								
	11								
	12								
	13								
	14								
	15								
	16								
	17								

ENROLLMENT OF NOS. 1 2 & 3 HEREON APPROVED BY THE SECRETARY OF INTERIOR MAR 6 1903

TRIBAL ENROLLMENT OF PARENTS

Name of Father	Year	County	Name of Mother	Year	County
1 Boland Perry	Dead	Sans Bois	Nancy Perry	Dead	Sans Bois
2 Pe-san-tubbee	"	" "		"	" "
3 No1			Sally Perry	"	" "
4					
5					
6					
7 No.1 on 1896 Roll as Isom Perry.					
8					
9					
10					
11					
12					
13					
14					Date of Application for Enrollment.
15					Sept 2/99
16					
17					

RESIDENCE: Chickasaw Nation ~~COUNTY.~~ **Choctaw Nation** **Choctaw Roll** *(Not Including Freedmen)* CARD NO.
POST OFFICE: Wapanucka, I.T. FIELD NO. 4451

Dawes' Roll No.		NAME	Relationship to Person First Named	AGE	SEX	BLOOD	TRIBAL ENROLLMENT Year	County	No.
void	1	~~Taylor, Stephen L~~	~~Named~~	~~25~~	~~M~~	~~I.W.~~			
void	2	~~" Mary Ann~~	~~Wife~~	~~19~~	~~F~~	~~3/4~~			
DEAD	3	~~" Edward McKee~~	~~Son~~	~~4mo~~	~~M~~	~~3/4~~			
	4	~~No.3 hereon dismissed under order of~~							
	5	the Commission to the Five Civilized							
	6	Tribes of March 31, 1905.							
	7								
	8								
	9		~~Nos 1&2 transferred to Chickasaw card #1656 Jany 13, 1903~~						
	10		No3 died prior to ratification of						
	11		Choctaw Chickasaw agreement Sept. 25, 1902.						
	12								
	13								
	14								
	15	~~Nos 1-2 transferred to Chickasaw card #1656~~							
	16	this January 13, 1903.							
	17								

TRIBAL ENROLLMENT OF PARENTS

	Name of Father	Year	County	Name of Mother	Year	County
1	~~W.A. Taylor~~		~~Non Citz~~	~~Eliz. Taylor~~	~~Dead~~	~~Non Citz~~
2	~~McKee James~~		~~Chick. Dist~~	~~Rhoena James~~		~~Chick Dist~~
3	~~No1~~			~~No2~~		
4						
5						
6						
7						
8						
9	No2 on Chickasaw Roll, Pontotoc Co, Page					
10	51 transferred to Choctaw Roll by Dawes					
11	Com.					
11	~~No2 on 1897 Chickasaw Roll as Mary James~~					
12	No.3 Enrolled December 14, 1900					
13	No 3 Died June 20, 1901. See affidavit of No1 filed Nov. 20, 1902					
14	10/21/1915 – No.2 transferred from Choctaw Card #62					Date of Application for Enrollment.
15						Sept 4/99
16					~~No2 enrolled Sept 7/98 re-~~	
17					enrolled Sept 4/99	

CANCELLED

RESIDENCE: Gaines COUNTY. **Choctaw Nation** Choctaw Roll (Not Including Freedmen) CARD NO.
POST OFFICE: South Canadian, I.T. FIELD NO. 4452

Dawes' Roll No.	NAME	Relationship to Person	AGE	SEX	BLOOD	TRIBAL ENROLLMENT Year	County	No.
14419	1 Massey, William W 51	First Named	48	M	1/8	1896	Gaines	8528
I.W. 435	2 " Alice Victoria 24	Wife	20	F	I.W.			14810
14420	3 " Oliver 22	Son	19	M	3/16			8529
14421	4 Daniel, Beatrice 19	Dau	16	F	3/16			8530
14422	5 Massey, Edmund 17	Son	14	M	3/16			8531
14423	6 " Benjamin H 12	"	9	"	1/16			8532
14424	7 " Jessie 9	Dau	6	F	1/16			8533
14820	8 " William W Jr 6	Son	3	M	1/16			8545
14425	9 " Earnest E 3	"	2mo	"	1/16			
14426	10 Daniel, William Wilson 1	Son of No4	9mo	M	3/32			
14427	11 Massey, Reby Louise 1	Dau	16mo	F	1/16			
	12 No3 is now the husband of Arizona							
	13 C. Massey on Choctaw card #5773							
	14 №11 Born May 28,1901 enrolled Oct 16 1902							
	15 ENROLLMENT							
	16 OF NOS. 1,3456791011 HEREON							
	17 APPROVED BY THE SECRETARY OF INTERIOR Apr 11 1903							

TRIBAL ENROLLMENT OF PARENTS

Name of Father	Year	County	Name of Mother	Year	County
1 Henry Massey	Dead	Non Citz	Louisa Massey		Gaines
2 James Crouch	"	" "		Dead	Non Citz
3 No1			Isabell Massey	"	Gaines
4 No1			" "	"	"
5 No1			" "	"	"
6 No1			Nancy Massey	"	Non Citz
7 No1			" "	"	" "
8 No1			No2		
9 No1			No2		
10 J.F. Daniel		Non Citizen	No4		
11 №1			№2		

ENROLLMENT OF NOS. 2 HEREON APPROVED BY THE SECRETARY OF INTERIOR Sep 12 1903

ENROLLMENT OF NOS. 8 HEREON APPROVED BY THE SECRETARY OF INTERIOR May 20 1903

12 No1 on 1896 roll as Wm Wilson Massey
13 No6 " 1896 " " Benjamin "
~~No8 " 1896 " " W^m W " Jr~~
14 ~~No9 Affidavit of birth to be~~
15 supplied: Filed Oct 26/99
16 Nos 1,3,4,5,6 and 7 admitted by Dawes Commission in 1896 as
17 citizens by blood: Choctaw case #1304: no appeal
~~No10 Born Oct 9th 1901: Enrolled July 2nd 1902~~
No.4 Now the wife of J.F. Daniel non citizen: Evidence of marriage filed July 2nd 1902

For child of No3 see NB (Apr 26 06) #194
" " " No4 " " " " " #1182
~~" " " " " " (Mar 3 05) #568~~
#1 to 9

Date of Application for Enrollment. Sept 4/99

For children of Nos 1&2 see NB (Mar 3 1905) Card #2, #628
For child of No 3

RESIDENCE: Red River COUNTY. **Choctaw Nation** **Choctaw Roll** *(Not Including Freedmen)* CARD NO. FIELD NO. 4453

POST OFFICE: Kullituklo, I.T.

Dawes' Roll No.		NAME	Relationship to Person First Named	AGE	SEX	BLOOD	TRIBAL ENROLLMENT Year	County	No.
I.W. 436	1	Harrison, Robert S [35]	First Named	33	M	IW			
12369	2	" Missie [27]	Wife	24	F	Full	1896	Red River	12264

ENROLLMENT OF NOS. 1 HEREON APPROVED BY THE SECRETARY OF INTERIOR Sep 12 1903

ENROLLMENT OF NOS. 2 HEREON APPROVED BY THE SECRETARY OF INTERIOR Mar 6 1903

TRIBAL ENROLLMENT OF PARENTS

	Name of Father	Year	County	Name of Mother	Year	County
1	J. V Harrison		Non Citz	Martha Harrison	Dead	Non Citz
2	Wallace Tushka		Red River	Kizzie Tushka		Red River

Evidence of marriage to be supplied:- License filed Nov 2/99

No2 on 1896 roll as Missie Tushka

~~No1- Ministers'[sic] certificate to be supplied:- Filed Nov 24/99~~

Date of Application for Enrollment.

Sept 4/99

No2 enrolled April 29/99 re-enrolled Sept 4/99

Choctaw By Blood Enrollment Cards 1898-1914

RESIDENCE: Gaines COUNTY. **Choctaw Nation** #4454 **Choctaw Roll** *(Not Including Freedmen)* CAR.
POST OFFICE: South Canadian, I.T. FIELD NO. 4

Dawes' Roll No.		NAME	Relationship to Person First Named	AGE	SEX	BLOOD	TRIBAL ENROLLMENT Year	County	No.
12370	1	Griffith, Louisa DIED PRIOR TO SEPTEMBER 25, 1902 78	First Named	75	F	1/4	1896	Gaines	4682
	2								
	3								
	4								
	5								
	6								
	7								
	8								
	9								
	10								
	11								
	12								
	13								
	14								
	15	ENROLLMENT							
	16	OF NOS. 1 HEREON APPROVED BY THE SECRETARY							
	17	OF INTERIOR MAR 6 1903							

TRIBAL ENROLLMENT OF PARENTS

	Name of Father	Year	County	Name of Mother	Year	County
1	Placeed Krebbs	Dead	Non Citz	Rebecca Krebbs	Dead	Gaines
2						
3						
4						
5						
6	No1 died July 10, 1900: Enrollment cancelled by Department May 2 1906					
7						
8						
9						
10						
11						
12						
13						
14						Date of Application for Enrollment.
15						Sept 4/99
16						
17						

RESIDENCE: Sans Bois COUNTY. **Choctaw Nation** **Choctaw Roll** *(Not Including Freedmen)* CARD NO.
POST OFFICE: Enterprise, I.T. FIELD NO. 4455

Dawes' Roll No.	NAME	Relationship to Person First Named	AGE	SEX	BLOOD	TRIBAL ENROLLMENT Year	County	No.
12371	1 Walls, Thomas J Sr 60	First Named	57	M	1/4	1896	Sans Bois	12666
I.W.437	2 " Catherine 37	Wife	38	F	I.W.	1896	" "	15139
12372	3 Collier Martha 19	Dau	16	"	1/4	1896	" "	12668
12373	4 Walls Jincy 16	"	13	"	1/4	1896	" "	12694
12374	5 " Pearl 13	"	10	"	1/8	1896	" "	12669
12375	6 " Guy 8	Son	5	M	1/8	1896	" "	12670
12376	7 " Annie 5	Dau	2	F	1/8			
12377	8 " Cassie R 3	Son	10mo	M	1/8			
12378	9 Collier Oma 1	Granddau	1mo	F	1/8			

No.8 Enrolled Oct. 10th 1900
No.3 is now the wife of J. O. Collier, a citizen of the United States: Feb 13,1902
No.9 born Jany 19, 1902: Enrolled Feby 13, 1902

ENROLLMENT OF NOS. 1345678&9 HEREON APPROVED BY THE SECRETARY OF INTERIOR Mar 6 1903

For child of No4 see MINOR (Apr 26 '06) Card No 1301

TRIBAL ENROLLMENT OF PARENTS

	Name of Father	Year	County	Name of Mother	Year	County
1	Jesse Walls	Dead	Kiamitia	Delilah Walls	Dead	Kiamitia
2	C. L. Allen		Non Citz	Betsy Allen		Non Citz
3	No1			Louvina Walls	Dead	Sans Bois
4	No1			" "	"	" "
5	No1			No2		
6	No1			No2		
7	No1			No2		
8	No1			No2		
9	J.O. Collier		noncitizen	No3		

No1 on 1896 roll as T. J. Walls Sr
No2 " 1896 " " Kate Wall
No2 as to marriage see testimony of Scott and Jesse Walls
No4 on 1893 Pay Roll, Page 85, No 879, Sans Bois Co., as Jensy Walls
No7 Affidavit of birth to be supplied Recd Feby 13-1902
No4 on 1896 roll as Jincy Wall

ENROLLMENT OF NOS. 2 HEREON APPROVED BY THE SECRETARY OF INTERIOR Sep 12 1903

#1 to 7
Date of Application for Enrollment.
Sept 4/99

For child of Nos 1&2 see NB (Mar 3'05) #317
No 3 " #1334

For child of No see NB (Apr 26 '06) No 1293

RESIDENCE: Sans Bois COUNTY. **Choctaw Nation** **Choctaw Roll** *(Not Including Freedmen)* CARD No.
POST OFFICE: Enterprise I.T. FIELD No. 4456

Dawes' Roll No.	NAME	Relationship to Person First Named	AGE	SEX	BLOOD	TRIBAL ENROLLMENT Year	County	No.
12379	1 Walls, Thomas J Jr 22	First Named	19	M	1/4	1896	Sans Bois	12667
12380	2 " Cecil Evert 1	Son	3mo	M	1/8			
I.W. 677	3 " Nellie Alice 17	Wife	17	F	I.W.			

ENROLLMENT OF NOS. 3 HEREON APPROVED BY THE SECRETARY OF INTERIOR Mar 26 1904

ENROLLMENT OF NOS. 1 & 2 HEREON APPROVED BY THE SECRETARY OF INTERIOR Mar 6 1903

TRIBAL ENROLLMENT OF PARENTS

Name of Father	Year	County	Name of Mother	Year	County
1 Thomas Walls		Sans Bois	Louvina Walls	Dead	Sans Bois
2 No.1			Nellie Alice Walls		intermarried
3 H. C. Bullard		noncitizen	Sarah Bullard	Dead	noncitizen

No3 transferred from Choctaw Card D 650 January 25, 1904
See decision of January 7, 1904
On 1896 roll as T. J. Walls, Jr
~~No1 is now the husband of Nellie Alice Walls on Choctaw Card #D.650. Evidence of marriage filed Aug. 22, 1901~~
Correct name of No1 is Thomas [?] Walls. See his testimony taken Aug 11-1901
No2 Born Sept. 15, 1902. Enrolled Dec 24, 1902

For child of Nos 1&3 see N.B. (Apr 26-06) Card #510

Date of Application for Enrollment.
Sept 4/99

P.O. is now Brooken I.T.

Choctaw By Blood Enrollment Cards 1898-1914

RESIDENCE: Gaines COUNTY. **Choctaw Nation** **Choctaw Roll** *(Not Including Freedmen)* CARD NO.
POST OFFICE: Leatherstone, I.T. FIELD NO. 4457

Dawes' Roll No.	NAME		Relationship to Person First Named	AGE	SEX	BLOOD	TRIBAL ENROLLMENT Year	County	No.
I.W. 438	1 Dunn, William B	37	First Named	34	M	IW	1896	Gaines	14460
12381	2 " Josephine	29	Wife	26	F	1/4	1896	"	3289
12382	3 " Tabitha J	6	Dau	3	"	1/8	1896	"	3290
12383	4 " Fannie M	5	"	1½	"	1/8			
12384	5 " James William	3	Son	2mo	M	1/8			
12385	6 " Ellen	1	Dau	3wks	F	1/8			

ENROLLMENT OF NOS. 1 HEREON APPROVED BY THE SECRETARY OF INTERIOR Sept 12-1903

Evidence as to status of No1 as an intermarried citizen Sept. 25, 1902, taken Oct. 29, 1902

ENROLLMENT OF NOS. 2 3 4 5 & 6 HEREON APPROVED BY THE SECRETARY OF INTERIOR Mar 6 1903

TRIBAL ENROLLMENT OF PARENTS

Name of Father	Year	County	Name of Mother	Year	County
1 William Dunn		Non Citz	Anna J Dunn		Non Citz
2 Wilson Massey		Gaines	Mary Massey	Dead	Gaines
3 No1			No2		
4 No1			No2		
5 No1			No2		
6 No1			No2		

For child of Nos 1&2 see NB (Mar 3,1905) Card #337
No1 on 1896 roll as W. B. Dunn
No3 " 1896 " " Betsy "
~~Nos 1-3 were admitted by Dawes~~
Com Case No 335
No1 admitted as W.B. Dunn
No3 " " Arbetha Jane Dunn
~~No4 Affidavit of birth to be~~
supplied filed Oct 26/99
No5 Enrolled May 24, 1900
Nº6 Born July 21, 1902: enrolled Aug 12, 1902

#1 to 4
Date of Application for Enrollment.
Sept 4/99

17 C.O.[sic] Canadian I.T

No1 So McAlester 11/1/04

Choctaw By Blood Enrollment Cards 1898-1914

RESIDENCE: Tobucksy COUNTY. **Choctaw Nation** **Choctaw Roll** *(Not Including Freedmen)* CARD NO.
POST OFFICE: Kiowa, I.T. FIELD NO. 4458

Dawes' Roll No.	NAME	Relationship to Person First Named	AGE	SEX	BLOOD	TRIBAL ENROLLMENT Year	County	No.
12386	1 Watts, Israel 53	First Named	50	M	1/8	1896	Tobucksy	13824

ENROLLMENT OF NOS. 1 HEREON APPROVED BY THE SECRETARY OF INTERIOR MAR 6 1903

TRIBAL ENROLLMENT OF PARENTS

Name of Father	Year	County	Name of Mother	Year	County
1 Philip Watts	Dead	Non Citz	Mary Watts	Dead	Atoka

Elizabeth Watts wife of No.1 on Choctaw card #D.590

Date of Application for Enrollment. Sept 4/99

RESIDENCE: Atoka COUNTY. **Choctaw Nation** Choctaw Roll (Not Including Freedmen) CARD NO.
POST OFFICE: Kiowa, I.T. FIELD NO. 4459

Dawes' Roll No.		NAME	Relationship to Person First Named	AGE	SEX	BLOOD	TRIBAL ENROLLMENT Year	County	No.
I.W. 841	1	Garner, Alexander T 30	First Named	27	M	IW			
12387	2	" Alice 22	Wife	19	F	1/32	1896	Atoka	5975
12388	3	" Gladys G 4	Dau	1	"	1/64			
12389	4	" Roy James 2	Son	3mo	M	1/64			
	5								
	6								
	7								
	8								
	9								
	10								
	11								
	12								
	13								
	14								
	15								
	16								
	17								

ENROLLMENT
OF NOS. 1 HEREON
APPROVED BY THE SECRETARY
OF INTERIOR MAY 21 1904

ENROLLMENT
OF NOS. 2 3 & 4 HEREON
APPROVED BY THE SECRETARY
OF INTERIOR MAR 6 1903

TRIBAL ENROLLMENT OF PARENTS

	Name of Father	Year	County	Name of Mother	Year	County
1	J. D. Garner		Non Citz	Angie Garner	Dead	Non Citz
2	Uriah Henderson	Dead	" "	Josephine Henderson		Chick Dist
3	No1			No2		
4	No.1			No.2		
5						
6						
7						
8						
9						
10						
11						
12						
13						
14						
15						
16						
17						

No2 on 1896 roll as Alice Henderson
No1 - Evidence of marriage to be
supplied:- Filed Dec 16/99
~~No3 Affidavit of birth to be~~
supplied:- Filed Oct 26/99
No.4 Enrolled November 7th, 1900
See testimony of №1 taken Oct. 30, 1902
~~Affidavits of Nos 1 and 2 as to the residence of №2 at the~~
date of her marriage to №1 filed May 18, 1903

Date of Application for Enrollment.
Sept 4/99

P.O. Alex IT 12/29/03

RESIDENCE: Chickasaw Nation ~~COUNTY.~~ **Choctaw Nation** Choctaw Roll CARD NO.
POST OFFICE: Wayne, I.T. (Not Including Freedmen) FIELD NO. 4460

Dawes' Roll No.		NAME		Relationship to Person First Named	AGE	SEX	BLOOD	TRIBAL ENROLLMENT Year	County	No.
I.W. 1016	1	Mozley, Benjamin F	46		43	M	IW	1896	Tobucksy	14814
15477	2	" Laura E	30	Wife	27	F	1/32	1896	"	8558
15478	3	" Lena B	10	Dau	7	"	1/64	1896	"	8559
15479	4	" Warren M	6	Son	3	M	1/64	1896	"	8560
15480	5	" Karl C	4	"	8mo	"	1/64			
15481	6	" Lois	1	Dau	4mo	F	1/64			

No5- Affidavit of birth to be supplied:- Filed Oct 26/99

Nº6 Born Dec. 15,1901: enrolled April 19, 1902

ENROLLMENT OF NOS. 2-3-4-5-6- HEREON APPROVED BY THE SECRETARY OF INTERIOR MAY 9 1904

TRIBAL ENROLLMENT OF PARENTS

	Name of Father	Year	County	Name of Mother	Year	County
1	K. T. Mozley	Dead	Non Citz	Mahaley Mozley	Dead	Non Citz
2	Uriah Henderson	"	" "	Josephine Henderson		Chick Dist

For child of Nos 1&2 see NB (Mar 3,1905) Card #338

All but No5 were admitted by Dawes Com., Case No 366? No appeal. Error: only No.1 admitted.

~~No1 admitted as Frank Moseley~~

No2 " " Laura E " } Error
No3 " " Lena " } Error
~~No4 " " Warren "~~ } Error

~~No2 '93 Tobucksy #594 as Mozly~~
~~" 3 " " 595 " "~~

~~No1 on 1896 roll as Frank S Mozely~~
No2 " 1896 " " Laura E Mosely
No3 " 1896 " " Lena "
~~No4 " 1896 " " Warren "~~

ENROLLMENT OF NOS. ---- 1 ---- HEREON APPROVED BY THE SECRETARY OF INTERIOR OCT 21 1904

Date of Application for Enrollment. Sept 4/99
→ 1 to 4

PO Noble, O.T. 4/8/07
P.O. Purcell I.T.
PO Maysville IT 12/27/04

Choctaw By Blood Enrollment Cards 1898-1914

RESIDENCE: COUNTY. **Choctaw Nation** **Choctaw Roll** *(Not Including Freedmen)* CARD NO.
POST OFFICE: FIELD NO. 4461

Dawes' Roll No.	NAME	Relationship to Person First Named	AGE	SEX	BLOOD	TRIBAL ENROLLMENT		
						Year	County	No.
	1							
	2							
	3							
	4							
	5							
	6 This No. lost ~~~~~ No card ever made out for it.							
	7							
	8							
	9							
	10							
	11							
	12							
	13							
	14							
	15							
	16							
	17							

TRIBAL ENROLLMENT OF PARENTS

Name of Father	Year	County	Name of Mother	Year	County
1					
2					
3					
4					
5					
6					
7					
8					
9					
10					
11					
12					
13					
14					
15					
16					
17					

CANCELLED

RESIDENCE: Sans Bois COUNTY. **Choctaw Nation** **Choctaw Roll** *(Not Including Freedmen)* CARD NO.
POST OFFICE: Enterprise I.T. FIELD NO. 4462

Dawes' Roll No.		NAME		Relationship to Person First Named	AGE	SEX	BLOOD	TRIBAL ENROLLMENT Year	County	No.
I.W. 439	1	Scott, James	55		51	M	IW	1896	Sans Bois	15018
12390	2	" Emily E	30	Wife	27	F	1/2	1896	" "	11122
12391	3	" Viola M	12	Dau	9	"	1/4	1896	" "	11123
12392	4	" Claude	7	Son	4	M	1/4	1896	" "	11124
12393	5	" Elbert	5	"	1	"	1/4			
12394	6	" Willie	1	Dau	1mo	F	1/4			
	7									
	8									
	9									
	10									
	11									
	12									
	13									
	14									
	15									
	16									
	17									

ENROLLMENT OF NOS. 1 HEREON APPROVED BY THE SECRETARY OF INTERIOR Sep 12 1903

ENROLLMENT OF NOS. 2 3 4 5 & 6 HEREON APPROVED BY THE SECRETARY OF INTERIOR Mar 6 1903

TRIBAL ENROLLMENT OF PARENTS

	Name of Father	Year	County	Name of Mother	Year	County
1	Peter Scott	Dead	Non Citz	Nancy Scott	Dead	Non Citz
2	Thos Walls		Sans Bois	Eliza Walls	"	Sans Bois
3	No 1			No 2		
4	No 1			No 2		
5	No 1			No 2		
6	No 1			No 2		
7						
8						
9						
10						
11						
12						
13						
14						
15						
16						
17						

No2 On 1896 roll as Emily W. Scott
No3 " 1896 " " Viola May "
~~No5~~
~~No6 Born Sept 28, 1901 and Enrolled October 26, 1901.~~

#1 to 5 inc.
Date of Application for Enrollment.
Sept 4/99

RESIDENCE: Chickasaw Nation ~~COUNTY.~~ **Choctaw Nation** Choctaw Roll (Not Including Freedmen) CARD NO.
POST OFFICE: Hewitt, I.T. FIELD NO. 4463

Dawes' Roll No.	NAME	Relationship to Person First Named	AGE	SEX	BLOOD	TRIBAL ENROLLMENT Year	County	No.
I.W. 440	1 Gill, Charles J 38	First Named	35	M	IW			
Dead	2 ~~" Josephine W~~	~~Wife~~	~~45~~	~~F~~	~~1/8~~	~~1896~~	~~Atoka~~	~~12628~~
12395	3 Merrill, Anna 16	S.D.	13	"	1/16	1896	"	8832
12396	4 Vieux, Minerva 13	" "	10	"	1/16	1896	"	12630
12397	5 " Louis 10	S.S.	7	M	1/16	1896	"	12629

No.2 Hereon Dismissed under order of the Commission to the Five Civilized Tribes of March 31, 1905.

ENROLLMENT OF NOS. 1 HEREON APPROVED BY THE SECRETARY OF INTERIOR Sep 12 1903

ENROLLMENT OF NOS. 3 4 & 5 HEREON APPROVED BY THE SECRETARY OF INTERIOR Mar 6 1903

TRIBAL ENROLLMENT OF PARENTS

Name of Father	Year	County	Name of Mother	Year	County
1 Henry P Gill	Dead	Non Citz	Sarah A. Gill		Non Citz
2 ~~Joseph Ward~~	~~"~~	~~" "~~	~~Eliz. Ward~~	~~Dead~~	~~Atoka~~
3 Warren Merrill	"	" "	No 2		
4 Louis Vieux	"	" "	No 2		
5 " "	"	" "	No 2		

For child of No.3 see NB (Apr 26 '06) Card No. 242
~~No2 on 1896 roll as Josephine Vieux.~~
~~No2 Died March 28, 1902; Proof of death filed Nov 1, 1902~~
See testimony of №1 taken Oct. 28, 1902
No.5 on 1896 Roll as Lewis Vieux
No.3 " 1896 " " Annie Merrill
~~Copy of divorce proceedings between No2 and her~~
former husband filed May 26, 1903

Date of Application for Enrollment. Sept 4/99

RESIDENCE: Atoka COUNTY. **Choctaw Nation** **Choctaw Roll** *(Not Including Freedmen)* CARD NO.
POST OFFICE: Kiowa, I.T. FIELD NO. 4464

Dawes' Roll No.	NAME	Relationship to Person First Named	AGE	SEX	BLOOD	TRIBAL ENROLLMENT Year	County	No.
12398	1 Thompson, Gertrude 24	First Named	21	F	1/32	1896	Atoka	12456
12399	2 " Eva 4	Dau	6mo	"	1/64			
	3							
	4							
	5							
	6							
	7							
	8							
	9							
	10							
	11							
	12							
	13							
	14							
	15							
	16							
	17							

ENROLLMENT
OF NOS. 1 & 2 HEREON
APPROVED BY THE SECRETARY
OF INTERIOR Mar 6 1903

TRIBAL ENROLLMENT OF PARENTS

Name of Father	Year	County	Name of Mother	Year	County
1 Uriah Henderson	Dead	Non Citz	Josephine Gill		Atoka
2 Henry Henderson		Chick Roll	No 1		
3					
4					
5					
6					
7					
8					
9					
10					
11					
12					
13					
14					
15			Date of Application ~~for Enrollment.~~		Sept 4/99
16					
17					

P.O. Hewitt I.T. 4/1/03

RESIDENCE: Sans Bois COUNTY. **Choctaw Nation** **Choctaw Roll** *(Not Including Freedmen)* CARD NO.
POST OFFICE: Enterprise, I.T. FIELD NO. 4465

Dawes' Roll No.	NAME	Relationship to Person First Named	AGE	SEX	BLOOD	TRIBAL ENROLLMENT Year	County	No.
I.W. 4017	1 Crowder, Caroline 59	First Named	56	F	IW	1896	Sans Bois	14368
	2							
	3							
	4							
	5							
	6							
	7							
	8							
	9							
	10							
	11							
	12							
	13							
	14							
	15							
	16							
	17							

ENROLLMENT
OF NOS. ~~~ 1 ~~~ HEREON
APPROVED BY THE SECRETARY
OF INTERIOR OCT 21 1904

TRIBAL ENROLLMENT OF PARENTS

Name of Father	Year	County	Name of Mother	Year	County
1 Chesley Wright	Dead	Non Citz	Louvina Wright	Dead	Non Citz
2					
3					
4					
5					
6 Affidavit of Nº1 as to former marriage and her					
7 correct maiden name filed July 29, 1903					
8					
9					
10					
11					
12					
13					
14					Date of Application for Enrollment.
15					Sept 4/99
16					
17					

RESIDENCE: Sans Bois COUNTY. **Choctaw Nation** **Choctaw Roll** (*Not Including Freedmen*) CARD NO.
POST OFFICE: Enterprise, I.T. FIELD NO. 4466

Dawes' Roll No.	NAME		Relationship to Person First Named	AGE	SEX	BLOOD	TRIBAL ENROLLMENT Year	County	No.
12400	1 Sirmans, Elsie	25	First Named	22	F	3/4	1896	Sans Bois	10670
12401	2 Rogers, Alice	6	Dau	4	"	3/8	1896	" "	10671
12402	3 Sirmans, Linnie	3	"	2mo	"	3/8			
12403	4 " Gelia	2	Dau	5mo	f	3/8			
	5								
	6								
	7								
	8								
	9								
	10								
	11								
	12								
	13								
	14								
	15								
	16								
	17								

ENROLLMENT OF NOS. 1 2 3 4 HEREON APPROVED BY THE SECRETARY OF INTERIOR MAR 6 1903

TRIBAL ENROLLMENT OF PARENTS

Name of Father	Year	County	Name of Mother	Year	County
1 Daniel Frazier	Dead	Sans Bois	Siney Frazier	Dead	Sans Bois
2 Henry Rogers	"	Non Citz	No1		
3 Otis Sirmans		" "	No1		
4 W^m^ O Sirmans		" "	No1		
5					
6					
7					

No1 on 1896 roll Elsie Rogers
Evidence of marriage between No1 and Wm Otis Sirmans filed Aug 14, 1901
No4 Enrolled Aug 23, 1901

#1 to 2 inc
Date of Application for Enrollment.
Sept 4/99

For child of No1 see NB (Apr 26 '06) Card No 1307
" children " " " " (March 3,1905) " #1010
No3 enrolled Oct 26/99

P.O. Brooken IT

Choctaw By Blood Enrollment Cards 1898-1914

RESIDENCE: Atoka COUNTY. **Choctaw Nation** **Choctaw Roll** (Not Including Freedmen) CARD NO.
POST OFFICE: Coalgate, I.T. FIELD NO. 4467

Dawes' Roll No.		NAME	Relationship to Person First Named	AGE	SEX	BLOOD	TRIBAL ENROLLMENT Year	County	No.
12404	1	Thompson, Nettie 21	First Named	18	F	1/32	1896	Tobucksy	863
Dead	2	~~" Richard C~~	~~Son~~	~~1~~	~~M~~	~~1/32~~			
	3								
	4								
	5	No. 2 Hereon Dismissed under order of							
	6	the Commission to the Five Civilized							
	7	Tribes of March 31, 1905.							
	8								
	9								
	10								
	11								
	12								
	13	ENROLLMENT							
	14	OF NOS. 1 HEREON APPROVED BY THE SECRETARY							
	15	OF INTERIOR Mar 6 1903							
	16								
	17								

TRIBAL ENROLLMENT OF PARENTS

	Name of Father	Year	County	Name of Mother	Year	County
1	John Bohreer		Non Citz	Susie Bohreer		Tobucksy
2	~~Robert Thompson~~	~~1896~~	~~Chickasaw~~	~~No1~~		
3						
4						
5						
6						
7	No1 is the wife of Robert Thompson on Chickasaw Card #667					
8	on 1896 roll as Nettie Bohren					
9	No2 born Nov 3d, 1900: Enrolled Nov 11th 1901					
10	~~No2 Died in July 1902: Proof of death filed Nov 13, 1902~~					
11	~~For child of No1 see NB (Apr 26 06) #1291~~					
12	" " " " " Chick NB (Mar 3-05) #667					
13						
14						Date of Application for Enrollment.
15						Sept 4/99
16						
17						

P.O. Kiowa I.T. 4/4/05

RESIDENCE: Chickasaw Nation ~~COUNTY.~~
POST OFFICE: Wayne, I.T.

Choctaw Nation

Choctaw Roll (Not Including Freedmen)

CARD NO.
FIELD NO. 4468

Dawes' Roll No.	NAME	Relationship to Person First Named	AGE	SEX	BLOOD	TRIBAL ENROLLMENT Year	County	No.
12405	1 Henderson, Roy 26		23	M	1/32	1896	Atoka	5974
IW 1132	2 " Lula 28	Wife	27	F	IW			

ENROLLMENT OF NOS. ~~~2~~~ HEREON APPROVED BY THE SECRETARY OF INTERIOR Nov 16 1904

ENROLLMENT OF NOS. 1 HEREON APPROVED BY THE SECRETARY OF INTERIOR Mar 6 1903

TRIBAL ENROLLMENT OF PARENTS

Name of Father	Year	County	Name of Mother	Year	County
1 Uriah Henderson	Dead	Non Citz	Josephine Gill		Atoka
2 G.M. Randolph		" "	Ollie Randolph		Non-Citizen

~~No1 is the husband of Lula Henderson on Choctaw Card #D808 Sept 25 1902~~

No2 transferred from Choctaw card #D-808 Oct 31, 1904: See decision of Oct 15, 1904

~~For child of Nos 1&2 see NB (Apr 26 '06) Card No 261~~
" " " " " " " (Mar 3 05) " " 339

Date of Application for Enrollment.
Sept 4/99

P.O. Purcell, I.T.

Choctaw By Blood Enrollment Cards 1898-1914

RESIDENCE: Sans Bois COUNTY. **Choctaw Nation** **Choctaw Roll** (Not Including Freedmen) CARD NO.
POST OFFICE: Enterprise, I.T. FIELD NO. 4469

Dawes' Roll No.	NAME	Relationship to Person First Named	AGE	SEX	BLOOD	TRIBAL ENROLLMENT Year	County	No.
12406	1 Henson, Lena 41	First Named	38	F	1/2	1896	Sans Bois	8
12407	2 Alexander Jane 17	Dau	14	"	3/4	1896	" "	11
12408	3 " Patsy 14	"	11	"	3/4	1896	" "	12
12409	4 " Sophia 8	"	5	"	3/4	1896	" "	13
12410	5 Henson, Mary M 3	"	5mo	F	3/4			
12411	6 " Sarah Elzada 1	Dau	3mo	F	3/4			
	7							
	8							
	9							
	10							
	11							
	12							
	13							
	14							
	15							
	16							
	17							

ENROLLMENT OF NOS. 1 2 3 4 5 & 6 HEREON APPROVED BY THE SECRETARY OF INTERIOR Mar 6 1903

TRIBAL ENROLLMENT OF PARENTS

Name of Father	Year	County	Name of Mother	Year	County
1 William Goforth	Dead	Chick Roll	Louisa Goforth		Choctaw Roll
2 Lone Alexander	"	Sans Bois	No1		
3 " "	"	" "	No1		
4 " "	"	" "	No1		
5 William Hanson[sic]		Non Citizen	No1		
6 " "		" "	No1		
7					
8					
9					
10					
11					
12					
13					
14					#1 to 4
15					
16					Sept 4/99
17					

No1 on 1896 roll as Sissy Alexander
No4 " 1896 " " Sophy "

No1 the wife of William Hanson, a non citizen
No5 Enrolled May 24, 1900
No6 Born Jany 29, 19021: Enrolled April 4, 1902

For child of No3 see NB (Apr 26-06) Card #342
" " " " 2 " " " " #652

Date of Application for Enrollment.

Choctaw By Blood Enrollment Cards 1898-1914

RESIDENCE: Atoka COUNTY. **Choctaw Nation** **Choctaw Roll** (Not Including Freedmen) CARD NO.
POST OFFICE: Owl, I.T. FIELD NO. 4470

Dawes' Roll No.	NAME	Relationship to Person First Named	AGE	SEX	BLOOD	TRIBAL ENROLLMENT Year	County	No.
12412	1 Jones, Louisa 53	First Named	50	F	1/2	1893	Atoka	1149
12413	2 Wolf Benjamin F 14	Son	11	M	1/4	1893	"	1150
12414	3 " Fannie 10	Dau	7	F	1/4	1893	"	1151
12415	4 " Lillie M 5	"	1½	"	1/4			
12416	5 " Ida 3	"	2mo	"	1/4			

ENROLLMENT OF NOS. 1 2 3 4 & 5 HEREON APPROVED BY THE SECRETARY OF INTERIOR Mar 6 1903

TRIBAL ENROLLMENT OF PARENTS

Name of Father	Year	County	Name of Mother	Year	County
1 Noel Jones		Atoka	Mary Jones	Dead	Atoka
2 Henry Wolf		Non Citz	No1		
3 " "		" "	No1		
4 " "		" "	No1		
5 " "		" "	No1		

First three on 1893 Pay Roll, Page 119, Atoka Co

Nos 4-5 Affidavits of birth to be supplied: Filed Nov 2/99

No.1 on 1896 Choctaw roll as Eliza James: page 180: #1320
No.3 " " " " " Fannie James " " #7321
No2 " " " " " Ben Hampton " 146 #6017
For child of No1 see NB (Apr 26-06) #1280
" " " " " " (Mar 3-05) # 340

Date of Application for enrollment
Sept 4/99

Choctaw By Blood Enrollment Cards 1898-1914

RESIDENCE: Sans Bois COUNTY. **Choctaw Nation** **Choctaw Roll** *(Not Including Freedmen)* CARD NO.
POST OFFICE: Russellville, I.T. FIELD NO. 4471

Dawes' Roll No.	NAME	Relationship to Person First Named	AGE	SEX	BLOOD	TRIBAL ENROLLMENT Year	County	No.
12417	1 Henry, Woodson 28	First Named	25	M	1/4	1896	Sans Bois	5064

ENROLLMENT OF NOS. 1 HEREON APPROVED BY THE SECRETARY OF INTERIOR MAR 6 1903

TRIBAL ENROLLMENT OF PARENTS

Name of Father	Year	County	Name of Mother	Year	County
1 Pat Henry	Dead	Creek Ind.	Martha Henry	Dead	Sans Bois

Date of Application for Enrollment.
Sept 4/99

RESIDENCE: Sans Bois | COUNTY. **Choctaw Nation** | **Choctaw Roll** (*Not Including Freedmen*) | CARD NO.
POST OFFICE: Sans Bois, I.T. | | | FIELD NO. 4472

Dawes' Roll No.	NAME	Relationship to Person First Named	AGE	SEX	BLOOD	TRIBAL ENROLLMENT Year	County	No.
I.W. 1535	1 Colbert, Susan 26		23	F	IW			
	2							
	3							
	4							
	5							
	6							
	7							
	8							
	9							
	10							
	11							
	12							
	13							
	14							
	15							
	16							
	17							

ENROLLMENT
OF NOS. 1 HEREON
APPROVED BY THE SECRETARY
OF INTERIOR Mar 14 1906

TRIBAL ENROLLMENT OF PARENTS

Name of Father	Year	County	Name of Mother	Year	County
1 Aleaney Dees	Dead	Non Citz	Alender Dees		Non Citz

~~No1 was formerly wife of Edmund Coley, 1893 Pay Roll~~ and 1896 Census Roll Choctaw Nation Sans Bois Co who died in 1899.

Granted Nov 14 1905

Evidence of marriage to be ~~supplied~~.

For children of No1 see NB (Apr 26-06) #1097

Date of Application for Enrollment. Sept 4/99

~~P.O. Bearden IT 10/9/05~~
P.O. Guertie I.T. 12/28/05

Choctaw By Blood Enrollment Cards 1898-1914

RESIDENCE: Sans Bois COUNTY. **Choctaw Nation** **Choctaw Roll** *(Not Including Freedmen)* CARD NO.
POST OFFICE: Enterprise, I.T. FIELD NO. 4473

Dawes' Roll No.		NAME	Relationship to Person First Named	AGE	SEX	BLOOD	TRIBAL ENROLLMENT Year	County	No.
12418	1	McIntosh, Catherine [39]		36	F	1/4	1896	Sans Bois	9008
12419	2	" George [24]	Son	21	M	1/8	1896	" "	9009
12420	3	" Turner [22]	"	19	"	1/8	1896	" "	9010
12421	4	" Jonah [17]	"	14	"	1/8	1896	" "	9012
12422	5	" Arthur [14]	"	11	"	1/8	1896	" "	9013
12423	6	" Amos [10]	"	7	"	1/8	1896	" "	9014
12424	7	" Nancy [9]	Dau	6	F	1/8	1896	" "	9015
12425	8	" Lona [6]	"	3	"	1/8	1896	" "	9016
Dead	9	~~" Dead Edward~~	~~Son~~	~~1~~	~~M~~	~~1/8~~			
12426	10	" Elias Thomas [2]	Son	11mo	SM	1/8			

No. 9 Hereon Dismissed under order of the Commission to the Five Civilized Tribes of March 31, 1905.

For child of No.1 see NB (March 3 1905) #1169

ENROLLMENT OF NOS. 12345678&10 HEREON APPROVED BY THE SECRETARY OF INTERIOR Mar 6 1903

TRIBAL ENROLLMENT OF PARENTS

	Name of Father	Year	County	Name of Mother	Year	County
1	John McKinney	Dead	Sans Bois	Sarah McKinney	Dead	Non Citz
2	Joe McIntosh		Colored Man	No1		
3	" "		" "	No1		
4	" "		" "	No1		
5	" "		" "	No1		
6	" "		" "	No1		
7	" "		" "	No1		
8	" "		" "	No1		
9	~~" "~~		~~" "~~	~~No1~~		
10	" "		" "	No1		

#1 to 9 inc
Date of Application for Enrollment. Sept 4/99

No1 on 1896 roll as Kitty McIntosh as to marriage to parents, see testimony of S.E. Lewis

~~No9 Affidavit of birth to be~~ supplied: Filed Jany 17, 1900

No10 Enrolled July 30, 1901. Affidavit returned for correction

No9 Died Oct 14, 1900: Proof of death filed Dec. 30, 1902

Choctaw By Blood Enrollment Cards 1898-1914

RESIDENCE: Atoka COUNTY. **Choctaw Nation** **Choctaw Roll** (Not Including Freedmen) CARD No.
POST OFFICE: Kiowa, I.T. FIELD No. 4474

Dawes' Roll No.		NAME	Relationship to Person First Named	AGE	SEX	BLOOD	TRIBAL ENROLLMENT Year	County	No.
I.W. 441	1	Pigott, Edward 56	First Named	53	M	IW			
14428	2	" Annie 50	Wife	47	F	1/8	1896	Atoka	10546
14429	3	" Mary A 14	Dau	11	"	1/16	1896	"	10547
	4								
	5								
	6								
	7								
	8								
	9								
	10								
	11								
	12								
	13								
	14								
	15								
	16								
	17								

ENROLLMENT OF NOS. 2 and 3 HEREON APPROVED BY THE SECRETARY OF INTERIOR Apr 11 1903

ENROLLMENT OF NOS. 1 HEREON APPROVED BY THE SECRETARY OF INTERIOR Sept 12 1903

TRIBAL ENROLLMENT OF PARENTS

	Name of Father	Year	County	Name of Mother	Year	County
1	John Pigott	Dead	Non Citz	Eliza Pigott	Dead	Non Citz
2	Joshua Norris	"	" "	Maranda Norris	"	Towson
3	No 1			No 2		
4						
5						
6						
7						

8 No1 Admitted by Dawes Com Case No 557. No appeal
9 Nos 2-3 " " " " " " 557
10 No3 Admitted as Mary Pigott
~~No3 On 1896 roll as May A Piggott~~
11 No2 " 1896 " " Annie "

Date of Application for Enrollment.
Sept 4/99

RESIDENCE: Sans Bois COUNTY. **Choctaw Nation** Choctaw Roll (Not Including Freedmen) CARD NO.
POST OFFICE: Enterprise, I.T. FIELD NO. 4475

Dawes' Roll No.	NAME	Relationship to Person First Named	AGE	SEX	BLOOD	TRIBAL ENROLLMENT Year	County	No.
12427	1 Walls, Jesse 29	First Named	26	M	3/4	1896	Sans Bois	12638
IW1133	2 " Pink 25	Wife	22	F	I.W.	1896	" "	15142
12428	3 " Bertha 8	Dau	5	"	3/8	1896	" "	12639
12429	4 " Elizabeth 6	"	3	"	3/8	1896	" "	12640
12430	5 " Edward 3	Son	2mo	M	3/8			
12431	6 " Lila 1	Dau	9mo	F	3/8			

ENROLLMENT OF NOS. ~~~~ 2 ~~~~ HEREON APPROVED BY THE SECRETARY OF INTERIOR Nov. 16 1904

For child of Nos 1&2 see NB (Apr 26 '06) #1194
" " " " " " " " (Mar 3 '05) #1365

ENROLLMENT OF NOS. 1 3 4 5 & 6 HEREON APPROVED BY THE SECRETARY OF INTERIOR Mar 6 1903

TRIBAL ENROLLMENT OF PARENTS

Name of Father	Year	County	Name of Mother	Year	County
1 Thos Walls		Sans Bois	Eliza Walls	Dead	Sans Bois
2 Jno Davenport		Non Citz	Mary Davenport		Non Citz
3 No1			No2		
4 No1			No2		
5 No1			No2		
6 №1			№2		

No1 on 1896 roll as Jessie Wall
No3 " 1896 " " Bertha "
~~No4 " 1896 " " Elizabeth "~~

As to marriage, see testimony of Thos. Walls

#1 to 4
Date of Application for Enrollment.
Sept 4/99

No5 enrolled Dec. 18/99. Affidavit irregular and returned for correction
~~Returned corrected and filed Feby. 20, 1900~~
No6 Born Feby 15, 1902, enrolled Nov. 7, 1902

Choctaw By Blood Enrollment Cards 1898-1914

RESIDENCE: Atoka COUNTY. **Choctaw Nation** **Choctaw Roll** *(Not Including Freedmen)* CARD NO.
POST OFFICE: Kiowa, I.T. FIELD NO. 4476

Dawes' Roll No.		NAME	Relationship to Person First Named	AGE	SEX	BLOOD	TRIBAL ENROLLMENT Year	County	No.
IW 1982	1	Houghton, Charles L 46	First Named	43	M	I.W.			
DEAD	2	~~" Leona~~	~~Wife~~	~~33~~	~~F~~	~~1/8~~			
15586	3	" Luther 19	Son	16	M	1/16			

5 Jan 4 1904: Decision of Commission enrolling Nos
6 1 and 3 rendered and dismissing No2
7 Record and decision forwarded Department
Feby 12, 1904
8 July 20, 1904 Decision of Commission enrolling
9 Nos 1 and 3 affirmed by Department
10 (I.T.D. 5774-1904)

ENROLLMENT
OF NOS. ~~~3~~~~~ HEREON
APPROVED BY THE SECRETARY
OF INTERIOR Sep 22 1904

ENROLLMENT
OF NOS. ~~ 1 ~~ HEREON
APPROVED BY THE SECRETARY
OF INTERIOR Sep 22 1904

TRIBAL ENROLLMENT OF PARENTS

	Name of Father	Year	County	Name of Mother	Year	County
1	Leonard L Houghton		Non Citz	Susie Houghton	Dead	Non Citz
2	~~J.N. Douglas~~	~~Dead~~	~~" "~~	~~Eliz. Douglas~~	~~"~~	~~Choctaw~~
3	No1			No2		

All admitted by Dawes Com Case No 193
No1 admitted as C. L. T. Houghton. Appeal dismissed C.D. 217

September 19, 1902 Post Office seems to be Berwyn I.T.
No2 died July 16, 1899: proof of death filed Dec. 11, 1902
No2 Dismissed Jany 4 1904.

Date of Application for Enrollment.
Sept 4/99

RESIDENCE: Gaines COUNTY. **Choctaw Nation** (Not Including Freedmen)

POST OFFICE: Bower, I.T. FIELD NO. 4477

	NAME		Relationship to Person First Named	AGE	SEX	BLOOD	TRIBAL ENROLLMENT Year	County	No.
1	Tiner, Newton	32	First Named	29	M	1/2	1896	Gaines	12004
2	" Dora	22	Wife	20	F	IW			
3	" Bertha	5	Dau	1½	"	1/4			
4	" Thomas	3	Son	3mo	M	1/4			

ENROLLMENT OF NOS. 2 HEREON APPROVED BY THE SECRETARY OF INTERIOR SEP 12 1903

ENROLLMENT OF NOS. 1 3 & 4 HEREON APPROVED BY THE SECRETARY OF INTERIOR MAR 6 1903

TRIBAL ENROLLMENT OF PARENTS

	Name of Father	Year	County	Name of Mother	Year	County
1	Leroy Tiner	Dead	Choctaw Roll	Mary J Tiner		Non Citz
2	Abe Powers	"	Non Citz	Mary Powers		" "
3	No1			No2		
4	No.1			No.2		

For child of Nos 1 and 2 see NB (Mar. 3,1905) #341

No1 on 1896 roll as Nude Tyner

No2 as to marriage, see testimony of No1 and John Heron

For child of Nos 1 and 2 see NB #574 (Apr 26;1906)

As to marriage of parents of No1 see enrollment of Mary J Tiner, now Mary J Hagwood. Same was presented by No1, found satisfactory but filed with card of mother

No3- Affidavit of birth to be supplied:- Filed Dec 14/99

No.4 Enrolled May 24, 1900

#1 to 3

Date of Application for Enrollment.

Sept 4

Kiowa 12/22/02

RESIDENCE: Atoka COUNTY. **Choctaw Nation** Choctaw Roll (Not Including Freedmen) CARD NO.
POST OFFICE: Kiowa, I.T. FIELD NO. 4478

Dawes' Roll No.	NAME	Relationship to Person First Named	AGE	SEX	BLOOD	TRIBAL ENROLLMENT Year	County	No.
12435	1 Hayes, Josephus 29		26	M	1/2	1896	Atoka	6037
DEAD	2 " Rhoda DEAD	Wife	24	F	I.W.	1896	"	14657
15860	3 " Addie F 5	Dau	2	"	1/4			
DEAD	4 " Thomas	Son	2mo	M	1/4			
12436	5 " James Elmer 1	Son	10mo	M	1/4			

ENROLLMENT OF NOS. 3 HEREON APPROVED BY THE SECRETARY OF INTERIOR Jun 12 1905

For child of No.1 see NB (Mar 3-05) Card #562
" " " " " " (Apr 26-06) " #503

No. 2 and 4 hereon dismissed under order of the Commission to the Five Civilized Tribes of March 31, 1905.

ENROLLMENT OF NOS. 1 & 5 HEREON APPROVED BY THE SECRETARY OF INTERIOR Mar 6 1903

TRIBAL ENROLLMENT OF PARENTS

Name of Father	Year	County	Name of Mother	Year	County
1 Zadoc Hayes	Dead	Wade		Dead	Non Citz
2 Jas Reeves		Non Citz	Sally Reeves	"	" "
3 No1			No2		
4 No1			No2		
5 No1			No2		

As to No2 See testimony of Edith Taney Wood and John Wood of Feb 9, 1905

No1- Proof of marriage of parents waived by Commissioner McKennon

No2- As to marriage, see testimony of No1 and Chas L Houghton

Nos 3-4- Affidavits of birth to be supplied

No2 on 1896 roll as Rhoda N Hayes

No5 Born August 15th 1901. Enrolled June 25th 1902

No.4 Died Dec 15,1900: Proof of death filed Dec 30, 1902

No2 died Oct 18,1901. Proof of death filed Dec 30, 1902

#1 to 4

Date of Application for Enrollment. Sept 4/99

P.O. Hewitt I.T. 1/28/05

Choctaw By Blood Enrollment Cards 1898-1914

RESIDENCE: Tobucksy COUNTY. **Choctaw Nation** **Choctaw Roll** *(Not Including Freedmen)* CARD No.

POST OFFICE: Kiowa, I.T. FIELD No. 4479

		NAME	Relationship to Person First Named	AGE	SEX	BLOOD	TRIBAL ENROLLMENT Year	County	No.
	1	Bell, Pink W 41	First Named	36	M	IW			
DEAD.	2	~~" Dell F~~	~~Dau~~	~~14~~	~~F~~	~~1/32~~	~~1896~~	~~Tobucksy~~	~~934~~

ENROLLMENT OF NOS. 1 HEREON APPROVED BY THE SECRETARY OF INTERIOR AUG 3 1904

No. 2 HEREON DISMISSED UNDER ORDER OF THE COMMISSION TO THE FIVE CIVILIZED TRIBES OF MARCH 31, 1905.

TRIBAL ENROLLMENT OF PARENTS

	Name of Father	Year	County	Name of Mother	Year	County
1	Gordon Bell	Dead	Non Citz	Martha A Bell	Dead	Non Citz
2	~~No1~~			~~Hattie Bell~~	~~"~~	~~Tobucksy~~

Protest of attorneys for Nations for enrollment of No1 filed July 29 1903. Original record and decision together with protest forwarded Department August 7 1903

All admitted by Dawes Com, Case No 923

See testimony of No1 as to marriage

Admitted by Dawes Com as P. W. Bell

No2 on 1896 roll as Della F. Belle

No.2 Died Sept 14,1900. Proof of death filed Dec. 30, 1902

June 21, 1904 Decision of Commission enrolling No1 approved by Department (See DC #21469-1904)

Date of Application for Enrollment. Sept 4/99

See Petition No W. 84

RESIDENCE: COUNTY. **Choctaw Nation** **Choctaw Roll** *(Not Including Freedmen)* CARD NO.
POST OFFICE: Jackson, I.T. FIELD NO. 4480

Dawes' Roll No.	NAME	Relationship to Person First Named	AGE	SEX	BLOOD	TRIBAL ENROLLMENT Year	County	No.
14942	1 Okchaya, Solomon 27	First Named	24	M	Full	1893	Jackson	534
	2							
	3							
	4							
	5							
	6							
	7							
	8							
	9							
	10							
	11							
	12							
	13							
	14							
	15							
	16							
	17							

ENROLLMENT
OF NOS. ~~~~ 1 ~~~~ HEREON
APPROVED BY THE SECRETARY
OF INTERIOR Oct 15 1903

TRIBAL ENROLLMENT OF PARENTS

Name of Father	Year	County	Name of Mother	Year	County
1 Wilson Okchaya	Dead		Wisey Okchaya	Dead	

No1 is the husband of Sibby Jones on Choctaw card #3932

On 1893 Pay Roll, Page 60, No 534, Jackson Co

All other information waived by Commissioner McKennon

In jail
See testimony of No1 taken Aug. 4, 1903

Date of Application for Enrollment. Sept 4/99

P.O. Caddo I.T. 8/31/03

RESIDENCE: Wade COUNTY. **Choctaw Nation** **Choctaw Roll** (*Not Including Freedmen*) CARD NO.
POST OFFICE: Bokoshe I.T. Dec. 16/02 FIELD NO. 4481

Dawes' Roll No.	NAME	Relationship to Person First Named	AGE	SEX	BLOOD	TRIBAL ENROLLMENT Year	County	No.
14821	1 M^c^Farland Benjamin 23	First Named	20	M	Full	1896	Wade	9230
	2							
	3							
	4							
	5							
	6							
	7							
	8							
	9							
	10							
	11							
	12							
	13							
	14							
	15							
	16							
	17							

ENROLLMENT OF NOS. 1 HEREON APPROVED BY THE SECRETARY OF INTERIOR May 20 1903

TRIBAL ENROLLMENT OF PARENTS

	Name of Father	Year	County	Name of Mother	Year	County
1	Thomas M^c^Farland	dead	Nashoba or Cedar	Bessie M^c^Farland		Cedar
2						
3						
4						
5						
6	In jail					
7						
8	All lacking information waived by Commissioner M^c^Kennon					
9						
10	On 1896 roll as Benj. M^c^Farland					
11	See additional testimony of Dec. 16, 1902					
12						
13						
14						Date of Application for Enrollment.
15	Bokoshe I.T. –Dec 16/02					Sept 4/99
16						
17						

Choctaw By Blood Enrollment Cards 1898-1914

RESIDENCE: Tobucksy COUNTY. **Choctaw Nation** **Choctaw Roll** *(Not Including Freedmen)* CARD
POST OFFICE: Savannah, I.T. FIELD NO. 4482

Dawes' Roll No.		NAME	Relationship to Person First Named	AGE	SEX	BLOOD	TRIBAL ENROLLMENT Year	County	No.
DEAD.	1	~~Dawson, John~~	~~Named~~	~~78~~	~~M~~	~~1/8~~	~~1896~~	~~Tobucksy~~	~~3301~~
12437	2	" Lela E 50	Wife	47	F	1/8	1896	"	3302
12438	3	" Effie 18	Dau	15	"	1/8	1896	"	3303
12439	4	" Aurelia 13	"	10	"	1/8	1896	"	3304
	5								
	6								
	7								
	8								
	9								
	10								
	11								
	12								
	13								
	14								
	15								
	16								
	17								

No. 1 HEREON DISMISSED UNDER ORDER OF THE COMMISSION TO THE FIVE CIVILIZED TRIBES OF MARCH 31, 1905.

ENROLLMENT OF NOS. 2 3 & 4 HEREON APPROVED BY THE SECRETARY OF INTERIOR MAR 6 1903

TRIBAL ENROLLMENT OF PARENTS

	Name of Father	Year	County	Name of Mother	Year	County
1	~~Dawson~~	~~Dead~~	~~Non Citz~~	~~Polly Dawson~~	~~Dead~~	~~Red River~~
2	R. S. McCarty	"	" "			Skullyville
3	No1			No2		
4	No1			No2		
5						
6						
7						
8	~~No2 on 1896 roll as Selah Dawson~~					
9	No4 on 1896 roll as Orilla Dawson					
10	No.1 Died May 3, 1902: Proof of death filed Dec. 30, 1902					
11	For child of No.3 see NB (Apr 26, 1906) Card No. 56					
	" " " " " " (March 3,1905) " " 342					
12						
13						
14						Date of Application for Enrollment.
15						Sept 4/99
16						
17						

Choctaw By Blood Enrollment Cards 1898-1914

RESIDENCE: Tobucksy COUNTY. **Choctaw Nation** **Choctaw Roll** (Not Including Freedmen) CARD NO.
POST OFFICE: So. M^c^Alester, IT FIELD NO. 4483

Dawes' Roll No.	NAME	Relationship to Person First Named	AGE	SEX	BLOOD	TRIBAL ENROLLMENT Year	County	No.
14943	1 Mitchell, Elmira 27		24	F	1/4	1893	Tobucksy	651
14944	2 Blosser, Pansy 7	Dau	4	"	1/8			

ENROLLMENT OF NOS. 1 and 2 HEREON APPROVED BY THE SECRETARY OF INTERIOR OCT 15 1903

N^o^1 is on Cherokee 1896 roll, page 295 #88 as Elmyra Blosser. Also on Cherokee card #D2626
~~N^o^2 is on Cherokee 1896 roll, page 113, #433. Also on Cherokee card #D2626~~
Joseph F Blosser father of N^o^2 is on Cherokee 1896 roll, page 113, #431, also on Cherokee 1894 ~~roll, page 140 #543, Cooescooe[sic] Dist, also on Cherokee Card #4308 Sept 26, 1902~~
N^o^1 is now wife of G.W. Mitchell Choctaw card #2411. Evidence of marriage filed March 5, 1903
See Testimony of N^o^1 March 5, 1903 making election for enrollment of herself and child as Choctaws.

TRIBAL ENROLLMENT OF PARENTS

Name of Father	Year	County	Name of Mother	Year	County
1 Osborne Pusley	Dead	Tobucksy	Sarah E M^c^Cay		Intermarried
2 J.D. Blosser		Non Citz	No1		

No1 on 1893 Pay Roll, Page 76, No 651 Tobucksy Co as Elemyra Pusley. For ~~evidence of marriage of parents, see enrollment of Sarah E M^c^Cay, her~~ mother.

No2 Affidavit of birth to be ~~supplied:- Filed Oct 26/99~~

~~No2 Father a Cherokee, see if she~~ is on Cherokee Rolls. No.

No.2 Father is on Cherokee Roll Card #4308.

Date of Application for Enrollment.
Sept 4/99

RESIDENCE: Skullyville	COUNTY.	Choctaw Nation	Choctaw Roll (Not Including Freedmen)	CARD NO.
POST OFFICE: Pecola[sic], I.T.				FIELD NO. 4484

Dawes' Roll No.	NAME	Relationship to Person First Named	AGE	SEX	BLOOD	TRIBAL ENROLLMENT Year	County	No.
I.W. 443	1 Karl, Frank A 25	First Named	22	M	IW			
12440	2 " Viola 23	Wife	20	F	1/8	1896	Tobucksy	7865
12441	3 " Earnest Harlan 2	Son	4m	M	1/16			

ENROLLMENT OF NOS. 1 HEREON APPROVED BY THE SECRETARY OF INTERIOR SEP 12 1903

ENROLLMENT OF NOS. 2 & 3 HEREON APPROVED BY THE SECRETARY OF INTERIOR MAR 6 1903

TRIBAL ENROLLMENT OF PARENTS

Name of Father	Year	County	Name of Mother	Year	County
1 Earnest Karl		Non Citz	Minnie Karl		Non Citz
2 Herman P Lyles		Tobucksy	Mary Lyles	Dead	" "
3 No1			No2		

No2 on 1896 roll as Viola Lyles
No2- As to marriage of parents, see testimony of Herman P. Lyles, Card ~~No 2376 and Robert Stephens~~
No1- Evidence of marriage to be supplied

No.3 Enrolled January 22, 1901
For child of Nos 1 and 2 see NB (March 3,1905) #343

Date of Application for Enrollment.
Sept 4/99

No2 enrolled June 7/99 re-enrolled Sept 4/99

RESIDENCE: Tobucksy COUNTY. **Choctaw Nation** **Choctaw Roll** (Not Including Freedmen) CARD NO.
POST OFFICE: South M^c^Alester, I.T. FIELD NO. 4485

Dawes' Roll No.	NAME	Relationship to Person First Named	AGE	SEX	BLOOD	TRIBAL ENROLLMENT Year	County	No.
12442	1 Duford, Willie 22	First Named	19	M	1/4	1893	Kiamitia	47
12443	2 " Albert 19	Cousin	16	"	1/4	1893	"	44
12444	3 McBee Ella 17	"	14	F	1/4	1893	"	45
12445	4 Duford Roxy 8	"	5	"	1/4			
12446	5 " Frankie 7	"	3	"	1/4			
12447	6 McBee, Pryor Edward 1	Son of No3	6mo	M	1/8			
I.W. 1425	7 Engleman, Mollie	Mother of ~~No.2~~	37	F	IW			

ENROLLMENT OF NOS. 7 HEREON APPROVED BY THE SECRETARY OF INTERIOR JUN 12 1905

ENROLLMENT OF NOS. 1,2,3,4,5,6 HEREON APPROVED BY THE SECRETARY OF INTERIOR MAR 6 1903

~~No3 is now the wife of George McBee,~~ a non-citizen. Evidence of marriage filed Dec 24, 1902

TRIBAL ENROLLMENT OF PARENTS

	Name of Father	Year	County	Name of Mother	Year	County
1	Mitchell	Dead	Kiamitia	Unknown		white woman
2	Edward Duford	"		Mollie Engleman		" "
3	" "	"	"	" "		" "
4	" "	"	"	" "		" "
5	" "	"	"	" "		" "
6	George McBee		Non Citizen	No.3		
7	Andrew Smith		" "	Sarah Smith		Non Citz

~~In 1882 No.7 married Ed Duford, a recognized and enrolled citizen by blood of the Choc. Nation, identified on 1893~~ Leased Dist. Payment Roll, Kiamitia Co Number 43 and who died in 1896

~~No.7 originally listed for enrollment on Choc card #D-427, Sept 4/99: transferred to this card May 15, 1905.~~ See decision of April 28, 1905

First three on 1893 Pay Roll, Pages 116-117 Kiamitia Co

Nos 4-5- Affidavits of birth to be ~~supplied:- Filed Oct 26/99~~

~~See Card No D427 as to marriage~~ of parents.

No.6 Born 20 June, 1902: application made Oct. 14, 1902

~~" " Proof of birth filed Feb. 5, 1903.~~

~~No3 is legal guardian of Nos 4 and 5, July 13, 1903~~

Date of application for enrollment Sept 4/99 #1 to 5 inc

RESIDENCE: Tobucksy COUNTY. **Choctaw Nation** **Choctaw Roll** *(Not Including Freedmen)* CARD NO.
POST OFFICE: Scipio I.T. FIELD NO. 4486

Dawes' Roll No.	NAME	Relationship to Person First Named	AGE	SEX	BLOOD	TRIBAL ENROLLMENT Year	County	No.
14168	1 Vail, Sophia 34	First Named	31	F	7/8	1896	Tobucksy	4012
14169	2 Crowder Mary S 13	Dau	10	"	7/16	1896	"	2319
14170	3 " Laura 11	"	8	"	7/16	1896	"	2320
14171	4 " John 10	Son	7	M	7/16	1896	"	2321
14172	5 Felton, Clarence 4	"	1	"	7/16			
I.W. 1345	6 Vail, John F 54	Husband	54	M	I.W.			

See Petition No W24 & 61

ENROLLMENT OF NOS. 6 HEREON APPROVED BY THE SECRETARY OF INTERIOR Mar 14 1905

ENROLLMENT OF NOS. 1 2 3 4 & 5 HEREON APPROVED BY THE SECRETARY OF INTERIOR Mar 19 1903

TRIBAL ENROLLMENT OF PARENTS

Name of Father	Year	County	Name of Mother	Year	County
1 Mitchell Nelson	Dead	Blue	Susan Nelson	Dead	Blue
2 John Crowder	"	Non Citz	No1		
3 " "	"	" "	No1		
4 " "	"	" "	No1		
5 John Felton		" "	No1		
6 William Vail		U.S. Citz.	Rebecca Vail		U.S. Citz.

For child of Nos 1 and 6 see NB (Mar 3,1905) Card #344

Nº1 is now the wife of John F. Vail on Chickasaw card #1498. Evidence of marriage filed Nov. 20, 1902.

No.6 admitted by Dawes Com on Dec. 2,1896 as an intermarried citizen of Choc Nation Case No. 254 as John Vail

No.6 originally listed for enrollment on Chickasaw card #1498 and transferred to this card Feb. 5, 1905. See decision of Jan. 20, 1905

No.6 married Levina Stidham, a recognized Chickasaw by blood Jan., 1878

She died in 1887 No.6 elects to be enrolled as a Choctaw by intermarriage

#1 to 5

Date of Application for Enrollment.

Sept 4/99

No6 P.O. Durant I.T. Box #95

RESIDENCE: Tobucksy COUNTY. **Choctaw Nation** **Choctaw Roll** *(Not Including Freedmen)* CARD NO.
POST OFFICE: South M^c^Alester, I.T. FIELD NO. 4487

Dawes' Roll No.	NAME	Relationship to Person First Named	AGE	SEX	BLOOD	TRIBAL ENROLLMENT Year	County	No.
13498	1 Sexton, Mary 26	First Named	23	F	Full	1896	Tobucksy	11276
	2							
	3							
	4							
	5							
	6							
	7							
	8							
	9							
	10							
	11							
	12							
	13							
	14							
	15							
	16							
	17							

ENROLLMENT
OF NOS. 1 HEREON
APPROVED BY THE SECRETARY
OF INTERIOR

TRIBAL ENROLLMENT OF PARENTS

Name of Father	Year	County	Name of Mother	Year	County
1 Dick Sexton		Jacks Fork	Susan Sexton		Jacks Fork
2					
3					
4					
5					
6					
7					
8					
9					
10					
11					
12					
13					Date of Application for Enrollment.
14					
15					Sept 4/99
16					
17 P.O. Atoka I.T.					

RESIDENCE: Gaines COUNTY. **Choctaw Nation** Choctaw Roll (Not Including Freedmen) CARD NO.
POST OFFICE: Wilburton, I.T. FIELD NO. 4488

Dawes' Roll No.		NAME		Relationship to Person First Named	AGE	SEX	BLOOD	TRIBAL ENROLLMENT Year	County	No.
12448	1	Nelson, George	32	First Named	29	M	Full	1896	Gaines	9597
I.W. 1426	2	" Mary Agnes	26	Wife	26	F	I.W.	1896	Sans Bois	14899
15929	3	" Rebecca	10	Dau	7	"	1/2	1896	Gaines	9598
15960	4	" Mabel	7	"	4	"	1/2	1896	"	9599
12449	5	" Beatrice	5	"	2	"	1/2			
12450	6	" George Jr	3	Son	1mo	M	1/2			
12451	7	" Osborne M	1	Son	5mo	M	1/2			

ENROLLMENT OF NOS. ~~ 4 ~~ HEREON APPROVED BY THE SECRETARY OF INTERIOR Nov 27 1905

ENROLLMENT OF NOS. ~~ 2 ~~ HEREON APPROVED BY THE SECRETARY OF INTERIOR Jun 12 1905

ENROLLMENT OF NOS. three HEREON APPROVED BY THE SECRETARY OF INTERIOR Aug 23 1905

ENROLLMENT OF NOS. 1 5 6 & 7 HEREON APPROVED BY THE SECRETARY OF INTERIOR Mar 6 1903

TRIBAL ENROLLMENT OF PARENTS

	Name of Father	Year	County	Name of Mother	Year	County
1	Simon P Nelson	Dead	Gaines		Dead	Gaines
2	Harmon Mickle	"	Non Citz	Joanna Mickle		Non Citz
3	No1			No2		
4	No1			No2		
5	No1			No2		
6	No1			No2		
7	№1			№2		

No.3 Granted Jun. 30, 1905

~~No.2 on 1896 roll as Mary A. Nelson~~

Nos 5-6- Affidavits of birth to be supplied:- Filed Nov. 2/99

No4 Granted Oct 5 - 1905

No3 on 1893 Roll- Gaines Co 402

~~Nos 2,3 and 4 denied by Dawes Commission in 1896~~

Choctaw Case #1137: No appeal

№7 Born March 1, 1902; enrolled Aug. 26, 1902

#1 to 6 inc
Date of Application for Enrollment.
Sept 4/99

P.O. address So. McAlester I.T.

Choctaw By Blood Enrollment Cards 1898-1914

RESIDENCE: Tobucksy COUNTY. **Choctaw Nation** Choctaw Roll (Not Including Freedmen) CARD NO.
POST OFFICE: Simpson, I.T. FIELD NO. 4489

Dawes' Roll No.	NAME	Relationship to Person First Named	AGE	SEX	BLOOD	TRIBAL ENROLLMENT Year	County	No.
12452	1 Winlock, Rufus 41	First Named	38	M	Full	1896	Gaines	12985
12453	2 Johnson Elizabeth 27	Wife	24	F	"	1896	"	12986
12454	3 Winlock Bennie 5	Son	2	M	"			
12455	4 Johnson John S 1	Son of No2	1	M	"			
14822	5 Winlock, Bettie 1	Dau	3mo	F	"			

~~The mother of No5 is Eliza Jones on~~
Choctaw card #3108. See copy of testimony of
No.1 taken July 27, 1903.

ENROLLMENT OF NOS. 1 2 3 4 HEREON APPROVED BY THE SECRETARY OF INTERIOR Mar 6 1903

ENROLLMENT OF NOS. HEREON APPROVED BY THE SECRETARY OF INTERIOR

TRIBAL ENROLLMENT OF PARENTS

Name of Father	Year	County	Name of Mother	Year	County
1 Silas Winlock	Dead	Wade	Siney Winlock	Dead	Tobucksy
2 Nelson	"	Cedar	Susan Nelson	"	"
3 No1			No2		
4 Alexander Johnson	1896	Sans Bois	№2		
5 No.1			No.2		

~~No3 Affidavit of birth to be~~
supplied:- Filed Oct. 26/99
For child of No.2 see NB (Mar 3, 1905) #616
~~No2 on 1896 roll, Page 290 No 11275 as~~
~~Lucy Silmon Tobucksy Co.~~
No.2 is now the wife of Alexander Johnson on Choctaw card #2968: Jany 11, 1902
Nos 1 and 2 divorced. Evidence of marriage between №2 and
~~Alexander Johnson filed April 17, 1902. Evidence of divorce between №s 1 and 2~~
~~№4 Born April 9, 1901: enrolled April 17, 1902~~ ~~filed April 17,1902~~
No.5 Born Sept. 13, 1902: Proof of birth filed Dec. 23, 1902 <Illegitimate> #1 to 4
For child of No2 see NB (Apr 26 '06) Card No 174

Date of Application for Enrollment.
Sept 4/99

Choctaw By Blood Enrollment Cards 1898-1914

RESIDENCE: Tobucksy COUNTY. **Choctaw Nation** Choctaw Roll (Not Including Freedmen) CARD NO.
POST OFFICE: South M^c^Alester I.T. FIELD NO. 4490

Dawes' Roll No.	NAME	Relationship to Person First Named	AGE	SEX	BLOOD	TRIBAL ENROLLMENT Year	County	No.
12456	1 Stanton, William H 30		27	M	1/32	1896	Tobucksy	11269
I.W. 678	2 " Inez J 26	Wife	23	F	I.W.	1896	"	15034
12457	3 " Serena P 9	Dau	6	"	1/64	1896	"	11270
12458	4 " Arthur G 6	Son	3	M	1/64			
12459	5 " Lettie I 3	Dau	1mo	F	1/64			
12460	6 " Lola Blanch 1	Dau	1mo	F	1/64			
	7							
	8 ENROLLMENT							
	9 OF NOS. 2 HEREON APPROVED BY THE SECRETARY							
	10 OF INTERIOR Mar 26 1904							
	11 Decision Prepared No 2 Nov. 27 '03							
	12							
	13							
	14							
	15 ENROLLMENT							
	16 OF NOS. 1 3 4 5 & 6 HEREON APPROVED BY THE SECRETARY							
	17 OF INTERIOR Mar 6 1903							

TRIBAL ENROLLMENT OF PARENTS

Name of Father	Year	County	Name of Mother	Year	County
1 William Stanton	Dead	Tobucksy	Ann Stanton	Dead	Non Citz
2 John S. Orr		Non Citz	Mary Orr		" "
3 No1			No2		
4 No1			No2		
5 No1			No2		
6 No1			No2		
7					
8					
9					
10					
11		No1 on 1896 roll as Wm H. Stenton[sic]			
12		No1- as to proof of marriage of			
13		~~parents see enrollment of sister~~ Tabitha Rozelle			
14					Date of Application for Enrollment.
15		No2 admitted as an intermarried citizen by Dawes Commission: ~~Choctaw Case #806: no appeal.~~			Sept 4/99
16		No6 Born March 22, 1902: enrolled June 10, 1902			
17		Intermarried Status Nov 24 '03			

Choctaw By Blood Enrollment Cards 1898-1914

RESIDENCE: Sans Bois COUNTY. **Choctaw Nation** **Choctaw Roll** *(Not Including Freedmen)* CARD NO.
POST OFFICE: Stigler, I.T. FIELD NO. 4491

Dawes' Roll No.	NAME	Relationship to Person First Named	AGE	SEX	BLOOD	TRIBAL ENROLLMENT Year	County	No.
12461	1 Carney, Ella 27	First Named	24	F	3/4	1896	Sans Bois	2072
12462	2 Baum, Hester 8	Dau	5	"	3/8	1896	" "	855
DEAD.	3 ~~Carney, Nora~~ DEAD.	~~"~~	~~1~~	~~"~~	~~7/8~~			
12463	4 " Nettie 3	"	22mo	"	7/8			
12464	5 " Albert 1	Son	4 "	M	7/8			
	6							
	7							
	8							
	9 No. 3 HEREON DISMISSED UNDER							
	10 ORDER OF THE COMMISSION TO THE FIVE CIVILIZED TRIBES OF MARCH 31, 1905.							
	11							
	12							
	13							
	14							
	15 ENROLLMENT							
	16 OF NOS. 1, 2, 4&5 HEREON APPROVED BY THE SECRETARY							
	17 OF INTERIOR MAR 6 1903							

TRIBAL ENROLLMENT OF PARENTS

Name of Father	Year	County	Name of Mother	Year	County
1 Forbis Jones	Dead	Gaines	Eliza Jones	Dead	Gaines
2 Phil Baum	"	Non Citz	No1		
3 ~~Albert Carney~~		~~Sans Bois~~	~~No1~~		
4 " "			No.1		
5 " "			No.1		
6					

7 No1 on 1896 roll as Ellen Cooper
8 No2 " 1896 " " Hester Burn
No3 Died April 16th 1901: Evidence of Death filed July 21st 1902
9 ~~No.4 Born Feby 16, 1900: application made Dec. 23, 1902. Proof of birth filed 2/2/1903~~
10 No.5 " Aug 28, 1902: " " " 23, 1902. Proof of birth filed 2/2/1903
11 No.1 is now wife of Allen Carney on Choc. Card 5423, 12/23 '02
12
13 For child of No1 see NB (Apr 26-06) Card #429
14 " " " " " " (Mar 3-05) " #1102

Date of Application for Enrollment.
15 Sept 4/99
16
17 P.O. Quinton IT 4/12/05

Choctaw By Blood Enrollment Cards 1898-1914

RESIDENCE: Tobucksy COUNTY. **Choctaw Nation** **Choctaw Roll** (Not Including Freedmen) CARD NO.
POST OFFICE: Krebbs, I.T. FIELD NO. 4492

Dawes' Roll No.		NAME	Relationship to Person	AGE	SEX	BLOOD	TRIBAL ENROLLMENT Year	County	No.
12465	1	Simpson, John 62 ✓	First Named	59	M	1/2	1896	Tobucksy	11311
12466	2	" Minia 42 ✓	Wife	39	F	Full	1896	"	11312
12467	3	Smith, Wisley ✓ 18	Ward	15	M	"	1896	Gaines	11253
	4								
	5								
	6								
	7								
	8								
	9								
	10								
	11								
	12								
	13								
	14								
	15								
	16								
	17								

CITIZENSHIP CERTIFICATE ISSUED FOR NO. 1-2 AUG 4 1903

SHIP CERTIFICATE OR NO 3 AUG 24 1903

ENROLLMENT OF NOS. 1 2 & 3 HEREON APPROVED BY THE SECRETARY OF INTERIOR MAR 6 1903

TRIBAL ENROLLMENT OF PARENTS

	Name of Father	Year	County	Name of Mother	Year	County
1		Dead	Non Citizen	Tilda	Dead	Choctaw
2	Sweeney Frazier	"	Gaines	Mary Frazier	"	Tobucksy
3	Abel Smith	"	Tobucksy	Patsy Frazier	"	"
4						
5						
6						
7						
8	No.2 on 1896 Roll as Maimie Simpson					
9						
10						
11						
12						
13						
14						
15						
16						
17						Sept 4, 1899

RESIDENCE: Tobucksy COUNTY. **Choctaw Nation** **Choctaw Roll** *(Not Including Freedmen)* CARD NO.
POST OFFICE: Holleman, I.T. FIELD NO. **4493**

Dawes' Roll No.		NAME	Relationship to Person First Named	AGE	SEX	BLOOD	TRIBAL ENROLLMENT Year	County	No.
I.W. 842	1	Holleman, William G (35)		32	M	I.W.	1896	Tobucksy	14611
12468	2	" Gillie A 31	Wife	28	F	1/4	1896	"	5331
12469	3	" Gracie R A 10	Dau	7	"	1/8	1896	"	5332
12470	4	" Thomas C 7	Son	4	M	1/8	1896	"	5333
12471	5	" Juanita M 5	Dau	2	F	1/8			
12472	6	" William Givens 1	Son	1mo	M	1/8			
	7								
	8	For child of Nos 1 and 2 see NB (Mar 3, 1905) #345							

ENROLLMENT OF NOS. 1 HEREON APPROVED BY THE SECRETARY OF INTERIOR May 21 1904

Notify A.S. M^c^Kennon So M^c^Alester I.T.

ENROLLMENT OF NOS. 2 3 4 5 & 6 HEREON APPROVED BY THE SECRETARY OF INTERIOR Mar 6 1903

TRIBAL ENROLLMENT OF PARENTS

	Name of Father	Year	County	Name of Mother	Year	County
1	J.B.R. Holleman	Dead	Non Citz	Rebecca Bragg		Non Citz
2	Jas. S. Davis		" "	Annie Davis		Tobucksy
3	No1			No2		
4	No1			No2		
5	No1			No2		
6	No1			No2		

No1 on 1896 roll as Wm G. Holleman
No2 " 1896 " " Gilly A "
No3 " 1896 " " Grace P "
No5- Affidavit of birth to be supplied:- Filed Oct 26/99
No1- Evidence of marriage to be supplied:- Filed Oct 26/99
No6 Enrolled Sept 26, 1901
Affidavits of Nos 1 and 2 as to residence at date of their marriage filed May 29, 1903

#1 to 5 inc
Date of Application for Enrollment.
Sept 4/99

P.O. Savanah I.T. 5/27/05

Choctaw By Blood Enrollment Cards 1898-1914

RESIDENCE: Tobucksy COUNTY. **Choctaw Nation** Choctaw Roll (*Not Including Freedmen*) CARD NO.
POST OFFICE: Krebbs, I.T. FIELD NO. 4494

Dawes' Roll No.	NAME		Relationship to Person First Named	AGE	SEX	BLOOD	TRIBAL ENROLLMENT Year	County	No.
12473	1 Bond, Daniel A	43	First Named	40	M	Full	1896	Tobucksy	928
12474	2 " Cillin	45	Wife	42	F	"	1896	"	929
12475	3 Hampton, Nellie	19	Ward	16	"	"	1896	"	5374
12476	4 Bonaparte, Simpson	16	"	13	M	"	1896	"	930
12477	5 " Jacob	13	"	10	"	"	1896	"	931
12478	6 Jackson, Amanda	13	"	10	F	"	1893	Gaines	277
	7								
	8								
	9								
	10								
	11								
	12								
	13								
	14								
	15								
	16								
	17								

ENROLLMENT
OF NOS. 1,2,3,4,5 & 6 HEREON
APPROVED BY THE SECRETARY
OF INTERIOR Mar 6 1903

TRIBAL ENROLLMENT OF PARENTS

Name of Father	Year	County	Name of Mother	Year	County
1 Robert Bond	Dead	Tobucksy	Ye-me-to-na		Tobucksy
2 Me-she-mah-tubby	"	"	Mary		"
3 Forbis Hampton	"	Gaines	Jennie Hampton	Dead	Gaines
4 Louis Bonaparte	"	Tobucksy	Louisa Bonaparte	"	Tobucksy
5 " "	"	"	" "	"	"
6 Wallen Jackson	"	Gaines	Sallissie James		Gaines
7					
8					
9					
10					
11					
12					
13					
14					
15					
16					
17					

No1 on 1896 roll as Daniel Bond
No6 on 1893 Pay roll, Page 29, No 277
~~Gaines Co, as Mandy Jackson~~
№6 is a duplicate of Andy Jackson on Choctaw card #4915

For child of No6 see NB (Apr 26 '06) #1310

Date of Application for Enrollment.
Sept 4/99

Choctaw By Blood Enrollment Cards 1898-1914

RESIDENCE: Tobucksy COUNTY. **Choctaw Nation** Choctaw Roll (Not Including Freedmen) CARD NO.
POST OFFICE: Hartshorne, I.T. FIELD NO. 4495

Dawes' Roll No.	NAME	Relationship to Person First Named	AGE	SEX	BLOOD	TRIBAL ENROLLMENT Year	County	No.
12479	1 Bond, Yimmetonah 90	First Named	87	F	Full	1896	Tobucksy	14224

ENROLLMENT
OF NOS. 1 HEREON
APPROVED BY THE SECRETARY
OF INTERIOR MAR 6 1903

TRIBAL ENROLLMENT OF PARENTS

Name of Father	Year	County	Name of Mother	Year	County
1 E-ma-thla-tubbee	Dead	Tobucksy	Ta-ho-ko-na	Dead	Choctaw

On 1896 roll as Yimmitona

Date of Application for Enrollment. Sept 4/99

RESIDENCE: Tobucksy COUNTY. **Choctaw Nation** **Choctaw Roll** *(Not Including Freedmen)* CARD NO.
POST OFFICE: Hartshorne, I.T. FIELD NO. 4496

Dawes' Roll No.	NAME	Relationship to Person First Named	AGE	SEX	BLOOD	TRIBAL ENROLLMENT Year	County	No.
12480	1 Bond, Rhoda 45	First Named	42	F	Full	1896	Tobucksy	933
12481	2 Bonaparte, Nabert 22	Son	19	M	"	1896	Atoka	1857

ENROLLMENT OF NOS. 1 & 2 HEREON APPROVED BY THE SECRETARY OF INTERIOR MAR 6 1903

TRIBAL ENROLLMENT OF PARENTS

Name of Father	Year	County	Name of Mother	Year	County
1 Robert Bond	Dead	Tobucksy	Yimmetonah		Tobucksy
2 Louis Bonaparte	"	"	No1		

No2 on 1896 roll as Nebert Bonaparte; also on 1896 roll, Page 24, No 932, Robert Bonaparte, Tobucksy Co.
No.2 is husband of No.1 on Choc Care 4873

Date of Application for Enrollment. Sept 4/99

RESIDENCE: Gaines COUNTY. **Choctaw Nation** **Choctaw Roll** *(Not Including Freedmen)* CARD NO.
POST OFFICE: Vireton, I.T. FIELD NO. 4497

Dawes' Roll No.	NAME	Relationship to Person First Named	AGE	SEX	BLOOD	TRIBAL ENROLLMENT Year	County	No.
12482	1 Kincade, Tennessee 67		64	F	Full	1896	Sans Bois	7443
DEAD	2 ~~Williams, Lizzie 20~~	~~Dau~~	~~17~~	~~"~~	~~"~~	~~1896~~	~~" "~~	~~12648~~
12483	3 King, Anderson 2	G.Son	2	M	"			

5 No 2 hereon dismissed under order of
6 the Commission to the Five Civilized
7 Tribes of March 31, 1905.

ENROLLMENT
OF NOS. 1 & 3 HEREON
APPROVED BY THE SECRETARY
OF INTERIOR Mar 6 1903

TRIBAL ENROLLMENT OF PARENTS

Name of Father	Year	County	Name of Mother	Year	County
1 Ti-hay-cubbee	Dead	Sans Bois	Cha-fa-ho-key	Dead	Sans Bois
2 ~~Allen Williams~~	~~"~~	~~" "~~	~~No1~~		
3 Isaac King	1896	" "	No.2		

7 No1 on 1896 roll as Tennessee Kingcade
8 No3 Born Aug 31, 1900: Enrolled Dec 23, 1902
No2 Died 1900: Proof of death filed Dec. 23, 1902.
9 See affidavit of Isaac King as to birth of No.3 filed Jany 28, 1903
10 also as to his marriage to No 2

#1 & 2
Date of Application for Enrollment.
Sept 4/99

Choctaw By Blood Enrollment Cards 1898-1914

RESIDENCE: Gaines COUNTY. **Choctaw Nation** **Choctaw Roll** *(Not Including Freedmen)* CARD NO.
POST OFFICE: Vireton, I.T. FIELD NO. 4498

Dawes' Roll No.	NAME	Relationship to Person First Named	AGE	SEX	BLOOD	TRIBAL ENROLLMENT Year	County	No.
12484	1 Hancock, Solomon 46	First Named	43	M	Full	1896	Sans Bois	5121
12485	2 " Susan 26	Wife	23	F	"	1896	" "	5122
12486	3 " William 5	Son	1	M	"			
12487	4 " Jefferson Lee 1	"	2mo	M	"			
	5							
	6							
	7							
	8							
	9							
	10							
	11							
	12							
	13							
	14							
	15							
	16							
	17							

ENROLLMENT OF NOS. 1 2 3 & 4 HEREON APPROVED BY THE SECRETARY OF INTERIOR Mar 6 1903

TRIBAL ENROLLMENT OF PARENTS

Name of Father	Year	County	Name of Mother	Year	County
1 Albert Hancock	Dead	Sans Bois	Bicey Hancock	Dead	Sans Bois
2 Harry Kincade	"	" "	Tennessee Kincade		" "
3 No1			No2		
4 No1			No2		
5					
6					
7					
8					
9					
10					
11					
12					
13					
14					
15					
16					
17					

No4 Born Sept 9, 1902; enrolled Nov. 12, 1902

For child of Nos 1&2 see NB (Apr 26 '06) Card #486

#1 to 3

Date of Application for Enrollment. Sept 4/99

RESIDENCE: Chickasaw Nation ~~COUNTY.~~ **Choctaw Nation** Choctaw Roll (Not Including Freedmen) CARD NO.

POST OFFICE: Center, I.T. FIELD NO. **4499**

Dawes' Roll No.	NAME	Relationship to Person First Named	AGE	SEX	BLOOD	TRIBAL ENROLLMENT Year	County	No.
12488	1 Dunagan, Lula [28]	First Named	25	F	1/16	1896	Tobucksy	3322
12489	2 " Thomas C [11]	Son	8	M	1/32	1896	"	3323
12490	3 " Mildred A [8]	Dau	5	F	1/32	1896	"	3324
12491	4 " Maggie G [6]	"	2	"	1/32			

ENROLLMENT OF NOS. 1 2 3 & 4 HEREON APPROVED BY THE SECRETARY OF INTERIOR Mar 6 1903

TRIBAL ENROLLMENT OF PARENTS

	Name of Father	Year	County	Name of Mother	Year	County
1	William Stanton	Dead	Tobucksy	Annie Stanton	Dead	Non Citz
2	D. N. Dunagan		Non Citz	No1		
3	" " "		" "	No1		
4	" " "		" "	No1		

No1 on 1896 roll as Lula Dunegann
No2 " 1896 " " Clay "
No3 " 1896 " " Mabel "
No1- As to marriage of parent see enrollment of Tabitha Rozelle
No4- Affidavit of birth to be supplied:- Filed:- Oct 27/99

Date of Application for Enrollment. Sept 4/99

For child of No.1 see N.B. (Apr 26,1906) Card No 211.

Choctaw By Blood Enrollment Cards 1898-1914

RESIDENCE: Tobucksy COUNTY. **Choctaw Nation** Choctaw Roll (Not including Freedmen) CARD NO.
POST OFFICE: Savannah, I.T. FIELD NO. 4500

Dawes' Roll No.	NAME		Relationship to Person First Named	AGE	SEX	BLOOD	TRIBAL ENROLLMENT Year	County	No.
12492	1 Ryan, Theron J	30		27	M	1/16	1896	Tobucksy	10762
12493	2 " Annie	30	Wife	27	F	1/4	1896	"	10765
12494	3 " Louisa B	8	Dau	5	"	5/32	1896	"	10763
12495	4 " Lola E	6	"	3	"	5/32	1896	"	10764
12496	5 " Roy C	3	Son	4mo	M	5/32			
12497	6 " Willamette	1	Dau	1mo	F	5/32			

ENROLLMENT OF NOS. 1 2 3 4 5 & 6 HEREON APPROVED BY THE SECRETARY OF INTERIOR MAR 6 1903

TRIBAL ENROLLMENT OF PARENTS

	Name of Father	Year	County	Name of Mother	Year	County
1	Thos Ryan	Dead	Non Citz	Lela Dawson		Tobucksy
2	Ben Lewis	"	Chick Roll	Mary Lewis	Dead	"
3	No1			No2		
4	No1			No2		
5	No1			No2		
6	No1			No2		

No2 on 1896 roll as Nannie Ryan
No3 " 1896 " " Eliza B "
No4 " 1896 " " Lula E "
~~No5- Affidavit of birth to be supplied:-~~ Filed Oct 27/99
No.6 Enrolled July 15, 1901
For child of Nos 1&2 see NB (Apr 26-06) Card #770
" " " " " " " (Mar 3 '05) " #346

#1 to 5
Date of Application for Enrollment.
Sept 4/99